Praise for *Coming Clean*

"Purging this country of its two-century addiction to fossil fuels is the great task of our time. Here is the resource we have long needed."

"Strung out by   reats?
Coming Clean   e to
building a bett

                         'T

"Straight from   ergy
economy, Mike   el prices
soaring, his pra   endously
important. I es   nake this
revolution hap

"A thoroughly e   lilemma.
Brune's empow   om the
energy bullies le

                         G *POINT*

"This is a valuab   istainable, resilient energy. As Brune puts it, 'Join us: it's fun over here.'"

      — R. JAMES WOOLSEY, ENERGY-INDEPENDENCE EXPERT,
           FORMER CIA DIRECTOR

"An optimistic, realistic, pragmatic call to action. In this eloquent book, Mike Brune offers practical approaches, hope, and inspiration. A must-read for anyone who dreams of a sustainable, just, and peaceful future."

— JOHN PERKINS, AUTHOR OF *CONFESSIONS OF AN ECONOMIC HIT MAN* AND *THE SECRET HISTORY OF THE AMERICAN EMPIRE*

"At last! A road map to a clean energy future. As Michael Brune says, embracing clean energy is not an obligation, it is an opportunity."

— VAN JONES, AUTHOR OF *THE GREEN-COLLAR ECONOMY*

COMING
CLEAN

COMING CLEAN

BREAKING AMERICA'S ADDICTION TO OIL AND COAL

MICHAEL BRUNE

Sierra Club Books
San Francisco

The Sierra Club, founded in 1892 by author and conservationist John Muir, is the oldest, largest, and most influential grassroots environmental organization in the United States. With more than a million members and supporters—and some sixty chapters across the country—we are working hard to protect our local communities, ensure an enduring legacy for America's wild places, and find smart energy solutions to stop global warming. To learn how you can participate in the Sierra Club's programs to explore, enjoy, and protect the planet, please address inquiries to Sierra Club, 85 Second Street, San Francisco, California 94105, or visit our website at www.sierraclub.org.

The Sierra Club's book publishing division, Sierra Club Books, has been a leading publisher of titles on the natural world and environmental issues for nearly half a century. We offer books to the general public as a nonprofit educational service in the hope that they may enlarge the public's understanding of the Sierra Club's concerns and priorities. The point of view expressed in each book, however, does not necessarily represent that of the Sierra Club. For more information on Sierra Club Books and a complete list of our titles and authors, please visit www.sierraclub.org/books.

Copyright © 2008 by Michael Brune

Published by Sierra Club Books,
85 Second Street, San Francisco, CA 94105

Sierra Club Books are published in association
with Counterpoint (www.counterpointpress.com).

SIERRA CLUB, SIERRA CLUB BOOKS, and the Sierra Club design logos
are registered trademarks of the Sierra Club.

Book and cover design by Blue Design (www.bluedes.com).

Library of Congress Cataloging-in-Publication Data

Brune, Michael
  Coming clean : breaking America's addiction to oil and coal / Michael Brune.
    p. cm.
  Includes bibliographical references and index.
  ISBN 978-1-57805-149-6 (alk. paper)
  1. Fossil fuels—Environmental aspects—United States. 2. Biomass energy—United States.
  3. Renewable energy sources—United States. 4. Green movement—United States. I. Title.
  TD887.F69B78 2008
  333.790973—dc22   2008026345

Printed in the United States of America on acid-free paper that contains 50 percent recycled fiber, of which a minimum of 30 percent is post-consumer waste.

Distributed by Publishers Group West
12 11 10 09 08
10 9 8 7 6 5 4 3 2 1

To Mary, my love,

and to darling Olivia, for bringing such joy and laughter

Contents

Acknowledgments

I grew up in a family of do-gooders, by which I mean to say that my parents often encouraged my two sisters, my brother, and me to try to make a positive difference in the world. My mother, Patricia Brune, is a public school teacher in New Jersey. My father, Robert, is a former mayor of Dover Township, New Jersey, and is passionate about energy and politics. Their commitment—to each other and to making the world a better place—inspired me to start writing this book.

I'm grateful to Jodie Evans, who first encouraged me to put this book together a few years ago. I had just become a father for the first time, was busy running Rainforest Action Network, and didn't take her suggestion too seriously at first. But without her persistence, and the support of RAN board chair Jim Gollin, I never would have started. Michael Marx and Safir Ahmed helped give the book its structure. I'm also indebted to my agent Julie Castiglia and to my tag-team editors at Sierra Club Books, Joan Hamilton and Diana Landau, who worked much harder than they should have. Sierra Club energy expert Fred Heutte and copyeditor Andrew Frisardi also made invaluable contributions.

Bill Twist, David Elliot, and the good folks at the Pachamama Alliance arranged for my trip to Ecuador. Matt Price and Larry Innes introduced me to First Nations leaders in Alberta. Mary Anne Hitt and Hillary Hosta put together a tour of West Virginia and taught me more about mountaintop removal mining than I ever wanted to know. Thank you, all.

My colleagues and friends Jennifer Krill, John Sellers, Steve Kretzmann, and Ilyse Hogue are some of the most creative people I know of that are working for social change. Their fingerprints are all over this book. Chelsea Sexton, Dave Bernikoff-Raboy, Heather Bernikoff-Raboy, Marc Geller, Sarah Connolly, Jodie Van Horn, and Nile Malloy gave valuable insights into plug-in hybrids, electric cars, and the other topics in the chapters on transportation.

Equally helpful were Danny Kennedy, David Hochschild, Adam Browning,

Elliot Hoffman, Dian Grueneich, Audrey Chang, John White, Art Rosenfeld, and Ralph Cavanagh, briefing me on the future of energy efficiency and renewable energy. Leila Salazar-Lopez, Shannon Coughlin, Heidi Quante, Andrea Samulon, Brihannala Morgan, and Alex Farrell helped me separate fact from fiction in the world of agrofuels.

Bill Barclay, Matt Leonard, Scott Parkin, Dana Clark, and Becky Tarbotton helped illuminate the specific role that corporate and public banks play in financing climate change. Thanks also to Brant Olson and Debra Erenberg for reviewing parts of the manuscript, to Branden Barber, Katie Steele, Joe Powers at Tesla, Kevin Koenig, Eric Schaeffer, Paul West, and Chandra Kirana for their help, and to the staff and board of Rainforest Action Network for their patience and support.

I'm deeply grateful to Somer Huntley for her back-breaking research and documentation, always done with a smile.

And most of all, I'm thankful for Mary and Olivia's love and encouragement.

It's Time to Refuel

There is one thing stronger than all the armies of the
world, and that is an idea whose time has come.

— Victor Hugo

I did a double take. On the magazine rack at my local grocery store was a photo of former Florida Marlins pitcher Dontrelle Willis. The photo had been altered so that the smiling baseball star was standing on the pitcher's mound, up to his thighs in water. You guessed it: *Sports Illustrated* had done its first cover story on climate change.

The cover announced, "As the Planet Changes, So Do the Games We Play." The article described how twice-a-day football practices were changing into once-a-night sessions due to the punishing Texas heat, and how the famous Hahnenkam downhill ski race in Kitzbuhel, Austria, had to be rescued by helicopters hauling in a hundred thousand cubic feet of snow. As sportswriter Alexander Wolff observed, "Global warming is not coming; it is here."

There can be little doubt that climate change has captured our attention. "Green" is "the new red, white and blue," according to *New York Times* columnist Thomas Friedman. Consider how the response to Al Gore's warnings on global warming has changed. After Gore made a passionate speech to a New York City audience in January 2005, a congressional leader mocked him by saying to a reporter, "Tell Al it's cold outside." Two years later, Gore won an Oscar and an Emmy, and he shared the Nobel Peace Prize; he now commands audiences of thousands around the world.

Americans are also voting with their checkbooks. In 2007, sales of hybrid vehicles increased by 38 percent, while total light-duty vehicle sales fell by 2.5 percent. In May 2008, record-high oil prices led cars to outpace pickup trucks as America's top-selling vehicles for the first time since 1992. A month later, General Motors announced that it would close four factories that make trucks and SUVs. Consumers can find smart replacements for almost any product, from energy-efficient refrigerators to superinsulated windows. One Web site, www.18seconds.org, counts the number of compact fluorescent light bulbs sold since January 1, 2007, tallying the coal not burned and pounds of CO_2 emissions prevented as a result of replacing incandescent bulbs with compact fluorescents. By June 2008, the site showed that more than 160 million bulbs had been purchased, saving an estimated 16.9 billion pounds of coal and more than 72 billion pounds of CO_2.

As Americans begin to take steps against climate change, polling shows that a solid majority of 60 percent believe that "we must take action now or it will be too late to stop it." Nearly three quarters of all Americans support moving away from oil and coal in favor of clean-energy sources. You might think that such a groundswell would prompt corporate and political leaders to take action. Businesses even have a saying for it: "The customer is always right." But there is a game being played. Business and political leaders love to paint themselves as environmental champions, but too few of them take meaningful action.

General Electric's "Ecomagination," for example, promises to "imagine and build innovative solutions that benefit our customers and society at large." Thanks to its purchase of Enron Wind at a bankruptcy auction in 2002, GE is the largest manufacturer of wind turbines in the country. How ironic, then, that GE is also one of the largest financiers of dirty energy and a leading manufacturer of massive turbines for coal-fired power plants, which warm the planet more than any other source of electricity.

Ford Motor Company's ads tout the firm's "Bold Moves," and its chairman gives speeches about his lofty environmental goals. What the company doesn't talk about, however, is that Ford's fuel economy has been below the industry norm for thirty-three consecutive years, and that its overall fleet averages fewer miles per gallon than the Model-T more than eighty years ago. Bold, indeed!

Corporate leaders aren't the only ones standing in the way of progress, however. In late May 2007, I attended an all-day hearing at the Environmental Protection Agency's (EPA) state headquarters in Sacramento, California. At issue was whether the agency would allow California to implement regulations it had finalized in 2004 to reduce greenhouse gas emissions from vehicles. The regulations required automakers to reduce greenhouse gas emissions by about 30 percent by 2016. More than a dozen other states subsequently adopted this standard, the most aggressive in the country.

The Bush administration opposed the state's law. It took the EPA a full eighteen months to even schedule a hearing on the issue, rousing the ire of political leaders on both sides of the aisle. Republican governors Arnold Schwarzenegger of California and Jodi Rell of Connecticut (which had followed California's lead on the legislation) placed an op-ed in the *Washington Post* the week before the hearing. "It's bad enough that the federal government has yet to take the threat of global warming seriously," they said. "But it borders on malfeasance for it to block the efforts of states such as California and Connecticut that are trying to protect the public's health and welfare."

This was truly an odd moment for California. The state had a law that united most of the business community. It would reduce vehicle exhaust, improve residents' health, save consumers' money, and cut greenhouse gas emissions. It was bipartisan and would reduce our dependence on oil and help the economy. Yet the only federal agency explicitly charged with protecting the environment was throwing up one roadblock after another.

More than fifty people—scientists, academics, business and political leaders—testified that day in favor of cleaner air. Two individuals (both representing the auto industry) testified in opposition. By the time it was my turn, it was clear that the panel had heard enough hard science and statistics for the day. I tried a direct approach.

I told the panel that, as the parent of a toddler, I was concerned about the world that today's children would inherit. By the time my daughter graduates from high school, up to 70 percent of coral reefs could be destroyed, unless we take strong action. By the time my daughter is in her midtwenties, up to a quarter billion people in Asia and Africa could face severe, life-threatening water shortages. When she reaches her midforties, more than 80 percent of all species in the Amazon would be threatened with extinction—all due to climate change. "How much more evidence do we need before taking action?" I asked. I urged the panel to stand up for what every person in the room knew was right.

As it turns out, the EPA leaders were unwilling to allow a state to limit its own pollution. In late December 2007, the Bush administration ruled in favor of the automakers, ignoring even the recommendations of EPA staff, one of whom told a reporter, "the most appropriate action is to approve the waiver."

Our failure to secure energy independence is not a partisan issue. Under the last several administrations, with both Democrat- and Republican-controlled Congresses, our reliance on dirty energy has grown. America has fought wars for oil. Coal companies are blasting apart entire mountains in Appalachia for "cheap" energy. Congress allows oil companies to gouge Americans at the pump but awards billions in annual subsidies to those same companies. And every year, the planet gets hotter.

The famed abolitionist and statesman Frederick Douglass once said, "Power concedes nothing without a demand. It never did, and it never will." It's time for a national intervention, because although many Americans are working individually to break our addiction to oil and coal, our business and political leaders are keeping us hooked.

Why We're Hooked

One reason it's hard to think about breaking our addiction to oil and coal is that we Americans owe our contemporary lifestyle to the ingenious ways both substances have been used. Let's face facts: without coal and oil, we wouldn't enjoy the conveniences that many of us take for granted. We mustn't overlook the determination and creativity of the engineers, entrepreneurs, and most of all, laborers who have helped raise the quality of life for millions of Americans.

Coal powered the Watt steam engine, which helped launch the industrial revolution. The discovery of oil in Titusville, Pennsylvania, in 1859 brought light and heat into homes and eventually allowed people to drive from one end of the continent to the other. Both fossil fuels were present in seemingly boundless quantities, could be transported cheaply, and most importantly, could easily ignite. Today, nearly half of our electricity comes from coal, while oil is used for everything from pharmaceuticals and plastics to fertilizer, cosmetics, and about 97 percent of our transportation fuels.

Times have changed, however, and the costs of our fossil-fuel habit cast a huge and spreading shadow on the benefits. Coal is the world's biggest and fastest-growing source of greenhouse gas emissions. In the United States each year, pollution from coal-fired power plants kills an estimated twenty-four thousand Americans prematurely—more than homicides and AIDS combined—and causes thousands more heart attacks, asthma flare-ups, and respiratory disorders. Strip mining in Appalachia has leveled more than 450 mountains, killing streams, wasting landscapes, and wrecking homes and communities. More than a hundred thousand Americans died mining coal in the last century, and safety violations still abound at underground mines across the country.

America's desperate hunger for oil is one of the largest contributors to the U.S. budget and trade deficits. Oil companies pollute our air and water and gouge Americans at the gas pump. Oil exploitation destroys rainforests and other wild lands, infringes on human rights, subverts democracy, and poisons communities. For decades, our oil dependence has twisted foreign policy, causing the United States to underwrite corrupt and unjust regimes. Saudi Arabia, one of our chief sources of oil, doesn't allow women to drive, vote, or walk in the streets without an escort. Gays are imprisoned and tortured because of their sexual orientation. Its citizens lack real voting rights, its newspapers lack independence, and human rights reformists are often thrown in jail. Yet, under an agreement dating back to 1945, the United States provides military protection for the corrupt Saudi monarchy in exchange for guaranteed access to Saudi oil. What's going on here? Our energy policies should advance American values, not undermine them.

Breaking Our Addiction

Fortunately, change often happens in response to crisis. This is true in evolutionary biology, as species adapt to their environment; it's also true in human relationships. Personally or collectively, we can grow by facing and solving our problems, once we admit that we have them. We actually learn through conflict.

When you think about it, many of us first experience this in our families or close friendships. How many of us have had to personally intervene—sitting down with someone we deeply love and explaining how his or her destructive behavior has hurt him or her and others? Come to think of it, how many of us have *been* sat down by a spouse or partner who said the same thing to us? Be honest now.

It's hard to intervene, and it's even more difficult to be sat down yourself, but when we can take feedback, reflect on it, and change what we do, we become better people. This is true for individuals, for corporations, and for society. We can grow by confronting our problems and trying to solve them.

My own organization, Rainforest Action Network (RAN), has undertaken corporate-size interventions for years. In the late 1990s, RAN led a coalition of organizations that persuaded Home Depot to stop selling wood from endangered forests around the world. It took more than two years to convince Home Depot to change its ways, but to its credit the company made a commitment and has honored it. Today, Home Depot can track nearly every single two-by-four and sheet of plywood from stump to shelf and attest that it didn't come from an endangered forest.

RAN has also pushed other Fortune 500 companies to green their practices, including FedEx Kinko's, Goldman Sachs, Lowe's, Citi, Bank of America, and others. Sometimes it takes just one letter to convince a corporate executive to drive change. One note to Kinko's, for example, convinced the company to prohibit the use of paper made from old-growth forests in its stores.

Other companies require more persuasion. RAN coordinated nearly a thousand protests against Home Depot's old-growth wood sales, placed ads in the *New York Times* and *Atlanta Journal-Constitution*, and worked with shareholder activists and popular groups such as R.E.M. and the Dave Matthews Band to push the company forward. Some CEOs may have to be prodded, but many other executives realize that their customers, shareholders, and employees increasingly do not want to buy from, own, or work for a company that makes its profits from plundering the environment.

Know Your Power

As Americans begin to work collectively to address the challenges posed by climate change, we have momentum on our side. Conditions are perfect for an energy revolution in this country. Melting glaciers, wars in the Middle East, persistently high gas prices, and chronic air pollution should provide ample motivation. If they don't, there's the unhealthy trade deficit and the charges of corruption, cronyism, price gouging, obscene profiteering, and environmental malfeasance leveled against Big Oil and King Coal.

It's also a brave new world for political activism. Paul Hawken, visionary entrepreneur and author of *The Ecology of Commerce* and *Blessed Unrest*, believes that Americans concerned about the environment and social justice are part of the largest, most powerful, and most unified movement in the history of the world (thanks to the Internet). New technology makes it much more difficult for public leaders in the Beltway or the boardroom to escape public scrutiny.

Not long ago, campaigners would have needed to hire a videographer, a translator, and a local guide to document human rights abuses in Nigeria, Indonesia, or Ecuador. It would have taken months to edit the footage and write the report, and tens of thousands, if not hundreds of thousands, of dollars to bring this documentary film to a wide audience. Today, we can ship a video camera anywhere in the world, and with a steady hand and a couple hours of editing time, put a video on YouTube, where it can be watched, for free, by millions.

How far can we go with these new tools and this movement of unprecedented size and connectivity?

We can change the energy pathway for the entire country, that's how far. We can help Detroit and other automakers go emissions-free, or watch them go out of business. We can replace dirty coal with solar, wind, and energy efficiency, using bulldozers not to construct new coal plants but to tear the most polluting ones down. We can take on the agribusiness industry and shine a spotlight on dangerous biofuels, because the world's poor shouldn't have to compete with automobiles for food.

In the late 1800s, the mining industry and railroad barons wrote laws that exploited workers, communities, and our air and water. One hundred years later, some of those laws are still on the books, but we can make new laws and set new standards now for sustainability and justice will that serve us for the next hundred years.

A Deeper Form of Patriotism

Imagine what this country can do if we fully dedicate ourselves to breaking our addiction to fossil fuels. If we become truly determined and fiercely committed, and insist that our leaders do likewise, we can create the clean and socially just economy that we deserve.

Americans' fundamental sense of fairness and justice led us to end slavery, ban child labor, and secure women's right to vote. American ingenuity and determination cured polio worldwide, mapped the human genome, and have put sixty thousand songs and videos in the palms of our hands. We invented jazz, rock and roll, baseball, and the Philly cheesesteak. Our self-reliance and individual sacrifice has, until recently, enabled each generation to do better than the one before it. And this country's historic respect for the messy processes of democracy and peaceful dissent has helped America enact civil rights legislation, promote human rights internationally, and end unjust wars.

How were these things accomplished? Often it was through the work of quiet heroes—ordinary Americans accomplishing extraordinary things. Citizen engagement has brought this country out of its darkest hours and helped us fulfill our promises of justice and equality to millions.

Remember, the Clean Air Act, the Clean Water Act, the Wild and Scenic Rivers Act, and the Environmental Policy Act were all signed by Richard Nixon. Nixon could hardly be accused of being a commie pinko tree-hugging hippie, and it's doubtful that he was a deep ecologist afraid to come out of the closet. He signed those bills because the public pushed him to do so.

It took organizers and committed Americans who believed in these basic ideas and who took action to make the world a better place. Those actions were often simple and mundane activities—talking to neighbors, making phone calls, handing out flyers—but the results changed the country and set an example for the world. Can we do it again?

Coming Clean

No doubt you've been told to change your light bulbs, properly inflate your tires, turn down the thermostat, and vote every year or so. Those are all useful ways to help create a clean-energy future. But they're not nearly enough. Let me be blunt: if we only take individual action and do nothing else to save our climate, we're probably cooked. We need to aim higher by changing corporate America and challenging our political leaders.

Rather than hope that 125 million drivers will each buy the most fuel-efficient car possible, we can work together to convince Detroit to make *all* cars clean, not just a token few. Rather than harangue each of 300 million Americans to buy the best dishwasher, refrigerator, or dryer, we can join forces to set national standards for efficiency so that all appliances, buildings, and factories are as efficient as possible, reducing costs and emissions at the same time.

Coming Clean sets its sights on identifying ways that Americans can work together to achieve big wins that will break our addiction to oil and coal. There are plenty of books that focus on describing the human and ecological costs of fossil fuels or climate change. This is not one of them. There are other excellent books that survey and evaluate the range of technological solutions to our energy crisis. Not this one.

This is a book about action. At its core, *Coming Clean* is inspired by two hopeful notions: that as a society we possess practical and attractive solutions that can replace oil and coal, and that as individuals we possess the ability to work together to improve each other's lives. I'll share enough information in the first two chapters to reveal the true social and environmental costs of dirty energy, without getting bogged down in policy minutiae. The rest of the book is devoted not only to which remedies we can employ most effectively but to how we'll ensure that those solutions are implemented. Each chapter ends with a list of ways to get involved—at home, in the workplace, or as part of a church, community group, or student or other organization.

One of the first things an addict loses is perspective: our leaders have been so fixated for so long on getting access to more oil and coal that they've lost sight of the true costs of our dependency. So the first two chapters of this book reveal those sometimes hidden burdens. "Getting Our Fix" examines how we're invading the last intact forests, deep oceans, and wilderness areas to extract oil at ever greater economic, ecological, and human cost—often to Indigenous peoples. "Smokescreen" explores the misleading claim that coal, our leading source of electricity, can be made clean, and looks at the industry's impacts on Americans from the mountains of West Virginia to the streets of Chicago.

The rest of *Coming Clean* highlights what we need to do to break the hold that oil and coal have on America and the rest of the world. We'll start at the top, showing why we must change the rules in government and on Wall Street. Chapter 3, "Separate Oil and State," shows how the country can declare political independence from Big Oil and King Coal. Chapter 4, "Follow the Money," exposes the cash behind climate change, supplied by corporate banks and the World Bank—and how to redirect it toward a clean-energy future, with success stories of how banks have been pressured to develop smart environmental policies.

Chapters 5, 6, and 7 explore how to retool our national transportation system, which now swallows two-thirds of the oil we use. "Redesigning Mobility" begins on a Japanese bullet train and envisions how a diverse set of transit options will make traveling more fun, efficient, and far better for the climate. "Jump-Start Detroit" shows how individual persistence, technological innovation, and collective action can truly revolutionize the auto industry. "Growing Gas" separates fact from fantasy in the biofuels industry, identifying policies that will allow biofuels to help relieve oil dependence while minimizing their potential for harm.

Moving from fuel to electricity generation, chapters 8 and 9 bring good news about how to accelerate a clean-energy transition. "Greening the Grid" focuses on how solar and wind—the renewables with the most potential to scale up quickly—can start putting coal-fired plants out of business and create new green-collar jobs along the way. "Less Is More" details some of the easiest steps we can take to beat our addiction and save money, by promoting smart policies on energy efficiency.

The last chapter, "Power Shift," begins with a sobering reminder of just how hard the fossil-fuel industries will fight to hold their position, with ad campaigns, lobbying strategies, distortions, and dirty tricks. But the shift is on, and if we act effectively, it cannot be stopped. To fuel your inspiration, I'll offer a glimpse of how thoroughly a clean-energy economy can permeate our lives by the year 2030.

Breaking our addiction to oil and coal is both patriotic and principled. Yet many are losing confidence that we can meet this challenge. The essential purpose of *Coming Clean* is to present evidence that we can and to provide a hopeful, helpful, do-it-yourself guide to making it happen. Big Oil and King Coal may have armies of lobbyists, lawyers, foreign diplomats, and even military advisors, but Americans know that we can do better for ourselves, our country, and our fellow humans. As the writer Arundhati Roy says, "Another world is not only possible, she is on her way. On a quiet day, I can hear her breathing."

CHAPTER 1

Getting Our Fix

The True Cost of America's Oil Habit

*The fact that oil is beginning to get more expensive
more quickly will contribute to the realization of how
dysfunctional our current pattern is. Take the tar sands
of western Canada. For every barrel of oil they extract
there, they have to use enough natural gas to heat a
family's home for four days. And they have to tear up
four tons of landscape, all for one barrel of oil. It is
truly nuts. But you know, junkies find veins in their toes.
It seems reasonable, to them, because they've lost
sight of the rest of their lives.*

—AL GORE

We were a couple hundred feet or so above the canopy in the Ecuadorian Amazon jungle, and I felt the urge to shout—whether with joy or alarm, I wasn't sure. Squeezed into a tiny, four-seat plane, up front with the pilot, I was enthralled by the divine view of a lush green carpet of magnificent forest that extended in every direction as far as the eye could see. Below, the muddy waters of the Rio Bobonaza meandered through the dense rainforest. Soon I'd be digging my feet into the wet soil, smelling the musty rain, and maybe spotting some toucans, macaws, perhaps a king vulture or two.

We had taken off from the town of Shell (this was oil country, after all), and by now not a hint of industrial society could be seen. There was no smog, gridlock, fast food restaurants, or strip malls, only the deep and seemingly impenetrable rainforest. We were flying over the traditional territory of the

Shuar, Achuar, and Kichwa peoples and could occasionally spot signs of their huts and villages from the air. This part of Amazonia is one of the most wondrous and biologically diverse forests on the planet, with thousands of plant and animal species unique to the region, including howler monkeys, pink river dolphins, jaguars, three-toed sloths, parrots, guacamayos, and more.

I looked forward to meeting both the human and wild inhabitants of this captivating landscape, but I found it difficult to fully enjoy the flight—for we weren't here on holiday, but to challenge one of the world's wealthiest and most powerful oil companies. With me in one plane were Bill Twist and Dave Elliot of the Pachamama Alliance, which works to protect Ecuador's rainforests. A second plane carried Hermann Edelmann from Pro-Regenwald, a German environmental group, and Randy Hayes, the founder of my own organization, Rainforest Action Network. We were visiting the Kichwa community at Sarayaku, located deep in the rainforests of southwest Ecuador, near the Peruvian border.

Just after liftoff, as we left the frontier town behind, we passed dozens of bulldozers, tractors, and piles of garbage. Magnificent rainforests were being disfigured by new roads penetrating deeper and deeper into the rainforest—with logging, oil drilling, and other industrial operations soon to follow. Without strong pressure and decisive leadership, these forests and their residents would be sacrificed like so many other parts of the Amazon—all for just a little more wood or oil.

Soon we banked left and followed the path of the river, descending quickly. Within seconds we were under the treetops, then just fifteen feet over the water. I began to shift uncomfortably in my seat: did the pilot forget that we weren't in a float plane? Just as I was about to say something, a turn in the river revealed a dirt runway ahead, beginning right at the river's edge. After an impressively smooth landing, the plane rolled to a stop, and what appeared to be the entire village of several hundred men, women, and children gathered around the plane. They had all come to welcome us.

Sarayaku is ground zero in the Kichwa people's battle to stop a massive oil drilling project within their native territory, led by Burlington Oil Resources, since acquired by Houston-based ConocoPhillips. More than half of the oil Ecuador produces is shipped to the United States, where it meets about 1 percent of U.S. demand. To put this another way, America consumes its daily oil imports from Ecuador in less than twenty minutes. Any oil found in Kichwa territory would be a fraction of that amount.

Our visit, in March 2004, came just weeks after Ecuador's government had threatened to use military force to repress any resistance by the Kichwa, who have always opposed this project. The Kichwa have seen how similar oil projects nearby have introduced deadly new diseases, poisoned water supplies, decimated forests, and divided communities.

Shortly after landing, we all gathered under a thatched canopy, little children smiling shyly behind their parents' legs. One by one, for several hours, elders and other community leaders described how the oil company's plans would threaten their way of life. "You must make this case known," said one of them, Ricardo. "We are a Kichwa people. The jungle is our market. We live and eat off the jungle. We fish here. Our children play in these rivers. In the plane, you saw the river and the beautiful state of our forests. This is our home."

As people who had lived in the region for centuries, the Kichwa were incredulous that their refusal to allow oil drilling was not taken seriously. "We don't want oil, okay?" another leader declared. "We've been saying this for twenty years, but nobody listens. We live in the twenty-first century now, and somebody must know that we have rights that must be respected."

After the meeting, we were led on a tour of the village, past a solar-powered infirmary, two schools, and at the end of the tour, surprisingly, a volleyball court. One hour and buckets of sweat later, our largely California-based crew walked off the court in humbling defeat, much to the delight of our mostly fourteen-year-old opponents.

As I lay under a mosquito tent that night, I thought about how to describe what I'd seen and heard that day to my wife back home in California. We were expecting our first child later that summer, and all day long I had found myself imagining what I'd do if I was a father in the Kichwa community. I'd want to protect my family, that much was clear. No matter where they live, almost all parents share the instinct to do whatever it takes to keep their kids safe. But not all parents face the same challenges. It's one thing to hold your child's hand as you cross the street, or to install safety latches on your kitchen cabinets. It's another thing altogether to stare down an oil company and risk a military invasion.

Americans love an underdog. I think that most of us, if we had the option, would support a peaceful community against a corporate bully or corrupt government every time. But when it comes to energy policy in the United States, we're not given much choice. Americans aren't asked whether it's right to plunder the Amazon—or finance terrorism—to keep our country awash in oil. Instead, politicians mostly cater to the demands of multinational oil corporations and do very little to hold them accountable for damages to the environment or to human dignity. It's clear that our leaders don't usually calculate the true cost of our oil addiction—which is even more expensive than you might think.

The High Price of Peak Oil

Around the globe, conflicts like the one at Sarayaku are becoming more frequent. The reason is simple: the world's appetite for oil continues to grow at the same time as our reserves of easily obtained oil are steadily decreasing. As a result, oil companies are digging deeper and reaching farther into previously untouched areas to find every remaining pocket of oil. Increasing oil consumption by China and India heightens this tension even further.

Unless we change course, the trends are not in our favor. Global oil consumption is projected to increase from 86 million barrels of oil per day in 2007 to 118 million barrels of oil daily in 2030. As we seek to burn more and more oil, many geologists and other experts believe that, very soon, less and less of it will be produced each year. If this occurs without planning for how to equitably distribute a dwindling resource—and without a crash program to implement oil-free solutions—we'll be in a world of hurt. This is the threat of "peak oil."

Peak oil theorists are like global-warming scientists: ridiculed at first, then politely dismissed, they now see their viewpoints gaining traction. The intellectual ancestor of today's peak-oil scientists is M. King Hubbert, a geologist and petroleum engineer who shocked the industry with his prediction in 1956 of a pending decline in U.S. oil production. Hubbert worked for Royal Dutch Shell for thirty years, later teaching at Stanford University and University of California, Berkeley, and putting in time at the U.S. Geological Survey (USGS).

Hubbert developed an analysis that showed how the growth and decline of oil production in a nation would be like that of an individual oil well. He surmised that the discovery of new oil would rise, peak, and fall in a roughly bell-shaped curve, and that a nation's actual production of oil would follow a similar pattern approximately forty years later.

At the time of Hubbert's prediction in 1956, the United States was the largest oil producer in the world. Observing that American oil discoveries reached their zenith in 1930, Hubbert estimated that U.S. oil production would peak around 1970, then gradually fall. And that's exactly what happened. U.S. oil production topped out at 9.6 million barrels per day in 1970, and has since declined to barely more than 5 million barrels per day, despite advanced engineering and state-of-the-art recovery techniques.

Noting how global oil discoveries peaked in the mid-1960s, and citing a bevy of other statistics, many experts foresee a similar growth-peak-decline curve for oil production globally. They include Kenneth Deffeyes, a Shell oil man and professor emeritus from Princeton University; Dr. Colin Campbell, a geologist who has worked for Amoco, Fina, BP, Chevron-Texaco, Shell, and Exxon, and who founded the Oil Depletion Analysis Centre in London; and Matthew Simmons, a Texas businessman and energy expert.

These experts believe, with little variation, that global peak oil production has either just occurred or will occur within the next several years. Deffeyes takes a whimsical but reflective view, writing, "I nominate Thanksgiving Day, November 24, 2005 as World Oil Peak Day. . . . We can pause and give thanks for the years from 1901 to 2005 when abundant oil and natural gas fueled enormous changes in our society. At the same time, we have to face up to reality: World oil production is going to decline, slowly at first, and then more rapidly."

Peak-oil theorists use several arguments. They begin with hard evidence, showing that for the past twenty to twenty-five years the world has been consuming oil far faster than it has been discovering it, thus depleting reserves more quickly than they can be replaced. Oil production has either leveled off or begun to decline in fifty-four of the world's largest sixty-five oil-producing countries. Many of the remaining countries, such as Saudi Arabia, Libya, and Iran, closely guard their data about remaining oil supplies. The lack of independent verification and transparency means that we simply don't know how much oil remains under their control.

Others are skeptical that the world will reach peak oil production any time soon. They profess faith that the industry will always discover new technologies, efficiencies, and ways to drill profitably, particularly if oil prices remain high. "This is not the first time that the world has 'run out of oil.' It's more like the fifth," scoffs Daniel Yergin, author of the Pulitzer Prize–winning book *The Prize: The Epic Quest for Oil, Money, and Power,* and chairman of Cambridge Energy Research Associates. This is a fair comment. The decline of oil production has indeed been prophesied since soon after the first commercial oil well was established in Titusville, Pennsylvania, in 1859, and plenty of times since then.

However, in a telling sign of the scarcity of conventional oil sources, the oil industry itself has cut its investment in exploring new oil sources. In the last decade alone, the share of major oil companies' exploration and production budget that has gone to exploration has declined from 30 to only 12 percent—most likely because oil executives know that most of the large reserves that can be profitably exploited have already been discovered. "Despite the fact that we're in the highest oil-price era, the level of exploration is not increasing," notes Michael Rodgers, senior director at PFC Energy. "The reason . . . is that, in so many regions of the world, the fields have gotten so small that even though you might be able to drill a well and get a positive rate of return, the incremental value doesn't mean a lot." But there are plenty of places, like Sarayaku, already explored and targeted, and clearly worth the effort to the companies seeking oil there. And as product gets scarcer and prices rise still more, the cost-value equation could shift again.

Deffeyes points out, too, that though U.S. refineries have been running at close to capacity for years, no new refineries have been built since 1976. "Oil tanker ships are fully booked," he adds, "but outdated tankers are being retired faster than new ones are being built." Sadad al-Huseini, the former head of exploration and production for Saudi Aramco, the national oil company of Saudi Arabia, says that global oil production likely reached its peak in 2006.

While it's debatable whether we've reached peak production, there's no question about the problems that will ensue when oil supplies do start to decline. Gasoline prices will rise, affecting working families and truckers in particular, as well as airlines and other sectors across the economy. Tens of billions more will be spent each year on military operations to safeguard access to oil in the Middle East, Latin America, and across Asia. Wars for oil will become more frequent, and may drag on for years. Human rights, human health, protection of wilderness areas, and other environmental concerns will be subordinated to meet America's energy demand. Wait—you think this is already happening? Imagine what will take place when less and less oil is available each year. And then consider a future in which China's and India's levels of oil consumption approach our own.

Whether peak oil is imminent or a few decades away shouldn't make much difference in how we respond to the threat. Oil is a finite resource. For every barrel of oil we discover, we now consume three, and global demand is expected to increase nearly 40 percent in the next few decades. You don't need to be a math expert to calculate that trouble lies ahead. Given this reality, it's not surprising that some policymakers are seeking to exploit parks and wilderness areas or to cut deals with unsavory governments to get access to every puddle of oil available. But like a junkie searching for veins in his toes, this irrational and desperate scramble for oil is corrupting the idea of what it means to be an American. Trying to drill our way out of our oil addiction could end up costing us not just our economic future but our souls.

> **Pass It On**
>
> For every barrel of oil discovered, we now consume three. Production has leveled off or declined in fifty-four of the largest sixty-five oil-producing countries, yet oil demand is expected to soar by nearly 40 percent in coming decades. Welcome to peak oil.

The Arctic Oil Equation

Consider the long-running debate over the Arctic National Wildlife Refuge (ANWR), the Alaskan wilderness area that is sacred to the native Gwich'in people and is a wildlife haven for caribou, grizzly bears, arctic wolves, and other species. Teams of corporate lawyers and oil-friendly officials have struggled mightily to drill in the region, while opposing lawyers and other passionate citizens are equally determined to keep the refuge pristine. As in the Amazon, the social and environmental costs of oil extraction in the Arctic are enormous compared to the actual benefit to society.

Ninety-five percent of all known oil reserves in Alaska have already been made available for exploration and production. Seeking access to the last remaining protected areas, drilling advocates argue that any incursion will impact only a tiny portion of the Arctic Refuge, as little as two thousand acres. This is, at best, misleading. Geological surveys indicate that oil in the Arctic Refuge, rather than being concentrated in one major field, may be scattered in thirty or more small deposits. And since the potential oil fields are more than thirty miles from the nearest pipeline and more than fifty miles from the nearest road, exporting oil from the refuge would require significant investments in new infrastructure across the melting landscape.

To actually produce this oil, proponents would have to defeat strong opposition in Congress, which has blocked repeated back-door attempts to attach drilling proposals to unrelated defense and budget bills. The oil industry would then have to overcome persistent legal challenges from environmental groups and indigenous communities. If exploration did proceed, thirty-two-ton "thumper trucks" would traverse the sensitive wildlands, sending jolts of seismic waves underground. In their wake, bulldozers and large rigs would roam over the delicate tundra, drilling exploratory and production wells throughout the refuge. Several dozen oil fields would need to be constructed, plus numerous airstrips, gravel mines, water reservoir excavations, water withdrawal sites, seawater treatment plants, utility lines, loading docks, dormitories, and garbage dumps across the landscape.

In addition, several hundred miles of seismic exploration trails and ice roads would have to be built, as well as countless more miles of pipelines and other access roads. Eventually the oil would be shipped to Prudhoe Bay and travel through the eight-hundred-mile Trans-Alaska Pipeline System to Valdez, to be loaded onto oil tankers that must navigate the rocky shoals of once-pristine Prince William Sound (where the *Exxon Valdez* ran aground in 1989) to ports in the Lower 48. Analysts estimate it would take at least ten years for the first drops of oil to reach our gas tanks. All this for much less oil than the United States consumes in a year.

Tar Sands: America's Next Tank of Gas?

If drilling efforts in the Amazon and the Arctic illustrate the high social and environmental risks that are incurred to produce small amounts of oil, the development of oily tar sands in the Canadian province of Alberta presents entirely different challenges. Everything about Canada's tar sands industry, from the size of its reserves to its impacts on human health and the environment, is extreme. Those reserves are large enough to potentially meet a portion of U.S. oil demand for years to come, which is a frightening prospect if you care about clean air and water and a stable climate.

"I've lived in Fort Chipewayn most of my life," recalls Allan Adam, chief of the Athabasca Chipewayn First Nation (ACFN), a native community of Alberta's boreal forests. "When we were kids, we were living out in the bush. My father taught us how to hunt, and my mother taught us how to dry meat and fish. We used to drink right from the Athabasca River."

But this was before the oil industry arrived to convert Canada's vast tar sands into a source of fuel. "We can't drink fresh water any longer. We have to bring it from the treatment plant. They say it's good for us, but we know better. Too many people here (in the communities at Fort Chipewayn and Fort McMurray) are getting sick—and it's because our water is being poisoned," Adam explains.

Residents of Fort Chipewayn, a town of about twelve hundred people, have been afflicted with an unusually high rate of debilitating illnesses, including rare cancers, lupus, leukemia, lymphomas, and autoimmune diseases. The region's former medical examiner, Dr. John O'Connor, has called for epidemiological studies to be completed before more permits to develop tar sands are approved, urging that such studies be started as quickly as possible. "For years the community has believed that there's lots of cancer," says Donna Cyprien, a local health director. "When they drank from the water, there was an oily scum around the cup. We now know there is something wrong." "The river used to be blue. Now it's brown. Nobody can fish or drink from it. The air is bad. This has all happened so fast," says Elsie Fabian, an elder in the native community.

Underlying the northeastern part of Alberta, Canada's tar sands cover an area larger than the state of Florida. They're quite different from a conventional oil site such as in Texas or Saudi Arabia, where the liquid oil flows easily when drilled. Here the "oil" is a thick, heavy substance called bitumen, mixed with dirt, rock, and minerals beneath the surface. The processes of mining and refining bitumen, which is then converted into oil for fuel, create waste and pollution on a scale that boggles the mind.

For every barrel of oil refined from Alberta's tar sands, four tons of dirt, rock, and bitumen must be dug up, producing enough waste to fill Yankee Stadium every two days. The mining, refining, and transport of tar sands oil is also extremely energy intensive, and thus a huge climate risk, producing almost three times as much greenhouse gases as conventional oil sources. In recent years, development of the tar sands is the largest contributor to the growth of climate-change pollution in Canada.

Approximately 20 percent of the bitumen can be excavated using strip mines, one of which, operated by Syncrude, is already the largest strip mine in the world. Another will soon be six miles in diameter. Dozens more strip mines are planned for the region.

The other 80 percent of the bitumen lies too deep for strip mining. At these sites, massive quantities of natural gas are piped in to produce steam, which is injected into the ground to heat up the bitumen and liquefy it so that it can be drilled. The process is highly inefficient: for every three barrels of oil produced, the energy equivalent of one is consumed in the process. Within the next few years, tar sands oil production will consume enough gas each year to heat every home in Canada. As Eric Reguly commented in the Canadian newspaper *Globe and Mail*, "Burning a clean fuel to make a dirty fuel is a kind of reverse alchemy, like turning gold into lead. It also leaves less gas for more sensible uses, like making electricity or heating your home."

Many who question the wisdom of mining tar sands look for justice to the United States, Canada's largest oil customer. Fed by ever-increasing U.S. oil demand, the production of oil from Alberta's tar sands has skyrocketed. At the end of 2007, about 1.3 million barrels of oil were produced each day. Expansion plans would bring production to over 2 million barrels per day by 2010, and nearly 3 million daily by 2015.

All that natural gas needed to produce oil from tar sands has to come from somewhere. To increase the flow of gas, Exxon, Shell, and others have proposed building the MacKenzie Gas Project, a 758-mile pipeline from the Arctic to eastern Alberta—much of it along the wild and scenic Mackenzie River. The Mackenzie Valley is part of the Canadian boreal forest, one of the largest intact forest ecosystems in the world, hosting healthy populations of grizzly bears, caribou, and millions of migratory birds.

The pipeline also would bisect the territory of the Dehcho First Nation, an indigenous community that has fought the proposal for decades. "People think of a pipeline like a garden hose in your yard," says Dehcho grand chief Herb Norwegian. "But a pipeline of this magnitude is like building a China Wall right down the valley, and the effects will be there forever and ever."

Furthermore, oil production in the tar sands is extremely water intensive, using from two to five barrels of water for each barrel of oil produced. Every year, up to 349 million feet of cubic water is allowed to be diverted from the Athabasca River in Alberta—more than twice the amount of water used each year by the residents of Calgary, Canada's third largest city. Mining tar sands depletes local freshwater aquifers, drains wetlands and muskegs, and produces massive amounts of waste associated with water treatment. Although oil companies are required to attempt to restore these natural systems, none has done so in nearly forty years of development. Much of the waste is sent to poisonous tailings ponds, many of them so large that they can be seen from outer space.

In September 2006, Chief Norwegian helped form the Keepers of the Water Coalition, an alliance of two dozen First Nations and other concerned citizens whose water is being poisoned and territories destroyed. The Keepers declaration stated, "Water is a sacred gift, an essential element that sustains and connects all life. It is not a commodity to be bought or sold. All people share an obligation to cooperate to ensure that water in all of its forms is protected and conserved with regard to the needs of all living things today and for future generations tomorrow."

They are resisting powerful forces, though. The province of Alberta and the federal government hope to increase production to 5 to 6 million barrels of oil per day by 2030, and several energy analysts predict that output could reach as high as 11 million barrels per day by 2047. To bring in still more natural gas and to export the oil that expanded tar sands would produce, another pipeline has been proposed, this one cutting through temperate rainforests in British Columbia's Great Bear Rainforest. Fifty-two angry First Nations communities along the coast have already sued to stop the plan.

Allan Adam views all this with a historical perspective. "We have all this oil in our back yard, yet there's no benefits coming to our community and our people are still being neglected. Not only that, but cancer rates have skyrocketed. It's not going to get better. It's just going to keep getting worse. People around here say that the oil industry is just the twenty-first-century version of General Custer. They're here to finish the job of what's been done to Indigenous people all over the continent."

The Bucket Stops Here

The problems associated with oil use—from extraction to combustion—aren't limited to other countries. America's dependence on oil is poisoning its own citizens. Federal officials estimate that approximately 90 million Americans live within thirty miles of one of the nation's 153 oil refineries. These refineries release millions of pounds of benzene, butadiene, formaldehyde, and other cancer-causing chemicals, as well as particulate matter, nickel, lead, sulfur dioxide, nitrogen oxides, and other pollutants linked to heart disease, severe asthma, and other respiratory ailments.

Although these refineries are subject to the Clean Air Act, enforcement has been, shall we say, lax. An investigative report by the Ecological Integrity Project and the Houston Galveston Association for Smog Prevention found that the U.S. EPA and state

Pass It On

In the United States, more than 90 million Americans live near oil refineries that release millions of pounds of cancer-causing chemicals, particulate matter, and other pollutants into the air each year.

governments routinely underreport toxic air emissions, and that the presence of certain cancer-causing chemicals in the air may be four to five times higher than what the EPA reports to the public.

More than half of the nation's refineries are located in Texas and Louisiana, including nine of the top ten carcinogen emitters. There and elsewhere around the country, refineries are often located in low-income communities and communities of color. In Port Arthur, Texas, dangerously high levels of ozone and benzene have been reported. Yet public officials often side with industry. Here's one uplifting statement: "This city is not going to change. It is a refinery town—tomorrow, next year, a hundred years from now. It will always be a petrochemical area," says Oscar Ortiz, the town's former mayor. Asked about the health impacts from the refineries' pollution, Ortiz replied, "We've all got to die of something."

Increasingly, communities are fighting back with an unlikely weapon: the humble, everyday, five-gallon bucket. Most people use these buckets as toolboxes, planters, even as makeshift drums on street corners. But more recently they've been put to a new and higher use: holding refinery owners accountable to local communities.

Here's how it works. Before the mid-1990s, residents concerned about releases of dangerous pollutants in their neighborhoods had to rely on costly air-sampling equipment brought in by government agencies to determine what they were breathing. In 1994, ailing citizens living near a Unocal refinery in Rodeo, California, filed a lawsuit to address excessive pollution from the site. Their lead lawyer was Edward Masry, who, along with his colleague Erin Brockovich, would soon be immortalized in an Oscar-winning movie. Masry realized that his clients in Rodeo had no economical way to monitor their air quality, so he hired an environmental engineering firm to design an inexpensive air-sampling device.

The engineers' solution was the five-gallon bucket. For about $75 citizens could draw a "grab sample" of air into a gas-sampling bag, seal it in the bucket, and send it to analysts for testing. Rodeo residents immediately put the buckets to use, and used the data on air quality in negotiations with the company. Two years later, Unocal settled the lawsuit, paying $80 million to the plaintiffs.

Denny Larson was a community organizer at the time. Today he is executive director of Global Community Monitor, an environmental justice organization, and has helped create "bucket brigades" in dozens of U.S. cities and at least nineteen countries around the world. Larson sees the bucket brigades as a key tool for community empowerment. No longer do citizens have to trust refinery operators to volunteer air-pollution data. Nor must they rely on government regulators and local politicians like Mayor Ortiz. Citizens can "use simple but effective and credible testing methods to document their toxic exposure.Armed with that information, they can fight to reduce their exposure to unnecessary pollution from large industrial sources," Larson says.

Dorothy Jenkins of New Sarpy, Louisiana, used the data from a local air sample to confront a manager of Orion Refining. "That was one of the greatest moments of my life," recalls Anne Rolfes, founder and director of the Louisiana Bucket Brigade and a colleague of Jenkins. "He was so smug and rude, insisting that there wasn't a problem, and she just slammed her air sample results down on the table and said, 'Then why did you violate the state benzene standard?'"

"People get so excited when they build the bucket, get the test results, and find out what they're breathing for the first time," Larson says. "Man, when they go after companies and regulators, you'd better not be in their way."

Freedom from Oil

As oil refining further degrades the environmental quality of poor communities, both inside and outside the United States, oil development often makes poor countries even poorer—an effect that Stanford University professor and author Terry Lynn Karl calls the "paradox of plenty." Many poor countries with large oil reserves become dependent on oil to fund their governments and increase public spending rather than developing stable and diversified economies. Increased oil prices create the illusion of prosperity in these countries; actually, they mask deeper troubles and destabilize governments that become too dependent on oil as a primary source of revenue. As a result, developing countries that have significant oil reserves are in worse economic shape than neighboring countries that don't have much oil. A report by Christian Aid states that poor countries dependent on oil revenues have a higher likelihood of "four great and interconnected ills. Oil, in these instances, becomes the key ingredient in a lethal cocktail of: greater poverty for the mass majority of the population, increased corruption, a greater likelihood of war or civil strife, [and] dictatorial or unrepresentative government."

From Alberta to the Amazon to the Arctic, the list goes on. Dependence on oil is causing human rights and environmental integrity to be trampled in Nigeria, Colombia, Burma, and many other countries. It's giving power to tyrants, as multinational oil corporations cozy up to corrupt, oil-rich governments in Sudan, Libya, Uzbekistan, and elsewhere. As the world's largest consumer of oil, the United States bears the greatest responsibility. And as oil grows scarcer, the human, economic, and ecological consequences of our addiction—whether it's a ballooning trade deficit, a destabilized climate, polluted air and water, or human rights violations—will only become more severe.

On the morning I left Sarayaku, as the sun was coming up and the howler monkeys were quieting down, I sat in the village and spoke with several of the Kichwa leaders. One gave me a handmade necklace: a gift, she said, for my pregnant wife. As we walked down to the riverbed where her own children were playing, she told me, "Our people will never be free as long as your country drinks oil like it is water. Until you stop, we will never truly be free."

Based on the most rosy industry forecasts, the oil under Sarayaku would meet U.S. demand for slightly more than a month. To get this oil, the Ecuadorian military would have to invade a peaceful community. Oil companies would threaten the water supply and wildlife upon which the Kichwa have depended for generations, and risk introducing deadly new diseases. If somehow that oil could be drilled profitably in such a hostile environment, oil companies would have to cut a pipeline through miles of pristine rainforest to load the oil onto a tanker for sale in the United States before it is refined into gasoline, belching more pollution into the air. Pumped into American gas tanks, each fifteen gallons would add an additional three hundred pounds of carbon dioxide to the atmosphere.

Here's a better idea: leave the oil there and prevent another community from getting mad at America. It wouldn't be that hard to do. We can easily save more oil than Sarayaku could produce if Congress or the president or any of the major automakers showed some courage and foresight. Just one solution—equipping all new vehicles with hybrid engines and other minor modifications—would save much more oil than we currently import from the entire Persian Gulf.

And we can go much further: by challenging every politician and corporate executive to get serious about climate change and clean energy. Personal responsibility is important—the choices we make about where we live, how we commute and heat our homes, and which vehicles we drive (or don't) can have an impact on how much oil our nation consumes. But the game is rigged, because we aren't given the best choices. Automakers have steadfastly refused to utilize the best technologies to clean up emissions. Airlines are slow to transition to more fuel-efficient models, and our mass transit systems have been underinvested and neglected for decades.

I believe that most Americans are fair-minded and compassionate. If more of us witnessed or understood the harm to families and natural systems that comes from wresting oil from the earth and bringing it to our country, we would demand more and better alternatives from our politicians and CEOs. Our choice is to act now to convert to a clean-energy economy, or to fight over every last barrel of oil that can be found—and suffer the consequences of burning it.

Take Action

Take it personally

1. Do your homework. To learn more about our oil addiction and the real price of oil, check out these books, movies, and Web sites:

   - Daniel Yergin's Pulitzer Prize–winning book *The Prize* is a comprehensive overview of the oil industry's pursuit of power.

   - *Blood and Oil,* by Michael T. Klare, is a perceptive analysis of the consequences of our oil addiction.

   - Stephen Gaghan's film *Syriana* explores power and corruption in Big Oil and the Middle East.

   - Kenneth Deffeyes's *Beyond Oil: The View from Hubbert's Peak* and James Howard Kunstler's *The Long Emergency* unpack the science and challenges of peak oil.

- The Rocky Mountain Institute's **Winning the Oil Endgame** is an optimistic treatise that advances a set of strategic solutions to our oil crisis.

- Visit www.oilwatch.org (Oilwatch), www.amazonwatch.org (Amazon Watch), www.priceofoil.org (Oil Change International), www.ienearth.org (Indigenous Environmental Network), and www.earthrights.org (EarthRights International) for up-to-date information on fights against Big Oil around the world.

2. Know your adversary. Oil companies are the richest corporations in the world, with plenty of spare change to hire the cleverest PR professionals. Visit Chevron's site, www.willyoujoinus.com, where a leading source of greenhouse gas emissions and human rights controversies is attempting to reposition itself as a company that cares. BP has adopted the brand "Beyond Petroleum"; check out its site at www.bp.com to see how one of the world's largest polluters uses an innovative marketing campaign and a small solar acquisition to mask its impacts.

Express yourself

Raise your voice in support of ethical policies that support human and environmental rights:

1. Contact the premier of Alberta, Ed Stelmach (or his successor), and urge him to adopt an immediate moratorium on expansion of Alberta's tar sands.

2. Write or call James Mulva, the current chairman, president, and CEO of ConocoPhillips, urging him to withdraw all plans to drill for oil within Kichwa territory in Ecuador.

3. Write to the CEOs of BP, Chevron, ConocoPhillips, Exxon, Shell, Total, and Occidental—some of the world's largest oil companies—to demand that they stop drilling for oil in endangered ecosystems and accept local communities' right of refusal to reject projects that will harm their health or livelihoods.

4. If you live near an oil refinery (or a coal plant or any other source of industrial pollution), take action to improve health and air quality in your community. You can work with Global Community Monitor, Communities for a Better Environment, and other organizations to hold polluters accountable; see the resources section for more information.

Stay engaged

As you learn more about the costs of our oil dependency, don't stop with one call or letter to a CEO. Stay involved! Suggest this book or others named above to your reading club. Host a movie night to screen **Syriana** or one of the powerful documentaries about oil exploitation, such as **Oil on Ice** (oil in Alaska) and **Crude Impact** (peak oil and the urgent need for action). Urge your family and friends, your employer, church group, or school to take action as well.

To reform the world's the richest and most powerful industry, we'll also need to weaken its control over our government (chapter 3), enlist the support of fossil fuel financiers (chapter 4), and change the industry's biggest markets (starting with the auto industry, chapter 6).

Challenging Big Oil will also require working collectively. Get to know the organizations that work on the issues mentioned in this chapter and support those whose aims and approach best match your interests. In the resources section you'll find an extensive list, along with brief descriptions and Web sites. They range from large, multi-issue environmental groups, like Rainforest Action Network or the Sierra Club, to local grassroots organizations with a tighter focus, like Keepers of the Water, introduced earlier.

CHAPTER 2

Smokescreen

The Dirty Side of "Clean Coal"

*You can fool all the people some of the time, and some
of the people all the time, but you cannot fool all the
people all the time.*

— ABRAHAM LINCOLN

Most Americans have never heard of Larry Gibson or Maria Gunnoe, but both have quickly become heroes of mine. It takes determination to stand up for what's right, but it really takes guts to do so while being violently threatened and harassed.

Gibson is a stout firecracker of a man whose voice shakes with passion when he talks about the coal mining that has been leveling the mountains around his home in West Virginia and throughout much of Appalachia. "I never thought I was poor until I went to the big city, in Cleveland," Gibson says. "Living here we had everything we needed—apple orchards, walnut trees—there were bears in the valleys, berries on the trees, even ginseng on the mountaintops. Now it's all gone."

One hot summer day, I visited Gibson to see what he was talking about. West Virginia boasts some of the country's most picturesque landscapes, from the whitewater rapids in the southeast to the Allegheny Mountains, the Monongahela National Forest, and the Ohio River Valley. Appalachia's forests are famously rich in the range of plant and animal life they support; like parts of central China, they still contain remnants of pre–ice age habitats. Driving the state's back roads, you remember why John Denver began one of his most famous songs, "Almost heaven, West Virginia . . ."

We took a short walk from Gibson's home in the town of Kayford toward the blast zone of a mountaintop-removal mining site. When we got to the edge, I had difficulty accepting what was in plain sight in front of me. I've had the sad experience of seeing plenty of ecological devastation—barren clear-cut forests, bleached and dying coral reefs, toxic waste incinerators, massive oil spills. Yet this scene was so jarring it took my breath away: an entire mountain being methodically blown apart.

Work had been halted for the day. Across the mine's entire thousand-acre expanse, not a single sound could be heard. Where we were standing, the forested ridge that once soared several hundred feet above was now an industrial waste zone that dropped five hundred feet below. All the trees were gone. "Most people think of coal mining as a process of removing coal from underneath a mountain," says Mary Anne Hitt, executive director of Appalachian Voices, a regional environmental organization. "Mountaintop removal entails removing the mountain from the coal."

In the distance, several dozen large piles of dynamite were organized in rows, ready for detonation. Following an explosion, giant bulldozers push what the coal industry calls overburden—trees, soil, rock, everything that isn't coal—over the edge into the valley below, burying the stream that once ran through the valley. Coal mining accounted for 65 percent of all explosives use in the United States in 2006. Throughout Appalachia, explosives can be set off within three hundred feet of a home, and blasting occurs all day, often seven days a week. The stories of what local residents have to endure will break your heart.

Pass It On

Coal mining accounted for 65 percent of all explosives use in the United States in 2006. Throughout Appalachia, explosives can be set off within three hundred feet of a home, and blasting occurs all day, often seven days a week.

As reported in the *Washington Post,* on the evening of August 19, 2004, Dennis Davidson came home from work as an inventory clerk and played catch in his family's front yard in Inman Hollow, Virginia, with his two sons, three-year-old Jeremy and six-year-old Zachery. His wife, Cindy, made dinner inside. After dinner, young Jeremy was so worn out that he crawled into his mother's lap, fell asleep, and was soon tucked into bed. At about 2:30 in the morning, a mining crew was working just 650 feet uphill from the Davidsons' home, leveling a road from the nearby strip mine to a coal-processing plant. A bulldozer operator dislodged a thousand-pound boulder and sent it careening down the hillside, directly into the house. The boulder tore through a bedroom wall, crashed through a closet, and came to rest at the foot of Zachery's bed. Zachery was scared but unhurt. His younger brother Jeremy was crushed instantly.

The scale and impact of mountaintop mining are terrible, yet many Americans don't even know about it. Mountaintop-removal coal mining has been described by opponents as "strip mining on steroids." The mines are located throughout West Virginia, eastern Kentucky and Tennessee, parts of western Virginia, and more recently, Maryland. In excess of 450 mountains have been leveled throughout Appalachia in just the last two decades. In that same period, more than seven hundred miles of rivers and streams have been completely buried. "The individual and cumulative impacts to both aquatic and terrestrial ecosystems are unprecedented," the U.S. Fish and Wildlife Service's West Virginia field office concluded in its September 2001 report.

Dynamite blasts routinely rattle the windows in Gibson's home. Unwilling to sell his land to coal companies, he's also been the victim of persistent harassment and intimidation. Gibson has been threatened, shot at, and had his car run off the road. His small home is now guarded by security cameras on the roof and on trees in his yard. One of his dogs was shot, and another escaped an attempted hanging. But Gibson grew up there, and he isn't leaving.

"What do you hold so dear in your own life that you won't put a price on it?" Gibson asks. "And when somebody comes to take it, what will you do? For me, it's this mountain and the memories I had here as a kid. I'm fighting for my life here, and I will never give up."

Gibson's not alone. An hour away in Bob White, West Virginia, I sat on the front porch of Maria Gunnoe's home as she described the horrors of mountaintop-removal mining operations directly to the east, south, and west of her home. The entire region is facing an onslaught of air and water contamination, landscape scars, mudslides, and floods from coal mining and processing. Since mountaintop mining began near her home several years ago, seven floods have ripped through her farm, destroying her barn and the bridge that connects to her property. Waste from the mining operation washes through the creeks in front of and behind her home, poisoning the water and soil.

"My family first settled this area over three hundred years ago. My grandparents lived right here. I was raised in this house," Gunnoe says. "We used to have the most beautiful garden over there, with the richest soil—up to your elbows! It's poisoned now. The well water is ruined, too. Ten coal trains pass by this house every day, and the blasting up in the mountains goes from daylight till dark."

Gunnoe has been fighting back, organizing with the Ohio Valley Environmental Coalition to stop the mountaintop mining around her home and throughout the region. "In doing this, I've had a little bit of everything done to me," she says. "I've been accused of all kinds of stuff. I've had sand put in my gas tank—it cost $1,200 to keep my truck on the road. Teachers make comments to my kids. It's not their place to tell my children that their water isn't poisoned by coal, when my children know they can't drink their water. I've had my tires cut, my dog shot. People spit on my truck all the time—big, gross tobacco juice spit. One of my dogs was shot and left in the parking lot where my kids catch the school bus.

"One thing about West Virginia people is, we're not the kind to give up and walk away. If we was the kind to give up and walk away, we would never have settled this area years and years ago. Because this was a very rough terrain—a very rough life here. But people loved it—people like my great-grandmother, people like my grandfather before me. They loved this land and tended this land. It's land that wasn't meant to be developed. It's a special land. God put it way up high so they'd leave it alone. I've had people tell me that God put the coal there for us to mine. I have to disagree with that. He buried it because it's so doggone nasty!"

I asked Gunnoe what she thought of "clean coal." Her jaw clenched. "Clean coal is the biggest lie that coal companies and the United States government have ever created. There's no such thing as clean coal. The two words together quite honestly anger me." She paused. "Wow—how can you steal a life from a family and clean it up? How can you rob people of who they are and where they are, and make that look like it's clean in any sense?"

The Seductive Myth of Clean Coal

The term *clean coal* has been used to describe a variety of industrial processes, everything from installing scrubbers mandated by law to making minor improvements in coal processing or burning techniques. Most commonly, "clean coal" describes a series of methods—most of which are in the small-scale, experimental stage—that attempt to reduce greenhouse gas emissions.

Here's the industry's theory: As coal is burned, carbon dioxide gas would be removed, either mechanically or through chemical processes. The gas would then be compressed and pressurized until it became a liquid with a consistency similar to oil. Then it would be sent through pipelines to carefully selected geologic sites and injected into the ground. If these potent greenhouse gases were held underground permanently, they wouldn't wreak havoc on the earth's climate.

But when you hear coal advocates describe "clean coal" as a way to fight climate change, put your BS detector on alert. The dirty secret of "clean coal" is that, after more than twenty years of government and industry research and billions in subsidies, not a single coal plant in the world can be called clean.

Pass It On

After years of research and billions in subsidies, not a single coal plant has ever effectively captured and stored all of its greenhouse gases.

Not a single power plant has ever captured all of its carbon dioxide emissions, much less compressed the carbon and stuffed it underground.

Moreover, the "clean coal" techniques that industry is talking about do not address most other forms of air and water pollution. They do not give the millions of Americans living near coal-fired power plants their basic human right to clean air and safe water.

They do not stop mountaintop removal and other unsafe and destructive forms of coal mining, nor do they prevent the creation of millions of tons of toxic waste.

And "clean coal" certainly does not address the steady decline of well-paying union jobs, nor the coal-mining industry's atrocious health and safety record. From 1985 to 2005, coal-mine production increased by 28 percent, while the number of coal-mining jobs decreased by 44 percent in that same period. In the coal fields I visited in West Virginia, many of the mountaintop-removal mining jobs were nonunion, paying significantly less than comparable union jobs. Meanwhile, more than a hundred thousand miners died in coal mines in the twentieth century, including twelve thousand from black lung disease as late as the years from 1992 to 2002.

Coal is also the dirtiest and most carbon-intensive fossil fuel, containing 70 percent more carbon per unit of energy than natural gas. Three tons of carbon dioxide are produced for every ton of coal that is burned. It is the largest and one of the fastest-growing sources of greenhouse gas emissions in the country. As climate change exacerbates droughts across the country, burning coal produces another problem: coal plants use far more water than all other forms of electricity besides nuclear power. If that's not bad enough, consider that the American Lung Association estimates that air pollution from coal-fired power plants kill an estimated twenty-four thousand people prematurely each year.

Despite all of this, industry executives and their political allies are propagating the "clean coal" myth in order to justify the largest proposed expansion of coal-fired power plants in more than half a century. Currently there are more than six hundred U.S. coal plants in operation. In 2007, a Department of Energy study listed 151 new coal plants that had been proposed. As a vision of our energy future, this is moving backward, not forward. As Jeff Goodell observes in *Big Coal: The Dirty Secret behind America's Energy Future*, coal was "supposed to be the engine for the industrial revolution, not the Internet revolution."

There's much at stake. More than a billion tons of coal is mined in the United States each year, producing nearly half our country's electricity. On average, every man, woman, and child in the United States uses about twenty pounds of coal each day. Our heavy reliance on coal to produce power gives the industry plenty of ammunition with which to bring American public opinion into line.

Of course the notion of "clean coal" is tempting. I'd vote for it myself if coal could be made genuinely clean and safe, from the mine to the processing plant to the generating station. But if you clear away the hype it just doesn't add up. "Clean coal" is an oxymoron, like clean dirt or healthy Twinkies. If America bets its energy future on the promise of "clean coal," the worst predictions of climate change are likely to come true. We will also increase the poisons in our water and air, imperil human health and safety, and do further irreparable harm to our natural heritage. Most important, we'll squander the best opportunity this country has ever had to create an energy-efficient economy that uses truly clean power.

Why, then, does "clean coal" have so many powerful and vocal advocates? It boils down to profits, politics, and relentless PR. The U.S. coal lobby is strong and has powerful friends in coal states on both sides of the aisle. This influence allows coal companies to flout safety regulations without fear of large penalties, to circumvent or roll back environmental regulations, and to secure billions of dollars of federal government subsidies. Big Coal has big friends on Wall Street, and in Democratic and Republican Party circles. And if these friends can't help change the dirty realities of the coal industry, they can certainly help polish its image.

Constructing the Lie

Coal-industry executives know how to go on the offensive when threatened. The industry has had to fight to maintain its market share and viability through much of the twentieth century, as coal was replaced, first by oil as a fuel for transportation, then by both oil and natural gas as a primary heating fuel.

Now coal competes with natural gas and renewables to generate electricity. As environmental health concerns have gained in prominence and climate change has become a national priority, threats to the coal industry's dominance have intensified.

In defense of Big Coal, an industry group called Americans for Balanced Energy Choices launched a new marketing campaign in 2004. On the group's Web site, an irrepressible twelve-year-old skateboarder in baggy pants extolled the wonders of the coal industry. It also commissioned a series of ads for its site, featuring a collection of cute kids as the coal industry's mouthpiece. In one ad, the same skateboarder sat in his room and said, "So my room can get a little dirty, but at least my environment's cleaner." In another, a young student in a lab said, "Kids are just better at technology than their parents. Like, by the time I graduate college, we'll be building clean coal power plants that are pollution-free."

I like a can-do, optimistic story and smart, perky kids as much as the next person. It would be great if somehow coal could be mined cleanly without threatening drinking water for millions. It would be wonderful if conditions were safe, unions restored, and workers paid salaries and benefits commensurate with the risk they take every day. It would be a comfort if coal's neurotoxins were eliminated, and it sure would help if burning coal somehow could not destabilize the planet's climate. While we're at it, it would also be great if babies didn't cry at night and eating ice cream gave us six-pack abs, but wishing things were true doesn't make them so.

The track record of some of the biggest boosters of "clean coal" reveals where the industry's true motivations lie. The president of the coal-friendly public relations firm Policy Communications, Jim Sims, was also director of communications for Dick Cheney's Energy Task Force in 2001. He is the head of the Western Business Roundtable and Partnership for the West, which recently took on the fight to oppose protection of polar bears in the Arctic. Sims keeps busy, also serving as president of Americans for American Energy, an organization that has fought to open up the Arctic National Wildlife Refuge to oil exploration.

Sims has allied with another notorious PR firm, Pac/West Communications, to form the Save Our Species Alliance. Named in Orwellian fashion, the alliance aims to gut the Endangered Species Act to benefit the logging, mining, ranching, and drilling industries. Pac/West also managed the campaign to promote the Bush administration's "Healthy Forest Restoration Act," which has resulted in extensive damage to the country's national forests. But don't worry; these organizations say they have our planet's best interests at heart.

If cute kids and powerful lobbyists can't sell clean coal, then maybe sex can. General Electric, a leading coal financier and manufacturer of turbines and other equipment for coal-fired power plants, gave pickaxes, miner's helmets, and not too much clothing to some sexy supermodels in a 2005 coal ad. The women in tank tops pose provocatively with jackhammers and drills, as bare-chested men preen under spotlights—while the soundtrack appropriates Merle Travis's classic anticorporate ballad "Sixteen Tons." The voiceover concludes, "Thanks to emissions-reducing technologies from GE Energy, harnessing the power of coal is looking more beautiful every day."

Too Much Hot Air

The central idea behind "clean coal" is that coal could be separated from its carbon dioxide, which could then be stored—forever—safely and effectively underground, where it wouldn't reach the atmosphere and contribute to global warming. The technique is called carbon capture and storage (CCS), carbon sequestration, and other names. My preferred term is "boondoggle." But whatever your preference, "clean coal" is a huge risk, a gamble that we can't afford to make.

Let's start with the promise of capturing carbon. Theoretically, this can be done in one of two ways. In one method, high-tech scrubbers would remove the CO_2 before it is released through a power plant's smokestack. Engineers are experimenting with capturing a portion of a plant's emissions, but to date haven't been able to capture all of even one plant's emissions. Another way to capture carbon is to build a new type of coal plant, called integrated gasification combined cycle (IGCC), in which the coal is refined, then heated and turned into a gas. In an IGCC plant, the CO_2 is removed during the "gasification" process, before the gas is burned and electricity is produced.

Both methods are costly in terms of fuel and funds. Using scrubbers on pulverized-coal plants to capture carbon emissions would increase the cost of electricity generation by 40 to 70 percent, according to the Intergovernmental Panel on Climate Change. (The wide range in cost estimates is attributable to a series of variables associated with the coal plant itself, including its size, overall efficiency, and so on, and also with the carbon-capture process.) According to the same report, an IGCC plant that captured its carbon would increase the cost of power production by 20 to 55 percent, primarily because IGCC plants produce fewer emissions and also require less energy to capture them. IGCC plants are more costly to construct, however.

Much of the increased cost to capture and compress carbon for either the IGCC or traditional coal plants method is due to the additional energy needed to separate and compress the carbon. IGCC plants that capture carbon require 14 to 25 percent more energy. Pulverized coal plants seeking to capture carbon need 24 to 40 percent more power. It's a coal company's dream: we would have to mine, refine, transport, and burn more coal just to create the energy to reduce the greenhouse gas emissions from burning coal in the first place. For every three to six coal plants currently in operation, an entirely new plant would have to be built to supply the extra power needed to capture the plants' carbon.

Just for a moment, let's set those issues aside and suppose that somewhere down the road these problems are solved and carbon can be captured inexpensively. Then the carbon needs to be stored somewhere. Compressed carbon can be shipped by pipeline and injected into either saltwater aquifers, into old oil and gas pits, or under the sea bed. One project in Norway injects approximately one million tons of carbon annually into a depleted oil field under the North Sea. A project in Saskatchewan has stored a total of five million tons of carbon in the past decade. In comparison, a single medium-sized coal plant typically emits about 3 million tons of carbon dioxide into the atmosphere each year.

Burning coal in the United States caused the release of more than 2 billion tons in 2006. If you think "clean coal" has a future in this country, then it would be wise to reflect upon the scale of carbon sequestration that would be required. In *The Future of Coal,* a 2007 analysis from MIT, the authors write,

"If 60 percent of the CO_2 produced from U.S. coal-based power generation were to be captured and compressed to a liquid for geologic sequestration, its volume would about equal the total U.S. oil consumption of 20 million barrels per day."

You read that correctly. To store less than two-thirds of the carbon dioxide produced by U.S. coal plants, we'd need to construct a new set of pipelines and tanker ships and then inject as much carbon into the ground as the amount of oil that is extracted around the world and then burned in America each year.

Again, let's set aside concerns about mountaintop removal and the expense and energy requirements of capturing and compressing carbon from coal plants. Let's also suppose that a new system of pipelines can be constructed around the country to allow the carbon to be transported and injected underground. Then safety issues loom: condensed carbon is buoyant underground and becomes lethal at concentrations of 15 percent or more. At concentrations of 25 percent or more, people can experience convulsions and lose consciousness after just a few breaths. In Cameroon in 1986, a natural release of poisonous CO_2 at Lake Nyos caused the deaths of more than seventeen hundred people.

One wonders who will want to live above these pockets of gas, and who will accept liability once leakages occur. "Clean coal" advocates frequently cite Texas as a location with abundant subterranean real estate, thanks to a century of pumping petroleum. But who would want to live over a carbon sequestration site? And can we trust coal companies or utilities to safely construct and monitor these sites, essentially forever? One coal company alone, Massey Energy, violated the Clean Water Act more than forty-five hundred times between 2000 and 2007. Utilities have resisted regulations that would protect human health and the environment for decades. We'd be smart to question their commitment to safety.

Pass It On

Nationwide, if 60 percent of greenhouse gas emissions were captured from U.S. coal plants, compressed into liquid form, and injected underground, that liquid carbon would equal the total quantity of oil the United States consumes on an annual basis.

Let's review. The coal industry touts "clean coal" as the way of the future, but most of the talk about "clean coal" ignores the damage caused by destructive coal mining and processing. Furthermore, not a single coal plant to date is capturing and sequestering all of its annual greenhouse gas emissions. The process of capturing carbon hasn't been perfected, but if it is, costs are expected to increase by 20 to 70 percent, while also increasing energy use at coal plants by 14 to 40 percent. Meeting the increased energy requirements will in turn cause more air and water pollution and increase demand for coal. The carbon can be compressed and piped to specific sites, but this will add still more costs and require construction of thousands of miles of new pipelines or shipping passages. The carbon can be sequestered underground, but to fully mitigate coal's climate impacts, we'd need to inject into the ground more carbon than the amount of oil that is drilled and extracted for American consumption each year. And if any of the carbon escapes from underground, a person breathing the air could be dead within two minutes.

But if this all works, will coal then be clean? Not even close.

Air America

"Run in place for three minutes," instructs Kidshealth.org. "Then place a straw in your mouth, close your lips around it, and try to breathe in and out—but only through the straw. . . . Now, narrow the straw by pinching it in the middle. That's what it feels like when someone tries to breathe during an asthma flare-up. During a flare-up, the airways narrow and become obstructed, making it difficult for air to move through them. Asthma can be very scary—and when not controlled, it can be life-threatening."

Approximately 20 million Americans suffer from asthma each year, including 6 million children. Asthma leads to 2 million emergency room visits and five thousand deaths each year in the United States. Asthma attacks can be triggered by many things: secondhand smoke, anxiety or excitement, allergic reaction to cats or dogs, mold, and other factors, such as air pollution. The American Lung Association estimates that more than 550,000 asthma attacks, 38,000 heart attacks, and 12,000 hospital admissions due to air pollution from coal-fired power plants help cause 24,000 people to die prematurely in America each year. Those premature deaths are twice as many people as die from traffic accidents each year, and more than half as many as are murdered.

Maureen Damitz works for the Respiratory Health Association of Metropolitan Chicago and is the proud mother of two boys, Jeff and Kyle. Both suffer from asthma. When Jeff, the older, was diagnosed soon after birth, the Damitzes did what many parents of children with asthma do. They educated themselves about how to respond in the event of an attack and took every precaution to prevent such attacks from occurring, by removing curtains and stuffed animals and pulling up the rugs in their Chicago home. "We followed all the rules and did everything we could," Maureen Damitz says. "But we can only do so much. We cleaned up our house, but someone needs to clean the air."

We're not talking just about asthma here. Each year, burning coal to make electricity creates more than 120 million tons of solid waste—about three times the amount of municipal waste produced in the entire country. Coal plants dump more than five dozen different types of hazardous air pollutants, as defined by the EPA, including poisons such as arsenic (100,000 pounds a year), lead (176,000 pounds), and chromium (161,000 pounds). Power plants also emit two-thirds of all sulfur dioxide and 22 percent of nitrogen oxides, which both cause acid rain and a range of respiratory disorders. Coal is also the country's largest source of poisoning from mercury—a potent neurotoxin that can cause severe birth defects, learning disabilities, lowered IQ, convulsions, and even death.

Particulate matter is another danger altogether. Airborne particles invisible to the naked eye burrow into the lungs, where they cause breathing difficulties, lung disease, and even cancer. Smaller particles can do even more damage by entering the bloodstream and contributing to cardiovascular disease. The American Heart Association published a study showing that air pollution can significantly increase the risk of ischemic strokes, which block the flow of blood to the brain and are a leading cause of death in the United States each year.

The burden of this pollution falls disproportionately on poor and minority communities. According to a 2002 report by a coalition of environmental organizations called Clear the Air, 68 percent of African-Americans live within thirty miles of a coal-fired power plant—the distance within which the worst effects of the pollution from a coal plant are expected to occur. The same report shows that 71 percent of African Americans live in counties that violate federal health standards for ozone and particulate pollution.

Chicago, where the Damitzes live, has some of the worst air pollution in the country. The city is ringed by aging coal-fired power plants. A Harvard University study released in 2001 estimated that the nine coal plants in northern Illinois caused three hundred premature deaths and more than fourteen thousand asthma attacks each year. Two of those plants, the Crawford and Fisk Generating Stations, are located within Chicago city limits in lower-income communities with large African-American and Latino populations. They were both built in the late 1950s and do not have the scrubbers or other pollution-control equipment mandated by law since the Clean Air Act was passed in 1970. In 2006, the two plants released more than fourteen thousand tons of sulfur dioxide and nearly four tons of nitrogen oxide.

A coalition of organizations has pushed to have the Crawford, Fisk, and other area coal plants equipped with modern equipment that would reduce their pollution. As a result, Fisk, Crawford, and other plants are due to be modified, but not until as late as 2017. Sam Villasenor, who campaigns for the Little Village Environmental Justice Organization, wants the plants shut down as soon as possible. "These plants should have been updated with scrubbers three decades ago, but they avoided regulation," he says. "Now they want us to be happy because they promise to fix them in ten years? These plants should be shut down now."

No New Coal

Remember those closed-door meetings of Vice President Cheney's Energy Task Force? Well, here's what they were up to. Coal consumption tripled in the United States between 1970 and 2000, and federal policymakers have called for a continued aggressive expansion of coal mining and combustion into the future. The 150 new coal-fired power plants proposed by industry and supported by the Bush-Cheney administration would emit more carbon dioxide than 178 of the world's 186 countries: an estimated 585 million tons every year for perhaps the next half-century. Although more than sixty of these plants were defeated in 2007 and early 2008, most are still on the drawing board, and of those, none would capture and store all of its greenhouse gas emissions. Only a handful will even experiment with this technology.

Perhaps it's time to consider Will Rogers' "first rule of holes": if you find yourself in one, stop digging. The Earth's climate has warmed slightly more than one degree in the past hundred years, and we are already seeing the melting of glaciers and polar ice caps, the warming of the deepest oceans, and species migrating to higher altitudes and latitudes. Severe droughts, severe storms, and severe floods are all increasing. The fourteen warmest years in recorded history have all occurred since 1990. We simply cannot afford an additional 3 million tons of annual greenhouse gas emissions every time a new coal plant goes online. And considering the toxic effects of air and water pollution, as well as the impact that coal mining and processing has on families across the country, isn't it time for at least a moratorium on new coal plants?

James Hansen thinks so. Dr. Hansen is director of NASA's Goddard Institute for Space Studies, an adjunct professor at Columbia University, and perhaps the country's most eminent climatologist. Hansen first drew national attention in a series of briefings and testimonies given to Congress in the late 1980s warning policymakers that the costs of responding to climate change would only increase as time passed. Although Hansen is a government scientist, he has been highly critical of the Bush administration's ideology on climate.

As the climate crisis has deepened, Hansen has become increasingly vocal. In 2006, he warned that humanity had about ten years to address climate change effectively, before feedback loops in natural systems (such as melting ice and thawing permafrost) caused runaway climate change that can't be stopped. In late February 2007, Hansen made a dramatic proposal calling for a complete moratorium on the construction of new coal-fired power plants, at least until carbon sequestration problems could be solved. Hansen further declared that any existing coal plant would need "to be bulldozed" within the next decade or two, if it could not capture and store its carbon in a safe and cost-effective way. Hansen's call for a moratorium has since been joined by dozens of other organizations and has been introduced as legislation in Congress.

It's time to unleash our country's ingenuity and put coal in our rearview mirror. Let's pass the Hansen Plan. Proposed new coal plants have already been rejected in Florida, Arizona, Oklahoma, Kentucky, North Dakota, and elsewhere. In October 2007, the Kansas Department of Health and the Environment became the first governmental agency to cite greenhouse gas emissions as the reason for rejecting an air permit for a proposed plant. This is a great start. We can defeat every proposal in the United States to build new coal-fired power plants.

We shouldn't stop there. As I'll describe in chapter 8, we have a historic opportunity to build a new economy powered by clean energy. If the myriad issues that currently make it hazardous, expensive, and inefficient to capture and store carbon are ever resolved, it's possible that this technology may play a role. A better bet is to retire the country's most polluting coal plants one by one, replace them with clean power and efficiency investments, and rejuvenate our economy in the process.

Consider the Four Corners Power Plant on the Arizona-Nevada border. In 2006 this was ranked top among coal plants in emission of nitrogen oxides, which destroy lung tissue and cause a long list of dangerous cardiovascular effects. The Four Corners Plant is also ranked eighteenth in greenhouse gas emissions among the country's power plants, and was thirty-eighth in mercury poisoning. It's located in a region that is ideally suited for solar energy. Wouldn't a concentrated solar farm paired with an aggressive regionwide program of rooftop solar systems be a better idea? Let's shut this dinosaur down.

How about shuttering the largest greenhouse gas emitter in the country? That's the Robert W. Scherer Power Plant in Georgia, jointly operated by Southern Company and Georgia Power. Retiring this plant and replacing it with renewable energy and aggressive efficiency measures would save 25 million tons of CO_2 annually, using 2006 figures. Southern Company also jointly operates (with Alabama Power) the second-ranked greenhouse gas emitter for 2006, the James H. Miller Jr. Electric Generating Plant in Alabama.

Here are some other coal plants asking to be mothballed:

- Bowen Power Plant: operated by Georgia Power, this was the top-ranked coal plant in sulfur dioxide emissions in 2006. It's also ranked number three in carbon dioxide emissions, and number fourteen for nitrogen oxides.

- Martin Lake Steam Electric Station: operated by Texas Utilities (commonly known as TXU), this plant released more mercury poisoning than any other coal plant in 2006. It was ranked number thirty-two in sulfur dioxide emissions, and number five in carbon dioxide pollution. TXU operates three coal plants that are among the nation's six worst for mercury emissions.

- Sherburne County Generating Plant: operated by Northern States Power Company in northern Minnesota, land of steady winds and community-based energy development. This plant is ranked number thirteen in total carbon dioxide emissions but is ranked number two by emission rate (pounds of CO_2 per megawatt hour). The plant is also ranked number twenty-two in nitrogen oxide emissions.

There are plenty more. If the city of Los Angeles dedicated itself to using electricity more efficiently, it could reduce greenhouse gas emissions as well as the health burden on Utah residents. The city owns the Intermountain Power Plant, which provides much of its power to Southern California but which is located in Utah's Sevier Desert and leaves its pollution in that state. Intermountain ranks among the top twenty polluting power plants in the country for carbon dioxide (number twenty in 2006), and nitrogen oxide (number twelve). In every region of the United States, there are coal plants whose time should be up.

It won't be easy. The coal industry has fought bitter battles against its own workers for more than a century, busting unions and routinely violating safety regulations. For decades, coal executives have defied scientists and citizens demanding clean air and water. The industry's close relationships in the White House, Congress, and statehouses across the country have been used to convince many policymakers that increased coal burning is a responsible energy choice. The myth of "clean coal" is a powerful one, and millions are being spent to sell it to American citizens.

But this emperor is wearing no clothes. We can recognize the myth as a distraction and a tease, and reject it. Even better, we can transition to clean energy sources that don't pollute our air and water and that provide sustainable jobs for working families across the country. We'll stop the expansion of the coal industry and start to downsize it. Big Coal has had a long reign, but it has no further place in a society that values sustainable jobs, clean air and water, and a stable climate.

Take Action

Take it personally

1. Do your homework. Check out these books and movies to learn more about the myth of "clean coal":

   - *Big Coal: The Dirty Secret behind America's Energy Future,* by Jeff Goodell, pays gracious respect for the technical and engineering accomplishments that have kept the lights on, but looks unflinchingly at the high costs of coal's "cheap" price.

   - *Coal: A Human History,* by Barbara Freese, elegantly recounts the story of coal's use from ancient times to today, describing how the mineral has helped and hurt society throughout history.

   - *Who's Got the Power?* a documentary by Casey Coates Danson, compares the benefits of energy efficiency and renewable power with the high cost of coal extraction and combustion.

   - *KilowattOurs,* by filmmaker Jeff Barrie, provides good background on how to promote a clean energy transition.

2. Know your adversary. Big Coal is ruthlessly effective and has hired some of the most talented PR firms in the business. Observe some of the masters of corporate doublespeak at www.americaspower.org. Learn how they deflect criticism, omit key information, and clothe a dirty and deadly industry in a shiny suit of feel-good patriotic optimism.

3. Know your power. Use the EPA's Power Profiler (at www.epa.gov/cleanenergy/energy-and-you/how-clean.html) to determine the energy mix for the power grid in your area. Type in your zip code to find out what percentage of your power comes from coal versus renewables and other power sources.

4. Visit www.ilovemountains.org to watch a Google Earth presentation of mountains that have been leveled throughout Appalachia. Type in your zip code and find out whether the power supplying your home or business was generated by a company that engages in mountaintop removal. You can also find out if your bank is financing destructive mining.

Express yourself

If you read an article or hear a radio broadcast in which someone offers the industry line that coal is being made clean, call or write to set the record straight. If politicians or corporate spokespersons cite the wonders of "clean coal," challenge them. Here are five questions you can ask elected officials:

1. Why do you support proposals for additional coal plants, knowing they will continue to poison our air, water, and families? (You might cite these facts: 6 million U.S. children have asthma; mercury poisoning threatens human health everywhere; coal is the largest source of air pollution and mercury.)

2. Since we know that coal accounts for approximately 40 percent of global greenhouse gas emissions, and is also one of the fastest growing sources of these emissions, is coal really the best investment in our future?

3. The nation's top climate scientist, Dr. James Hansen, has urged a moratorium on new coal development. Will you?

4. As the coal industry becomes more mechanized, well-paying jobs are disappearing, while energy efficiency and renewable energy can create more jobs per kilowatt of electricity. Isn't this a better investment for our economy and our country?

5. How much money have you taken from the coal industry since you entered politics?

Stay engaged

There are plenty of ways you can help make the transition from the dirtiest form of energy to clean, renewable power. Chapters 8 and 9 outline specific actions to advance clean energy and energy efficiency. We also need to support the rights of people whose health and way of life are endangered by mining and burning coal. See the resources section for information about organizations such as Coal River Mountain Watch, Ohio Valley Environmental Coalition, and others that focus on these issues.

CHAPTER 3

Separate Oil and State

Getting Fossilized Power Out of Politics

Sunshine is said to be the best of disinfectants.

— SUPREME COURT JUSTICE LOUIS D. BRANDEIS

I f you're like me, when you learn more about oil drilling in the Arctic, the illusion of "clean coal," or our government's anemic response to climate change, you shake your head and wonder what has happened to our country's leadership. America's energy policies bankroll our enemies, pollute our air and water, and imperil our economy. This is no secret. It's been talked about, debated, dissected, and then largely ignored by the leaders of both parties since the first oil shock in 1973. Every administration and every Congress since then has had the opportunity to break our addiction to dirty energy, but more often than not they end up making it worse.

Take climate change. A major report from the U.K. government concludes that not taking strong action on global warming "could create risks of major disruption of economic and social activity . . . on a scale similar to those associated with the great wars and economic depression of the early 20th century." The world's most respected scientists insist with increasing alarm that by 2050 the world needs to reduce its greenhouse gas emissions by at least 80 percent from 1990 levels to stave off wrenching changes to our planet and our way of life. The U.S. government has responded with policies that encourage more drilling, more mining, more burning, and more pollution. We're running in the wrong direction: total U.S. greenhouse gas emissions have actually increased by more than 17 percent since 1990.

If all it took to make progress were clever speeches, dense policy proposals, press conferences, and pilot projects, we would have licked our addiction to dirty energy years ago. Both Republican and Democratic politicians routinely make happy talk about energy independence and intone gravely on the risks of global climate change, yet very few propose and fight for solutions that match the problem in scale.

If Republicans were serious about these issues, they'd advocate making our economy more efficient, rather than building more coal-fired power plants. And if Democrats were truly committed to breaking our dependence on oil, they wouldn't be coddling an automobile industry in which the former top-selling vehicle, the Ford F-series truck, gets lower gas mileage than the Model T nearly a hundred years ago. The automobile fuel efficiency standards passed by Congress in 2007, hailed as a "breakthrough" by some, will improve gas mileage in America's cars, trucks, and SUVs by an average of less than one mile per gallon until 2020. At that time, we'll reach the fuel efficiency that China's drivers enjoy today. Are you inspired yet?

There's no mystery about what needs to happen to end our fossil-fuel habit, as you'll learn in the chapters that follow. We would save more oil than is rumored to be under the Arctic National Wildlife Refuge by using highly fuel-efficient replacement tires in every new American car, truck, and SUV. We'd save all the oil that America currently imports from the Persian Gulf by putting hybrid engines and other fuel-saving technologies in all our vehicles.

These steps are just a start. When America gets truly serious about creating a new energy economy, our country will restore its reputation for world leadership, clean up its air and water, rejuvenate its manufacturing base, create clean, well-paying jobs, and show that we can do more than just talk about a stable climate and energy independence.

But none of this will happen without political courage. To break free of oil and coal will require that politicians stand up to some of the richest corporations in the world. Large donations and the sophisticated campaign machinery behind the coal and oil lobby make that hard to do, so most politicians attempt to have it both ways—by talking a good game on clean energy, yet voting for only the mildest proposals. Don't let them fool you. Most of our top political leaders are not yet taking energy independence and climate change seriously. If they were, we wouldn't be in the mess we're in today.

Each of the chapters to come suggests specific ways to break our addiction to dirty energy. In the first part of this chapter, we'll explore the relationship between lawmakers and the corporations that earn enormous profits by cooking the planet. In the second half, you'll meet some people who are challenging those cozy ties. If we are serious about coming clean, holding our politicians accountable is a good place to start. Because to get clean energy, we'll need a clean government.

Friends with Money

Do you know why coal companies like Massey Energy can violate the Clean Air Act, Clean Water Act, and other state and federal regulations *thousands of times* and still be allowed to stay in business? Because they've bought friends in Congress—on both sides of the aisle. How do oil companies like Exxon and Chevron pollute our air, water, and climate, yet still get preferential treatment and subsidies? Because they've made large investments in the lucrative field of lawmaking, and they're cashing in.

You would think that an industry as prosperous as Big Oil wouldn't even ask for handouts from the federal government. You also might think that those in government who profess to be fiscally conservative, environmentally responsible, or dedicated to free markets would refuse to fund corporate welfare for dirty energy.

You might even believe that a functioning democracy would call utility owners to task. Utilities and coal companies spend millions on teams of lawyers to delay or avoid compliance with laws and safety standards. Have they forfeited any rights to gifts from American taxpayers? Not exactly.

Executives in the oil and coal sectors are keen, if cynical, observers of the political process; they know the benefits of having good buddies in high places. In 2006 alone, oil companies spent a total of nearly $75 million in lobbying expenses. Chevron spent $7.5 million. Exxon invested $14.5 million. All told, oil companies spent $574 million from 1998 to 2007 on politicians, political parties, and lobbyists, according to the nonprofit organization Center for Responsive Politics. Exxon was the oil industry's top spender in that period, lavishing more than $71 million, but the late Kenneth Lay, former

CEO of now-defunct Enron, might have been the poster child for political cronyism. "Kenny boy," as President George W. Bush was fond of calling him, and his wife gave $882,580 to federal candidates from 1989 to 2001, all but $86,470 of which went to Republicans. Lay personally donated $139,500 to Bush's campaigns for governor and the presidency, gave an additional $100,000 to Bush's inauguration in 2001, and raised at least an additional $100,000 from others for Bush's 2000 presidential campaign, making him a Bush "Pioneer" and one of the president's most valued fundraisers. Other Enron employees also supported Bush, donating $602,000 to Bush's campaigns for governor and the presidency, making the company Bush's top political patron.

Pass It On

From 1998 to 2007, oil companies invested a total of $574 million in lobbyists, politicians, and their political parties at the federal level. Exxon spent the most during this period, $71 million.

These were wise investments. Lay was appointed to the transition team for the Bush administration's Energy Department, helping to appoint two out of five members of the Federal Energy Regulatory Commission. Lay also met four times with Vice President Cheney's Energy Task Force, at one meeting delivering a memo with a series of policy recommendations. A subsequent investigation by Representative Henry Waxman found that "all or significant portions of Enron's recommendations" were adopted in seven of eight policy areas.

On April 17, 2001, Vice President Cheney met with Lay during the California energy crisis. In a memo, Lay advised, "The administration should reject any attempt to re-regulate wholesale power markets by adopting price caps." The next day, Cheney announced that the Bush administration would not support price caps on California's energy prices, a decision that ultimately made billions for Enron at the expense of the state's citizens.

There are plenty of examples of dirty-energy money driving politics. In the 2002, 2004, and 2006 election cycles, the oil industry doled out more than $70 million to politicians, more than 80 percent of which went to Republicans. In mid-2006, the U.S. House and Senate each voted on separate pieces of legislation to weaken the country's long-standing moratorium on oil drilling off America's coastlines. Of the top twenty recipients of oil industry cash in the 2006 election cycle (all of them Republicans), every one of them sided with the oil industry on those votes.

Cronyism and corruption between Big Coal and federal regulators is legendary. It ought to be criminal. Since 2001, mining companies have given more than $180,000 to Kentucky's Republican senator Mitch McConnell, a big friend of the coal industry. Soon after taking office, President Bush appointed McConnell's wife, Elaine Chao, to the post of secretary of labor, the department that oversees the Mine Safety and Health Administration (MSHA). Chao was a Bush Pioneer who raised more than $100,000 for his presidential campaign. Chao's deputy labor secretary, Stephen Law, also helped raise funds for the Republican Party.

One of McConnell's donors is mining executive Bob Murray, CEO of Murray Energy. Murray's company operates the Crandall Canyon mine in Utah, which gained notoriety in 2007 when six miners were killed in a shaft collapse. Another three workers tragically died in a subsequent rescue attempt. Federal inspectors had issued 324 violations at the mine since 2004, including 107 that were "significant and substantial." Meanwhile Murray's Galatia mine in southern Illinois was cited more than twenty-seven hundred times in just two years, and another Murray company—Ken American Resources—and four top managers have been convicted in a federal court of conspiring to violate federal mine safety rules.

Years earlier, in 2002, MSHA officials had brought Murray to the district office in Charleston, West Virginia, to discuss safety concerns. Murray shouted at the table full of MSHA officials, warning that he'd get the inspectors fired. "Mitch McConnell calls me one of the five finest men in America," Murray told the inspectors, "And the last time I checked, he was sleeping with your boss." Murray pointed at two inspectors: "They are gone."

Sure enough, one of the men, Tim Thompson, was soon transferred to a district with no jurisdiction over Murray's mines. He unsuccessfully appealed his transfer for three years before eventually accepting retirement. "The ironic part is, I'm a Republican," Thompson told the *Kentucky Herald-Leader*. "But I don't think you should bring up politics at a meeting like that, involving safety."

Human Resources

One of the most effective ways that fossil-fuel companies influence government is not with cash but by getting their own people into powerful government positions. People like Phil Cooney.

For about a decade, Cooney worked for the American Petroleum Institute (API), an oil industry trade association. He served as the "climate team leader" at API, which has fought tenaciously for more than fifteen years to resist any regulation of greenhouse gas emissions. A primary strategy was to sow seeds of doubt about whether climate change was real and whether U.S. action was justified.

The strategy worked—in part because of the media's "equal time" mandate. The *Seattle Times* reported on a study conducted by science historian Naomi Oreskes, prompted by a conversation with her hairdresser, who had said she wasn't worried about climate change because even the scientists didn't know what was happening. Oreskes set out to examine whether there was, in fact, much disagreement in the scientific community. In a random sampling, she selected a thousand research papers on global warming from 1993 to 2003. Not one study rejected the idea that the planet was warming and that humans were to blame. However, in a separate analysis of 636 articles covering climate change from 1988 to 2002 in the *New York Times, Washington Post, Los Angeles Times,* and *Wall Street Journal,* researchers found that 52.7 percent gave "roughly equal coverage" to the competing notions that climate change either is caused by humans or is simply a result of natural fluctuations.

Cooney was very good at his job, and in 2001, he followed the Bush administration into the White House, serving as chief of staff for the President's Council on Environmental Quality. In March 2001, EPA chief Christine Todd Whitman traveled to Italy for climate talks with European leaders, assuring them that the Bush administration would honor its campaign pledge to regulate greenhouse gas emissions. Concerned that Whitman might be successful in pressing the administration to keep its climate commitments, Cooney took the unusual step of organizing public criticism of a fellow Bush administration official. He asked for assistance from Myron Ebell, policy director for global warming at the Competitive Enterprise Institute (CEI), another organization fighting responsible action on climate change. For years, CEI has counted Exxon as a top funder. In a memo later obtained by Greenpeace, Ebell replied, "Dear Phil, Thanks for calling and asking for our help," proceeded to strategize about how CEI would call for Whitman's firing, and asked for support from the administration for a "strident and noisy" campaign. Whitman kept her job, but was effectively muzzled and ultimately resigned in 2003.

Two years later, in June 2005, internal White House documents were leaked to the *New York Times* showing that Cooney—not a scientist—had made a series of small but significant edits to U.S. scientific climate change reports in 2002 and 2003. At least 181 of those edits sought to downplay the significance of the scientific consensus on climate change. Another 113 attempted to sow doubts about the extent to which this change was caused by humans, or even to proclaim the benefits of global warming.

Cooney resigned almost immediately after this story broke. Two days later, he was hired by Exxon. In March 2007, Cooney resurfaced at a congressional hearing, expressing no regrets about how his policies distorted scientific findings and misled the public. "My sole loyalty was to the President and advancing the policies of his administration," he said.

Cooney's story was broadcast throughout the mainstream media, including National Public Radio and *Meet the Press*. The connections between corporate polluters and the White House were in plain view, at a time when U.S. citizens were facing gas prices near historic highs and the oil industry was enjoying record profits. Yet the billion-dollar federal subsidies to Big Oil—the richest industry in the world—went on.

Return on Investment

Consider the irony. Not only do oil and coal companies pollute our air and water and destabilize our communities and our climate, but we taxpayers pay them to do so. It's not enough that oil companies inflate gasoline prices while earning more profits than any industry in the history of the world—they're also world-class operators at squeezing billions in subsidies out of the government and at securing other tax breaks, regulatory loopholes, relaxed regulations, and reduced royalty payments. You almost have to admire the chutzpah.

Robert F. Kennedy, Jr., president of the Waterkeeper Alliance, says, "You show me a polluter, and I'll show you a subsidy. I'll show you a fat cat using political clout to escape the discipline of the free market and load his production costs onto the backs of the public." These are indeed fat cats. The top five oil companies brought in more than $800 billion in revenue in 2006, earning nearly $83 billion dollars in profits. In 2006, Exxon became the most profitable corporation in history, earning $39.5 billion in profits in a single year.

Coal and oil executives aren't hurting personally, either. John Drosdick, top oil man at Sunoco, brought in a tidy $46.2 million dollars in total compensation in 2006. Don Blankenship earned $34 million from Massey Energy the year prior, while Ray Irani, the chief executive of Occidental Petroleum, has averaged nearly $40 million for the past five years. The granddaddy of gilded executives, however, is the former chief executive of Exxon, Lee Raymond. On Capitol Hill in 2005, when Raymond was asked to account for record gas prices, he proclaimed his sympathy, telling lawmakers, "We're all in this together." The next year, Raymond retired with a parting gift from Exxon of nearly $400 million, including access to Exxon's jet, a car and driver, and a $1 million a year gig as a part-time consultant to the company.

More troubling is the cash these corporations get at the public trough. According to a 2007 analysis of federal policies by the environmental group Friends of the Earth, oil companies will receive more than $31.6 billion in handouts from Congress alone over a five-year period from 2007 to 2011. These include more than $16 billion in tax breaks, nearly $10 billion in reduced royalty payments, research and development subsidies totaling nearly $2 billion, plus an additional $4 billion or so in other accounting tricks. Friends of the Earth estimates that these figures could "dramatically increase over the next 25 years if current tax breaks are extended and if an estimated loss of up to $60 billion in royalty revenue from offshore oil drilling occurs."

Pass It On

Money in, money out: according to one analysis, oil companies received a total of $39 billion in U.S. federal subsidies in 2006, a year in which some of those same companies earned more in profits than any corporation in modern history. Coal companies received $8 billion in subsidies that same year.

Other analysts have a broader perspective. Doug Koplow is the founder of Earth Track, a Cambridge-based consulting firm that analyzes subsidies to natural resource industries. "While subsidies are most commonly thought of as cash payments to a particular person or corporation, this definition misses most of the ways in which governments transfer value to private entities," he wrote in a paper for the Organization for Economic Cooperation and Development. "A range of policies . . . offer politicians less visible ways to provide benefits to constituent groups."

Koplow estimates that total U.S. subsidies for the oil industry topped $39 billion in 2006 alone. This figure includes the cost of guarding the Alaska pipeline, providing accelerated depreciation benefits to lower taxes, and keeping oil shipping lanes open in the Persian Gulf. (The larger costs of the Iraq War are not included in his estimate.) According to Koplow, total U.S. federal energy subsidies in 2006 were $74 billion, of which fossil fuels received 66 percent, or $49 billion. Total investments in conservation: $2 billion. State and local subsidies to the fossil-fuel industries are not included in the calculations, nor are the billions in subsidies that the World Bank and other international financial institutions give each year. (I'll discuss those in the next chapter.)

To broaden the idea of subsidies even further: sometimes the biggest gift the government can give to an oil or coal company is to simply look the other way. It's a story Jack Spadaro knows well.

Mine Your Own Business

On a rainy Sunday morning in West Virginia in February 1972, a toxic waste impoundment from a nearby coal mining and processing facility collapsed, releasing an estimated 132 million gallons of black sludge in a twenty-foot wave into the raging waters of Buffalo Creek. Within minutes, 125 people were killed and four thousand homes were destroyed.

A young research engineer from the West Virginia School of Mines was sent to investigate. "Memories of those conversations are still with me," Jack Spadaro said in an interview. "Buffalo Creek wasn't necessary. The neglect, the disregard . . . of the mine operators caused it."

Spadaro subsequently helped write safety regulations aimed at preventing a repeat occurrence. Twenty-eight years later, disaster struck once again. In October 2000 in Martin County, Kentucky, another waste impoundment burst, releasing more than 300 million gallons of toxic sludge—almost thirty times the size of the *Exxon Valdez* spill in Alaska's Prince William Sound. Amazingly, no one was killed, although a seventy-five-mile plume of waste extended from the creek where the spill originated to the Ohio River. Water supplies for 27,623 people were contaminated. The EPA ruled it the worst environmental disaster in the history of the southeastern United States. Spadaro was asked to help lead an investigation of the spill for the Mine Safety and Health Administration (MSHA).

Less than a month after the Martin County spill, President George W. Bush was elected, in part because of his upset victory in West Virginia. Coal executives shelled out $3.65 million in the 2000 federal election, giving 88 percent to the Republican Party and its candidates. One executive, Bush Pioneer James H. "Buck" Harless, raised $275,000 for Bush's run, donated to his Florida recount campaign, and contributed $100,000 to his inauguration party. In turn, Bush nicknamed Harless "Big Buck" and invited him to join Ken Lay in the administration's transition team on energy. "We were looking for friends, and we found one in George W. Bush," Harless told the *Wall Street Journal*.

Two days before the inauguration, as Spadaro and his nine-person team were quickly building evidence of negligence on the part of Martin County Coal Company, a subsidiary of Massey Energy, the investigating team was suddenly given a new supervising officer, Tim Thompson. Thompson (who two years later would arouse the ire of Bob Murray) demanded that the investigation be closed within a week. Later that year, Harless was given a seat on the board of Massey Energy, the company ultimately responsible for the spill.

Can you guess how this story ends? Spadaro's team had to cut short its investigation. It recommended eight substantive violations on the part of Massey's subsidiary, which could have resulted in multimillion-dollar fines, demands for significant remediation measures, and potential criminal proceedings. Only two of those recommendations were approved by MSHA bosses, however. Spadaro and his team continued to press the case, charging that the MSHA had covered up negligence on the part of Massey. Spadaro was forced off the team, reassigned, demoted, and fired. He appealed his termination under whistleblower's protection, but eventually quit in disgust. The total fine issued by the Labor Department to Massey, for the worst environmental disaster in the history of the southeastern United States? Just $55,000.

It falls outside the scope of this book to explore the many other cases where energy policy has been corrupted by corporate cash (but see the resources section at the end of this book if you want to find more). Although the media and watchdog groups have exposed many such corporate giveaways, the net effect actually may have been to lower the expectations many Americans have for our government. It's easy to be cynical when a government that is ostensibly of, by, and for the people looks more like a government of, by, and for big business.

Empowering Democracy

It's time to get dirty-energy money out of politics and to end corporate welfare to the richest industries in history. Politicians need to show some backbone to help our country create a clean-energy future. Elected officials can step up and disavow campaign contributions, travel junkets, or other financial perks from the coal and oil industries. It's really quite simple: if we want our government to be independent of the fossil-fuel industry, then politicians have to prove they can't be bought. And if we want to move decisively to safe and sustainable forms of energy, then we should stop using taxpayer dollars to subsidize some of the oldest and dirtiest forms of energy.

Imagine what we could do with the fossil-fuel industry's $49 billion in annual subsidies. We could provide Head Start schooling for all eligible children in the United States (about $2 billion) and medical care for uninsured U.S. kids ($6 billion). Rather than dole out taxpayer dollars to Exxon and other oil companies, we could subsidize the rapid development of plug-in hybrid vehicles (more on this in chapter 5) or residential and industrial-scale solar arrays (see chapter 8). We can declare independence from oil and coal, and clean up government in the process.

An array of energetic public-interest groups is turning up the heat. Veteran energy strategist Steve Kretzmann has sparred with the oil industry in the halls of the World Bank and United Nations and around the world in Ecuador, Colombia, Nigeria, Kazakhstan, and beyond. *Rolling Stone* calls him a "whip-crack petroleum economics analyst." I first met Steve in 1995 when he was campaigning to save the life of Nigerian poet Ken Saro-Wiwa, who was imprisoned for criticizing the vicious Nigerian military dictatorship and the oil operations of Royal Dutch Shell. Tragically, Shell refused to intervene in Saro-Wiwa's case, and he and eight others were hanged in November of that year.

More recently, Kretzmann founded and now directs a new organization, Oil Change International (full disclosure: I'm on the board). Oil Change is focused on identifying and overcoming the political barriers to a transition to clean energy. Kretzmann describes how his approach has evolved over time. He says that while it is crucial to hold the oil industry accountable for human rights abuses, accelerating climate change, fomenting war, deepening poverty, and greedy pricing, "we must also confront the system that allows these injustices to occur. To create a clean energy future, we have to separate oil and state."

Oil Change wants to make it as easy as possible for people to persuade their elected officials to come clean. The organization's Web site helps you find out if your representatives are on the take from Big Oil. Next, the site guides you to immediately send a letter to congratulate the representatives who have refused contributions from Big Oil and encourage those who haven't to declare their independence. Oil Change staff members coordinate with people on the ground, too, helping them arrange face-to-face meetings with their representatives, or at least key staff members, in their home districts.

Joining Oil Change in this campaign is a broad alliance of organizations, including the Sierra Student Coalition, Energy Action Coalition, Global Exchange, Public Citizen, Greenpeace, Rainforest Action Network, the Ruckus Society, and many others. In the summer of 2006, these organizations were joined by thousands of MoveOn.org members, holding rallies at more than three hundred gas stations across the country that called for an "oil-free Congress" and a responsible energy policy. Each of the organizations is mobilizing members to contact their representatives and to show up at campaign rallies to urge candidates to refuse corporate donations from big polluters.

Along with the rising awareness and indignation of informed citizens around the country, this campaign is having an impact. In the 2006 congressional midterm election, every single candidate who refused to accept money from the oil industry won election. Four out of the top five largest recipients of oil money contributions in Congress were voted out of office in 2006.

"We can do this. We know how to power a society in a way that does not fuel global warming and war," Kretzmann insists. "At the end of the day, it's about politics. Once our political system isn't bought and paid for by the big energy giants, a whole world of possibilities will emerge."

Turning a Bright Light on Government

Cleaning up our government won't happen overnight. And there's bound to be some backlash from the oil and coal giants. To take them on, we'll need to be prepared with the most accurate, specific, and up-to-date information about how big money dominates the political process. A handful of organizations do this well, but no one illuminates the connections between money and politics better than a new group, MAPLight.org.

MAPLight.org was started by Dan Newman, who studied biomedical ethics and psychology before cofounding Say I Can, a speech-recognition firm. As a campaign volunteer and an observer of politics on the side, Newman grew frustrated by the influence of big money on the lawmaking process. "It's obvious to me how much corporate money is preventing change from happening, and how hard it is for citizens to band together and get anything done when they're competing against big campaign donations from special interests," he says. "So I started this Web site to give people specific examples of how the money and political system works."

MAPLight.org uses public information to make the political process more transparent by combining several distinct sets of data. The site shows who gave money to lawmakers in the U.S. Congress

Pass It On

In the 2006 congressional election, four of the top five recipients of oil industry contributions were defeated, whereas every candidate that refused all oil money won their election.

and the California state legislature (other states are to be added soon). Then it shows how those lawmakers voted on dozens of bills in the past several years. Finally, it reveals the positions taken on those bills by the donors themselves. Pick a bill, a legislator, or an issue, and you'll see a clear and consistent pattern of how big money and the political process intertwine.

Newman gave me a guided test drive to show how the Web site can be used. We picked a bill introduced by former congressman Richard Pombo (R-CA) to allow drilling in the Arctic Refuge. The bill actually passed in the U.S. House of Representatives in 2006 but stalled in the Senate. From the MAPLight.org home page, we clicked on "U.S. Congress," then "Bills," then entered into the search engine "American-Made Energy and Good Jobs Act," Pombo's creatively named bill to exploit the pristine wildlife refuge. We picked "major (multinational) oil and gas producers" and "oilfield service and equipment providers" to measure the influence they had over the eventual vote. Sure enough, the industry gave $10,863 to each legislator who voted for the bill.

We went a step deeper, and the story became even more interesting. Clicking the tab "Timeline of Contributions" revealed a surge in donations right before the vote took place in late May 2006. Two and a half weeks before the vote, Occidental Petroleum made a series of donations to Representatives Duncan, Weller, Bono, Neugebauer, and McCaul. All voted to drill in the Refuge. A few days later, Chevron kicked in contributions to Representatives Mica, Pickering, Ros-Lehtinen, Wilson, and Barton. They all voted for the bill, too. In the month before the vote, Pombo himself received donations from Shell (five separate ones), Exxon, Marathon, BP, and Chevron.

Is this a coincidence? Just because an oil company gave money to politicians does not necessarily mean that their votes were bought. But, as Newman says, "sometimes the money influences the vote, which means the money is making the difference rather than the strength of the policy or what constituents want. Other times, money goes to people who already support industry." Either way, democracy is weakened. If industry money can't buy votes, it can ensure that polluter-friendly candidates get more cash for their election campaigns. Even if no individual person changes his or her vote in direct response to a corporate donation, Congress as a whole can be bought.

The enormity of the challenge of restoring accountability in government can be daunting. Newman has a healthy perspective, however, reminding us that Americans have the power. "The desire for change among Americans is so broad," he says. "People know the political system is corrupt, and by giving people something visibly good they can do, we're showing that this corruption is a solvable problem. It's a political system that 'we the people' have created, and that 'we the people' can change."

Indeed we can. Year by year, support is growing for an end to corporate welfare for dirty energy. Following the defeats of four of the top five beneficiaries of oil industry donations in the 2006 election, Democratic leaders in Congress, having gained the majority, took action within the first hundred hours of the new session. Led by Speaker Nancy Pelosi, the House passed a bill to cut subsidies, restore oil royalty fees, and redirect as much as $15 billion toward renewable energy programs. Although the Senate narrowly defeated a similar provision in December 2007, it's clear that oil-industry subsidies are becoming a threatened species. It's only logical: if even the president admits that "America is addicted to oil," then it's time to stop paying the pusher.

Take Action

Take it personally

1. Find out how much money your federal, state, and local representatives are taking from Big Oil by visiting Oil Change International's www.priceofoil.org.

2. See how much your representatives in Congress receive from the coal industry and other special interests. Visit the Center for Responsive Politics Web site at www .opensecrets.org.

3. Observe the connections between money and politics at www.maplight.org.

4. Want more examples of the corrupting influence of corporate cash? Check out Robert F. Kennedy, Jr., *Crimes against Nature: How George W. Bush and His Corporate Pals Are Plundering the Country and Hijacking Democracy.* Or visit the Web site of the Natural Resources Defense Council (NRDC), at nrdc.org, for a comprehensive list of environmental rollbacks that the Bush administration engineered in its first term, with the help of a compliant Congress.

Express yourself

It's time for our political leaders to come clean. Contact your elected officials and urge them to:

- **Declare independence from dirty energy** by refusing to accept political contributions, gifts, or travel junkets from oil and coal companies.

- **Stop the giveaways!** Demand that they oppose all tax breaks, royalty reductions, subsidies, and gifts of taxpayer funds to oil and coal companies. No dirty money should be accepted by government officials, and no taxpayer money should be given to fossil-fuel companies in return.

- **Reinvest in America.** Every subsidy taken from oil and coal should be redirected toward energy efficiency and renewable power. Recommitting these funds will accelerate the transition to clean energy.

Stay engaged

Join the effort to separate oil and state by getting involved with one of the organizations mentioned above or in the resources section. Internationally, support the Publish What You Pay campaign (www.publishwhatyoupay.org)—an initiative that seeks to "help citizens of resource-rich developing countries hold their governments accountable for the management of revenues from the oil, gas, and mining industries." This coalition of more than three hundred organizations worldwide seeks to eliminate corruption by forcing corporations to disclose what they pay governments for their extraction rights.

CHAPTER 4

Follow the Money

How Your Bank Is Funding Climate Change, and What You Can Do about It

*Permit me to issue and control the money of a nation,
and I care not who makes its laws.*

— MAYER ANSELM ROTHSCHILD, BANKER

You might not know it, but there's a good chance that you're funding climate change. Do you have a credit card or checking account with Citi, JPMorgan Chase, or Bank of America? How about an investment fund, student loan, or even a home mortgage? These giant institutions aren't just the country's three largest consumer banks. They're also the largest financiers of the dirtiest and most carbon-intensive industries in America today. And they're bankrolling those industries with your money.

Banks are one of the best recyclers in America—of money that is. Every bank in the country takes consumer dollars in the form of ATM fees, credit card interest payments, savings and checking deposits, mortgage payments, and so forth, and then reinvests that money to earn a higher rate of return. Many of these investments or loans are helpful; the economy needs credit and liquidity in order to function properly.

But banks also direct hundreds of billions of dollars each year to oil and coal operations that blast mountains apart, drill in sensitive ecosystems, and destabilize our climate. Although fossil-fuel industries attract criticism for these practices, banks often enjoy almost complete anonymity—even though they're paying for and profiting from the entire operation.

It has become almost a cliché: follow the money. It was the famous advice that "Deep Throat," FBI insider Mark Felt, gave to *Washington Post* reporters Bob Woodward and Carl Bernstein during their Watergate investigation. In the film *JFK,* Donald Sutherland's mysterious character "X" advises Kevin Costner's Jim Garrison to "follow the money" to understand the motivations behind JFK's assassination. After the 9/11 attacks, one of the first things the Bush administration did was to freeze the financial assets of terrorist suspects and conduct financial investigations to determine who was behind the attacks. Whether you're a grassroots environmental group or a giant multinational oil company, financing keeps you afloat.

The role of banks in providing loans, advice, liquidity, and a range of financial services to dirty-energy companies must not be underestimated. Cleaning up our government won't be enough. To create a future in which we enjoy safe, secure, and sustainable energy, we also need Wall Street and the global financial system to stop the flow of easy money for the world's biggest polluters.

Banking on Addiction

The banks' press materials say all the right things. On Bank of America's Web site, Anne Finucane, the chair of the company's Environmental Council, states, "We . . . recognize that climate change and atmospheric pollution represent a risk to the ultimate stability and sustainability of our way of life."

In 2007, Bank of America announced a $20 billion commitment over ten years to address climate change. "Today, we have a tremendous opportunity to support our customers' efforts to build an environmentally sustainable economy," said CEO Ken Lewis in a press release. The company pledged to introduce a new credit card to help customers offset greenhouse gas emissions, a mortgage program with incentives for energy efficiency, and expanded advisory services to help clients take advantage of "carbon-offset" markets.

Two months after Bank of America's announcement, Citi raised the ante with a pledge to invest $50 billion over ten years in clean energy and reductions in the firm's own greenhouse gas emissions. "We believe very strongly that addressing climate change is one of the most important issues being faced by chief executives, investors and governments today," declared Michael Klein, Citi's co-president of markets and banking. Citi, Chase, and Bank of America each invest in some clean-energy technologies and have each pledged to reduce the energy use and resulting greenhouse gas emissions from their own offices and bank branches. (Citi says that it will cut its emissions 10 percent worldwide by 2011.)

With big numbers and promises such as these, what's the worry? Only that these policies are an easy distraction from a much bigger problem: the exponentially larger loans and investments that are profoundly damaging to our climate and our way of life. It's difficult to take a bank too seriously regarding climate change when it continues to finance the world's largest climate polluters. For example, while Bank of America was announcing its new climate change commitment, the company also extended credit to AES Corporation, which has sought to build new coal-fired power plants in four states. Bank of America funds Massey Energy, Arch Coal, and Alpha Natural Resources, three of the largest coal companies engaging in mountaintop-removal coal mining throughout Appalachia; Dynegy, which as I write is planning to build up to eight or more new coal-fired power plants across the United States; the world's largest coal company, Peabody Energy, which has poisoned the groundwater for Hopi and Navajo in Arizona and has plans to build an additional three coal plants; and many other companies and utilities seeking to expand markets for coal-fired power.

Pass It On

A single coal plant with financing from Citi, Chase, or Bank of America will produce more greenhouse gases in three weeks of operation than Citi's entire annual commitment to reduce emissions from its offices in a hundred countries around the world.

Similarly, Citi has provided financial assistance to American Electric Power, which has proposed new coal plants in West Virginia, Virginia, Ohio, Arkansas, and Oklahoma; Florida Power and Light, which proposed adding four coal plants; Southern Company, which operates two plants that are the largest emitters of greenhouse gases in the country; TXU Energy, whose coal plants include several that are among the nation's top emitters of greenhouse gases and mercury pollution; and plenty of other coal companies and operators of dirty-power plants.

And that's just for coal. Kenneth Derr, the former chairman of Chevron, sits on Citi's board of directors, and you can bet that Citi is knee-deep in controversial oil deals in the Amazon and beyond. As this book was written, Citi's largest shareholder was the Gulf Arab emirate of Abu Dhabi, the world's sixth-largest oil exporter. Another large shareholder is Prince Walid bin Talal of Saudi Arabia.

"Too many investors and companies are vested in not addressing climate change," declares Leslie Lowe, a program director at the Interfaith Center on Corporate Responsibility. "They have assets that will be devalued, personal holdings that will be devalued, and so they're fighting a rear-guard action to preserve those assets, or what we'd call 'business-as-usual.'"

The approach these banks take to addressing climate change would be amusing if it weren't so serious. It's a nice gesture for banks to use less energy at their branch offices. But compared to the extensive financing that companies like Citi offer to coal companies and utilities, this is like rearranging deck chairs on the *Titanic*. Consider this: A single medium-sized coal plant with financing from Citi will produce more carbon dioxide in just three weeks of operation than the reductions Citi plans to make annually in all of its offices around the world. And there are hundreds of coal plants in the United States alone. In a year, one large coal plant releases as much carbon as six hundred thousand cars and trucks.

Let's look more closely at Citi's 2007 $50 billion climate-change commitment. Citi will spend $31 billion over ten years for investment and financing in energy efficiency, renewables, and upgrading existing infrastructure, an average of $3.1 billion per year. Compare that to the $63 billion in Citi's corporate credit portfolio dedicated to the utilities and petroleum sectors in 2006 alone. That figure doesn't even include the income earned for underwriting stocks and bonds, advisory, and other services related to financing for these two sectors. Bank of America will spend an average of $1.8 billion per year to help corporate clients reduce greenhouse gas emissions. Meanwhile, the company extended $35.6 billion in credit to oil and utilities in 2006.

It might seem daunting to attempt to change the policies of institutions as large as Citi, Bank of America, or JPMorgan Chase. They're the three most powerful financial institutions in the world. Citigroup alone had almost $25 billion in profits in 2006, maintains offices in more than a hundred countries, and employs more than 320,000 people. Bank of America, one of the world's most recognized brands, has nearly six thousand branches within the United States and net assets of more than $1 trillion.

But it's been done before. Earlier this decade, a small collection of nonprofit organizations organized tens of thousands of volunteers to persuade Citi, Bank of America, JPMorgan Chase, and others to help protect threatened ecosystems and address indigenous rights. If we can get banks to protect biodiversity and human rights, then we can also compel them to join the fight to stabilize our threatened climate in more meaningful ways. Here's how we did it.

Inside a Campaign

I'm often asked how my organization determines which issues to prioritize. Deciding between different campaigns and potential corporate targets is a complex process at Rainforest Action Network (RAN). The first step involves detailed research: identifying the top causes of climate change, deforestation, or human rights abuses; specifying which industries or particular companies are most implicated in contributing to the problem; deciding whether there are reasonable steps those companies can take to address that problem, or effective national or international laws that can be applied or strengthened.

Other questions are more strategic: Is the company vulnerable to public pressure? If so, how? What is the psychological profile of its CEO and senior management team? What allies can be cultivated? Which constituencies can be mobilized? Can people get involved in ways that are both fun and meaningful? And then questions of funding and organizational capacity must always be answered, too.

No matter what the proposal, mounting a new campaign almost always provokes a friendly but fierce debate within the organization. In late 1999 and early 2000, as we were considering taking on the company then known as Citigroup, the discussion was particularly passionate. RAN had recently persuaded Home Depot to stop selling wood from endangered forests, a big victory that provided much-needed momentum to protect British Columbia's Great Bear Rainforest. *Time* magazine named it the top environmental story of 1999, and we were plotting our next move.

A major issue was whether we thought Citi could be pushed forward. And if so, how far would the company go? RAN had a staff of just a couple dozen people. Citi was about to become the world's largest bank and soon the world's most profitable corporation. Pick your problem area—logging, mining, oil and gas, large hydroelectric dams—and Citi was a top financier. Pick your favorite threatened ecosystem—California redwoods, the Amazon basin, tropical forests in central Africa and Southeast Asia—and Citi was also implicated in its destruction.

The breadth of its operations was both a danger and an opportunity—a huge David versus Goliath scenario. How could we possibly take on a company so large? On the other hand, Citi was a symbol of corporate-led globalization. If we could change the policies of the world's largest bank, the impact would be profound.

Ultimately it was Citi's size and global reach that convinced us to give the campaign a go. Perhaps just as importantly, it was the size of Citi's brand. For years Citi had spent hundreds of millions of dollars on a whimsical "Live Richly" advertising campaign designed to position the company as a friendly, full-service bank that protected not just your assets but your true interests in life. "Hugs are on a 52-week high," announced a typical Citi billboard. "The best blue chips to buy are the ones you dip in salsa," offered another. We loved the prospect of juxtaposing these feel-good corporate slogans with images of Citi-financed environmental decay and exploitation. James Gollin, a former investment banker with Nomura Securities and Morgan Stanley International and the current chair of RAN's board of directors, calls it "corporate jujitsu"—using the power of a company's brand against itself.

The more popular the brand, the easier it is to subvert. *Adbusters* magazine took on cigarette advertising to kids with its brilliant "Joe Chemo" campaign, which placed the mascot formerly used to sell Camel cigarettes in a hospital bed hooked up to life support. On the poster, a spoof of the surgeon general's warning reads, "The Surgeon General warns that smoking is a frequent cause of wasted potential and fatal regret." Another ad challenges the sexiness of alcohol advertising: "Absolute *[sic]* on Ice" features a toe tag on a dead body at the morgue with the text, "Nearly 50 percent of automobile fatalities are linked to alcohol. . . . A teenager sees 100,000 alcohol ads before reaching the legal drinking age."

Before we start a new initiative at RAN, we send a short note to the corporate executive whose policies (and mind) we want to change. Our letter in early 2000 to Citi CEO Sandy Weill was respectful but direct: we informed Mr. Weill that his company was damaging human rights and the environment, and asked that he join us to solve the problem collaboratively. Each time we send such a letter, we hope to inspire the CEO to simply do the right thing—to show that his or her company can do well by doing good, by taking responsibility for its environmental and social impacts.

Sometimes one letter is all it takes. Lowe's, the country's second-largest home-improvement retailer, agreed to phase out all wood products from endangered forests after a letter and meeting with RAN. Similarly, Kinko's responded to a letter by adopting the country's strongest policies to increase the recycled content of paper and eliminate purchases of wood from endangered forests.

Our note to Citi didn't quite have that effect, but it did lead to a meeting with Citi executives at its headquarters in New York. The goal was a comprehensive policy that would include strong environmental and social standards affecting forests, human rights, climate protection, labor standards, and more. "We wanted Citi to model what a responsible and equitable twenty-first-century bank could be," recalls Ilyse Hogue, former director of RAN's global finance campaign. "But we were light-years apart at that time." Years later, a Citi executive joked that it seemed RAN wanted an "intergalactic, universal policy that would abolish everything that we do."

We had been warned that this would be difficult. Michelle Chan, a campaigner with Friends of the Earth who pioneered financial advocacy with corporate banks in the mid- to late 1990s, had had some frustrating early encounters. "When we first started, banks didn't factor in most environmental issues, and certainly didn't have comprehensive policies," she said. "If we brought a controversial project to a bank, they would routinely try to pass any criticisms off to either the company involved or to the government. Our first challenge was simply getting banks to accept responsibility for their loans and investments."

It became clear that Citi wouldn't move voluntarily. It was time to make some noise.

Not with Our Money!

Challenging Citi to stop bankrolling bulldozers in the Amazon and elsewhere was an effort in which RAN was joined by hundreds of small groups around the country and thousands of concerned individuals around the world. Many were students—who were particularly important in this case because Citi needed them and their money. High school and college students are red meat for banks. Once a bank starts doing business with a young person, it won't let go. Banks aim to entice students with their first credit card, and then as time passes, ply them with student loans, auto loans, mortgages, investment accounts, retirement plans, and so on.

Each semester at high schools, universities, and colleges across the country, Citi employees would arrive on campus to sign up students as new credit card customers. It was a golden opportunity for our campaign. When Citi employees set up booths to attract fresh recruits, RAN volunteers would set up a table nearby with photos and fact sheets documenting the impact of the bank's loans on ancient redwood forests, national parks in the Amazon, and other endangered regions. (Not many applications for credit cards were submitted on the days we were there.)

But it wasn't just students who were involved. RAN staff members and volunteers would pass leaflets to Citi employees outside Citi's headquarters in New York. We quickly found insiders who were willing to give us valuable information. "I remember standing outside the Citigroup Center in January and being pleasantly surprised by how many people not only took the flyer from my frigid hands, but gave me a subtle thumbs-up, a smile, or told me how much they appreciated our campaign," remembers former RAN campaigner Dan

Firger with a laugh. "Not every employee was on our side, but it was gratifying to see how many really cared about what their company was doing."

We had successfully reached out to employees before. Often a public campaign will inspire employees within a company to take action. These employees want to keep their jobs, but also wish to work for an employer that's doing right by people and the planet. When we were pressuring Home Depot to stop selling wood from endangered forests, I began to receive calls from a Home Depot worker who wanted to help. He was concerned that his two daughters wouldn't have rainforests to visit when they got older. He gave me information about the sources of Home Depot's wood, and one day shared the access codes to the intercom at every one of Home Depot's stores. Weeks later, volunteers could be heard on the intercom at Home Depot stores across the country saying, "Attention, Home Depot shoppers, we want to draw your attention to the doors in aisle 16 which were made from wood that has been ripped from the heart of the Amazon basin. In aisle 12 . . ."

As the Citi campaign continued, we placed an advertisement in the *New York Times*. The headline "Did you know someone is using your credit card without your authorization?" ran above pictures of clearcut forests, oil pipelines, and pollution-belching smokestacks. The ad informed customers that Citi was quietly using their money to fund dozens of controversial projects, and urged them to cut up their Citi credit cards and send them to RAN. We began to receive thousands of cut-up cards in the mail.

Eventually dozens of organizations were pressuring the company from all sides, including Amazon Watch, International Rivers Network, the Ruckus Society, and the Service Employees International Union. Students mocked Citi director and former treasury secretary Robert Rubin at a speech at Columbia University. Activists hung a banner at Citi's headquarters reading, "Hey, Citi, not with my money!" Local residents used civil disobedience to blockade Citi branches in Iowa, New York, Florida, California, Washington, D.C., and elsewhere. Volunteers cut up Citi credit cards and held protests at Citi branches around the country.

A group of investors led by Trillium Asset Management and Friends of the Earth represented key shareholders who wanted change. Shareholder resolutions were filed. International leaders came to speak at Citi's annual shareholder meetings at Carnegie Hall. At one meeting in April 2002, Lily la Torre, a leader from the Peruvian environmental organization Racimos de Ungurahui, implored Citi to withdraw its support for an oil pipeline that would cut through primary rainforests. She invited CEO Sandy Weill to visit her community to learn directly about the effect the pipeline would have. Weill declined.

When informed that Weill would take a summer vacation in Tuscany, we placed an ad in the *International Herald Tribune* with pictures of the Citi CEO joined by President Bush and World Bank CEO James Wolfensohn. The headline read, "Put a Face on Climate Change and Forest Destruction."

A turning point came early in 2003 when Weill, a Cornell University alumnus, came to give a speech at his alma mater's business school. Cornell's students were well prepared. They arranged for RAN founder Randy Hayes to address students the night prior to Weill's speech, and invited Weill to a "Randy versus Sandy" debate. Again, Weill declined. The next day, as Weill approached the lecture hall, three banners were unfurled, urging him to do the right thing. During his remarks, several students held signs inside the room protesting Citi's dirty investments. One read, "Destroying Old Growth Forests Isn't Cool!"

Weill finished his speech, and took questions from the audience. The first student, Brihannala Morgan, stood up and thanked Weill for coming, and then challenged him on his company's lack of a responsible environmental policy. Before the audience, she introduced Weill to Hayes, who said, "I'd like to work together with you to bring environmental responsibility to Citigroup, and I'd also like to invite you to join me in an academic debate on this subject, perhaps to be held right here at Cornell." Weill declined once again to engage, but assured the audience that he took these issues seriously.

The next questioner stood up, thanked Weill again for coming, and asked another tough question. Five of the eight questions asked weren't from students eager to suck up for a fast-track summer internship. They were from kids asking why Weill's company was sacrificing their future. Eventually the chief executive admitted that his company could and should do more. He mentioned the ad in the *International Herald Tribune* the previous year, and how embarrassed he was to have his grandson ask him what he was doing to make climate change worse. He promised the audience that Citi would take quick action.

A couple of weeks later, we received word that Citi was willing to negotiate. At the time, RAN was running advertisements on cable television in New York, in which Ali McGraw, Daryl Hannah, Susan Sarandon, and Ed Asner were pictured cutting up their Citi credit cards, interspersed with images of oil spills and blackened tree stumps. "Stop bankrolling bulldozers," growled Asner. On the eve of Citi's 2003 shareholder meeting, RAN agreed to pull the ads and suspend all campaign activities—in exchange for a commitment by Citi to set a new global standard for environmental responsibility by a bank.

Two months later, in June 2003, Citi joined with international banks Barclays, ABN AMRO, and WestLB in launching the Equator Principles—a set of voluntary guidelines that minimize or eliminate some of the adverse social and environmental impacts of the projects banks fund. All four banks had been the target of public-pressure campaigns in the preceding eighteen months. As of early 2008, nearly fifty banks have adopted the principles, covering more than 90 percent of all project finance deals around the world.

In January 2004, Citi went a step further by announcing that it would deny funding for logging in tropical rainforests, enact special restrictions on extractive industries operating in critical ecosystems worldwide, stop financing illegal logging activities, and enhance consultation with indigenous communities. The announcement was covered by CNN, the *Wall Street Journal,* the *New York Times,* and other outlets. Within four months, Bank of America adopted similar standards, followed by JPMorgan Chase and the investment banking firm Goldman Sachs. "This was a great paradigm shift; today communities around the world are being given the tools to 'follow the money' if they want to stop destructive projects," says Ilyse Hogue. "Grassroots citizens stood up and together we finally got banks to admit culpability and accept responsibility for their loans and investments."

It was an important victory and a hard-earned one. We never knew what prompted Citi to change its mind and take action to help protect endangered ecosystems. It could have been a colleague who bent Sandy Weill's ear, or a shareholder. Perhaps it was the confrontation at Cornell, the ad in the *International Herald Tribune,* or the thousands of letters and e-mails the company received. I'd like to think it was all these things and more, but also that Weill and his team stepped forward because it was simply the right thing to do.

Our agreements with Citi and the other banks closed a chapter, but the story continues. Each bank has acknowledged that climate change is a critical issue facing society. Each has pledged to reduce energy use at their own facilities and to study other potential solutions. However, not one bank has committed to phase out loans and investments in activities that cook the planet. Not yet, anyway. We still have some work to do.

Perverse Subsidies

Corporate banks such as Citi, Chase, and Bank of America are just one part of the problem. Public financing institutions are also bankrolling climate change by diverting taxpayer funds toward the fossil-fuel industry. For example, the World Bank Group has provided more than $8 billion to the oil industry since 1992. In the last ten years, the U.S. Export-Import Bank and the Overseas Private Investment Corporation have given more than $21 billion in loans and loan guarantees to U.S. corporate interests for refineries, pipelines, and power plants in more than forty countries around the world. The beneficiaries of these loans are companies such as Halliburton, Exxon, Bechtel, and others. Why not invest in clean energy and efficiency projects instead?

Ending corporate welfare for the world's biggest climate polluters is a topic that could unite all Americans and bring us into community with the rest of the world. Whether it's the government subsidies discussed in the preceding chapter or loans from public banks, we shouldn't use taxpayer dollars to enrich already profitable corporations, or to keep America hooked on dirty energy. In the United Kingdom, it is the right-wing Conservative Party that is calling for an elimination of such "perverse subsidies." David Cameron, the party's leader, said, "This is a vital issue—we have a responsibility in this generation to make sure we provide a greener and cleaner planet for our children. We cannot go on as we are in terms of the way we run government and live our lives."

For years civil society groups and grassroots activists have lobbied the World Bank and other financial institutions to stop funding destructive investments. Here's the story of how they almost convinced the World Bank to stop lending to dirty oil and coal projects, and why they won't give up.

World Bank on Trial

Tensions were high in a crowded conference room at the World Bank offices in Prague, Czech Republic, in late September 2000. The next day the city would be filled with tens of thousands of European citizens calling for fundamental reform—or the complete abolishment—of the World Bank and International Monetary Fund (IMF). James Wolfensohn, the World Bank president, gathered several nonprofit leaders around the table to hear their concerns. They represented a diverse network of organizations that criticized the World Bank and IMF for deepening poverty, causing widespread social and environmental instability, and "turning slowdowns into recessions and recessions into depressions," as described by former World Bank chief economist and Nobel Prize winner for economics Joseph Stiglitz. Wolfensohn knew he had to do something.

Established in 1945, the World Bank (officially known as the World Bank Group) is a collection of five international agencies whose original mandate was to assist with postwar reconstruction. Today the bank uses public funds to provide financing and advice to countries and corporations alike, ostensibly to improve living standards and alleviate global poverty. However, the bank's loans and investments—particularly in the fossil-fuel sectors—and the conditions that they place on those loans too often produce the opposite result. In developing countries from Cameroon to Colombia, communities assailed World Bank–financed projects as benefiting only oil corporations and corrupt government officials, not the poor. Between 1992 and 2005 the World Bank Group committed over $28 billion to fossil-fuel projects—seventeen times more than its financing for renewable energy and energy efficiency.

By the time the meeting in Prague was held, discontent with corporate-led globalization was at a fever pitch. Protests criticizing the World Trade Organization in Seattle and the World Bank and IMF in Washington were generating worldwide media coverage. To the surprise of many

Pass It On

Between 1992 and 2005 the World Bank Group committed over $28 billion to fossil-fuel projects—seventeen times more than its financing for renewable energy and energy efficiency.

community leaders in the room, Wolfensohn offered a radical solution. He proposed that the World Bank appoint an independent blue-ribbon panel to reassess whether World Bank investments in extractive industries were justified, given their questionable ability to promote sustainable development and alleviate global poverty. An agreement was made to move forward with this plan.

An independent team known as the World Bank Extractive Industries Review (EIR) was established, led by Dr. Emil Salim, Indonesia's former minister for the environment. "The World Bank was criticized that its oil, gas, and mining portfolio was not contributing to poverty alleviation and sustainable development," Salim told me years later. "I was to set up a multi-stakeholder process to discuss [whether this was true]."

Salim's team was given a multimillion dollar budget and a mandate to incorporate input from all sides. Conferences involving a wide range of stakeholders were held in Europe, Africa, Asia, and North and South America in 2002 and 2003, where industry executives, nongovernmental organizations, indigenous communities, labor unions, and others gave testimony. The team also had special private meetings with numerous governments and with Royal Dutch Shell, Exxon, Chevron, and some of the world's largest mining corporations. Six studies were commissioned and site visits were conducted to examine firsthand the impact of World Bank activities on communities, local economies, and the environment.

"Many of us were skeptical from the outset. No one knew what the EIR's recommendations would be, nor even whether they'd be accepted in good faith," recounts Oil Change International's Steve Kretzmann. "But that misses the point. The World Bank essentially agreed to put the fossil-fuel industry on trial, and created a process where all the evidence could be carefully considered."

For many people, this was an extraordinary opportunity to share their views in an official forum. Representatives from Indigenous organizations around the world met in Oxford, England, to formulate a collective response. The Indigenous Peoples' Declaration on Extractive Industries stated, "Our futures as indigenous peoples are threatened in many ways by developments in the extractive industries. . . . Our experience shows that exploration and exploitation of minerals, coal, oil, and gas bring us serious social and environmental problems, so widespread and injurious that we cannot describe such development as 'sustainable.' Indeed, rather than contributing to poverty alleviation, we find that the extractive industries are creating poverty and social divisions in our communities, and showing disrespect for our culture and customary laws."

In December 2003, more than three years after Wolfensohn agreed to conduct the review, the EIR released its official report, *Striking a Better Balance*, which strongly recommended that the World Bank improve its governance and accountability, respect human rights, and strengthen social and environmental performance standards. The fourth and final recommendation asked the bank to phase out all oil and coal activities: "The WBG should phase out investments in oil production by 2008 and devote its scarce resources to investments in renewable energy resource development, emissions-reducing projects, clean-energy technology, energy efficiency and conservation, and other efforts that delink energy use from greenhouse gas emissions. . . . The WBG has for the last few years not invested in new coal mining development. This should continue."

The World Bank's managers were in a tough spot. They had created this independent team, after all, but were hesitant to follow its strong recommendations. A collection of Nobel Peace Prize winners turned up the heat in a letter to the bank, saying, "War, poverty, climate change, greed, corruption, and ongoing violations of human rights—all of these scourges are all too often linked to the oil and mining industries. Your efforts to create a world without poverty need not exacerbate these problems."

Nine months and countless meetings and conference calls later, the bank's management officially responded. They chose to disagree by agreeing, stating that the bank "welcomes the Review" and agrees with "the majority of its recommendations." The bank announced, however, that it would not accept the recommendation to phase out oil and coal investments. Instead, it promised: "Our future investments in extractive industries will be selective."

One wonders what the bank's definition of "selective" might be. Wolfensohn continued making loans to the fossil-fuel industry in the last year of his presidency. After leaving the bank in 2005, Wolfensohn was replaced by

Paul Wolfowitz, one of the architects of the Iraq War. Appointed by the Bush administration, Wolfowitz certainly didn't change the bank's policy on extractive industries. According to the Bank Information Center, the International Finance Corporation, which is part of the World Bank, increased its loans to corporate oil and gas companies by 35 percent from 2005 to 2007. "A significant portion of these investments are for projects involving export of oil and gas to Europe and the US, thereby subsidizing these countries to prolong their dependence on fossil fuels," says Bank Information Center's Heike Mainhart-Gibbs. In early 2008, the International Finance Corporation agreed $450 million in loans to a massive, four-thousand-megawatt coal plant in India.

Robert Goodland, an advisor to the EIR team, believes the World Bank missed an unusual opportunity: "We . . . strongly recommended the WBG extend their then-current moratorium on lending for coal, to phase out of oil lending by 2008, and to ramp up the transition to renewables." Instead, the World Bank went in the opposite direction by significantly increasing its loans to the oil and coal industries. Goodland called the bank's response to the EIR a "monumental blunder" that would impact the developing world most, as increased loans to the oil and coal industries intensified the climate change risks on the world's poorest people.

"I have been disappointed in the way the World Bank responded," says Salim. "Oil and coal industries are rich and strong enough to finance their own activities. The World Bank should not make the strong stronger, but should instead push renewable energy, which is very behind in its development."

In the end, the EIR gave a guilty verdict on World Bank financing of extractive industries—but the bank's managers have suspended the sentence. Actually, that's not true. They've thrown out the verdict, absolved the accused, and added an extra billion or two to make sure there were no hard feelings.

Funding the Future

Undeterred, citizens groups and grassroots leaders have renewed their efforts to end public giveaways to the fossil-fuel industry. In coordination with allies working to secure climate-friendly policies at corporate banks, an international movement on financial activism is emerging. One such collaboration is End

Oil Aid, a coalition of organizations led by Oil Change International, which has developed a Web site, www.endoilaid.org, which allows visitors to determine how much each public lending agency (U.S. or global) gives in "oil aid" each year. Since 2000, it has found, more than $60 billion has been transferred from public coffers.

Meanwhile, Congressman Maurice Hinchey (D-NY) has introduced the End Oil Aid Act (H.R. 1886), to prohibit the use of taxpayer dollars to subsidize the overseas operations of the oil industry. And in the U.K. Parliament, a petition signed by fifty members calls on the government to produce a climate-change strategy that phases out support for oil and gas projects.

Activists continue to pressure corporate banks in creative ways. In Washington, D.C., two Bank of America customers dressed up as polar bears and withdrew their life savings of $27,000 in protest of their bank's role in accelerating climate change through its loans to the coal industry. At Kayford Mountain, West Virginia, local residents held up a giant banner adjacent to a mountaintop-removal site, reading, "Mountaintop Removal—Funded by Bank of America." In all, demonstrations were held at more than a hundred Citi and Bank of America locations in November 2007 to protest the companies' financing of coal and other "investments of mass destruction." Three months later, in February 2008, Citi, JPMorgan Chase, and Morgan Stanley released the "Carbon Principles," a new set of lending guidelines on coal-plant financing. The principles don't ban funding for new plants outright, but they do compel utilities to account for potential increases in coal prices, demands for carbon sequestration, and a cap on greenhouse gas emissions due to climate change.

Grassroots pressure clearly is having an impact, but people don't have to wear polar bear suits to promote clean-energy financing. Pinstripes work just as well. Meeting the demand for environmentally conscious lenders are banks such as ShoreBank Pacific, which bills itself "the nation's first environmental bank." ShoreBank Pacific loans money from its "EcoDeposits" program to businesses and organizations seeking to reduce their environmental footprint. All loans are evaluated by an internal science team that helps the bank's clients improve their environmental performance.

New Resource Bank, founded in San Francisco by Peter Liu, seeks to define full-service environmental banking. Its offices have achieved "gold" status in the Leadership in Energy and Environmental Design program (LEED); its employees are reimbursed for using mass transit; and the firm has made loans to organic farmers, green-home builders, clean technology firms, and other environmental entrepreneurs. "There was a real need in the business community for a green lender, and also for a bank to make a difference," Liu says. New Resource Bank has no coal- or oil-company clients, and it partners with homeowners and solar providers to help install residential solar arrays with no money down. To attract depositors from the Bay Area and beyond, New Resource Bank refunds fees from any ATM in the country.

Credit unions are another important alternative to commercial banks that finance climate change. A credit union is a nonprofit, cooperative financial institution that is owned and operated by its members. Most have some common bond that unites all members, be it a profession, geographic location, or religious affiliation. Credit unions don't have the same quarterly financial pressures as do most corporate banks, and do not provide corporate financing or financial services to companies such as Exxon, Peabody Coal, Shell, or others. They are bound by mandate to give lending preference to their members and are better structured to finance small-scale renewable energy projects and small-business ventures that are too early-stage or localized for the commercial banks.

"Follow the money" is more than a catchphrase. It's how you can predict the future. "The surest indication of what kind of energy infrastructure our country will have in the next ten to fifteen years is to look at where commercial banks are directing their corporate financing," says Bill Barclay, a finance expert at Rainforest Action Network. It won't do to have the world's largest financial institutions continue to bankroll dirty energy. Literally trillions of dollars of investments in transportation, energy, and other sectors need to be redirected to clean and sustainable technologies. We need our banks to help lead the clean-energy revolution or get out of the way.

Take Action

Take it personally

Tell your bank to fund the future:

1. **Stockholders:** If you own shares in Citi, Bank of America, JPMorgan Chase, or other banks, exercise your authority: you're an owner of the company. Contact your bank's managers and urge them to redirect bank financing in the energy sector to clean businesses. Attend your bank's annual shareholder meeting to tell its officers what you think in person (or send a proxy). Contact As You Sow, Trillium Asset Management, and other shareholder advocacy groups for more information.

2. **Investments:** Are your mutual funds, cash investments, or private banking accounts managed by Citi, Chase, Bank of America, or even Goldman Sachs, Merrill Lynch, or others? Contact these banks and tell them to stop investing in oil and coal, or you'll move your money to someone who will. Find some friends who invest with such banks as well, and multiply your leverage. Visit www.ran.org for more information.

3. **Credit cards, mortgages, and loans:** Banks have an opportunity, and responsibility, to prohibit any investment in industries that threaten to destabilize our climate. Compare your bank's social and environmental performance with those of New Resource Bank, ShoreBank Pacific, and other green financial institutions and consider which deserves to manage your accounts.

4. **Credit unions:** To find a credit union near you, visit www.creditunionsonline.com.

Express yourself

We can't reduce our dependence on oil and coal if the world's largest banks supply those industries with whatever financing they need, for any project, anywhere. Regardless of where your personal accounts are held, make your views heard:

1. If the World Bank had heeded the recommendations of its own Extractive Industries Review, we wouldn't still be giving billions in taxpayer dollars to some of the world's richest corporations. Join the campaigns of Oil Change International and the Bank Information Center to end aid to the oil and coal industry.

2. Want to know who's funding climate change? Take a look at America's three largest banks: Citi, Bank of America, and JPMorgan Chase. Join the campaigns of Rainforest Action Network, Friends of the Earth, Co-op America, and others to bring ethics to the banking industry.

3. Nearly fifty banks have signed the Equator Principles establishing social and environmental guidelines that help protect endangered ecosystems and community

rights. However, there is no similar code of conduct regarding climate change. Check out what the international coalition Bank Track is doing to redirect the global banking industry to put clean energy first. More information can be found at the group's Web site, www.banktrack.org.

Stay engaged

Let's put our money to work creating a sustainable energy economy. For an elaboration of what that economy might look like, check out the International Forum on Globalization's (IFG) *Alternatives to Economic Globalization,* a summary of which can be found at the IFG Web site, www.ifg.org/alt_eng.pdf. In the resources section here you'll find more organizations to support and other sources of information.

CHAPTER 5

Redesigning Mobility

Moving America in a Post-Oil Economy

My other car is a bus.

— BUTTON CREATED BY THE AMERICAN
PUBLIC TRANSPORTATION ASSOCIATION

There are people who like trains, and then there are Train Lovers. I'm probably in the former camp. I didn't have train sets growing up, nor did I harbor dreams of being a conductor someday. I mostly ride commuter trains to and from work, and as long as they run on time, are relatively clean and comfortable, and get me to where I need to go, then they're all right with me.

But that was before I got on board the *shinkansen*, a high-speed bullet train that links Japan from north to south. After my colleague Brant Olson and I took the train from Tokyo to Kyoto in August 2006, I became a convert: bullet trains are the most technologically sophisticated, stylish, and efficient way to travel. We simply must get them here in the States.

The *shinkansen* isn't your grandfather's locomotive. Painted a pristine white, with sleek aerodynamic noses, the trains reach speeds of more than 180 miles per hour. New trains entered into service in mid-2007 improve speeds by inclining at turns, and also use 19 percent less power. On the horizon are magnetic levitation trains—which float several millimeters over the railways, held by an electromagnetic force. These trains have safely traveled over 350 miles per hour in Japanese test runs. A nineteen-mile demonstration line is currently in operation at the Pudong International Airport in Shanghai, China.

Overall, Japan's rail system is among the best in the world, with trains that are quick, clean, and convenient. For an island nation smaller than the state of California, Japan has more than twelve thousand miles of tracks and more than twenty-six thousand runs daily, connecting Japan's biggest cities to its most remote towns. Introduced in 1964 for the Tokyo Olympics, the *shinkansen* is wildly popular: it has more than eight hundred thousand riders *every day.* Compare those figures with Amtrak, the twenty-one-thousand-mile intercity rail system in the United States, which has a daily ridership of more than seventy thousand. Japan's high-speed railway is also the safest form of transport in the world: in more than forty years of operation, not a single fatality has occurred.

And traveling this way is a breeze, from start to finish. Unlike the airport experience, with its long lines, boarding passes, frequent delays, and baggage hassles, getting on and off Japan's trains is as smooth as can be. We arrived at Tokyo Station about eight minutes before our scheduled departure and quickly bought tickets that identified our car number and assigned seats. Clear signs (in Japanese and English) directed us to the correct track; another set of signs pointed out where to stand to board our particular car. At the precise minute it was due, the train quietly sped into the station. Also impressive was the boarding process: even though these trains can hold more than one thousand passengers each, the boarding process at any particular stop takes no more than ninety seconds, as passengers board fifteen separate cars, each with a door at the front and back.

On the train, unlike being in an automobile, there was no fighting traffic and getting tense behind the wheel. Here, we could walk around, go to the dining car, play cards, read, listen to music, or get a beer—it was good times on the rails! The biggest challenge to riding the *shinkansen* is learning how to look out the window. The ride is super smooth, and you don't realize how fast you're traveling until you look outside. If you look at the ground immediately outside the train, you can get dizzy as it zooms by at a couple hundred miles per hour. The secret is to look a ways into the distance, where your eyes can adjust and you can relax and watch the world go by.

We sped past Mt. Fuji and the bright lights of Nagoya on our way south. A little more than two hours after leaving Tokyo, we pulled into Kyoto Station, a postmodern wonder of glass and steel, complete with an eleven-story hotel, an amphitheater, a public park on the roof, and more than a dozen restaurants, which, on this summer night, were packed with young people. First unveiled in 1997, the station has become a social and commercial center for the entire city.

After checking into our hotel across the street, we headed into town rested and relaxed. Our plan was to down a few beers and see if we could find that Kyoto Protocol on climate change somewhere. We'd heard they needed an American to sign it.

Step Out of the Car, Please

Two-thirds of the oil that is consumed in the United States each year is devoted to transportation. If America is to ever have a real shot at breaking its fossil-fuel addiction, we'll need to get around much more efficiently. Certainly, a component of that is pushing automakers to manufacture fuel-efficient vehicles, which I'll discuss in the following chapter. It won't be sufficient to build better cars, however. We'll also need to find elegant and effective ways to get people out of those cars whenever it's appropriate, without sacrificing the comfort and convenience to which we've grown accustomed.

Let me first calm any unfounded fears. This chapter isn't pushing some kind of utopian dreamworld in which our energy problems would be solved if everyone could pedal their bicycles to Home Depot and strap sheets of drywall to their backpacks. Nor am I suggesting that if people in rural Utah or western Pennsylvania would just take a bullet train to the office, life would be dandy. Rather, this is about giving ourselves more options to get from one place to another. And it's about making those options more practical and attractive at the same time. Some of the solutions are reachable in the long term, others right away.

Let's start with some givens. Convenient public transit is not yet available to many Americans or just isn't practical where they live and work. Americans in twenty, thirty, or more years will most likely still have cars in many areas. And let's face it, cars can be fun. They not only symbolize freedom; for many people, they *are* freedom. Jack Kerouac captured this in his classic book *On the Road,* and when Bruce Springsteen sings, "Just roll down the window and let the wind blow back your hair," he's referring to the distinctive pleasures of someone savoring life—in a car. Learning to drive is a formative experience for many Americans. How many of us can remember when we first got our license, or the first car that was truly our own, when we could finally go anywhere we wanted, anytime?

But if we're a car culture, some things about that culture must change, as climate change becomes a greater threat, oil dependence deepens, and Americans spend more time in traffic with each passing year. We can't eliminate cars in the near future, but we can definitely create more attractive alternatives. This is the challenge: finding a way to decrease our need for cars and increase our quality of life at the same time. Put another way, how do we make other transportation options more attractive than the automobile, so that everybody wins?

We'll look at some practical solutions in this chapter. Some of these fixes will be immediate, such as embracing car shares, or increasing funding for buses, bike paths, and light rail. Others may take up to a decade or more, such as rejuvenating Amtrak by establishing a new, home-grown system of American trains. Still other remedies, such as rethinking the layout of our communities, could take even longer. Each solution will require significant investment from the public and private sectors—but isn't that a better way to spend our dollars than on corporate handouts for oil and coal?

How to Run a Railroad

In the end, you get what you pay for. The reason Japan's trains are so efficient and popular is that the Japanese government has invested heavily to modernize its railway infrastructure. Beginning in the 1950s, Japanese citizens saw the development of a rapid public train system as integral to uniting the country and accelerating its economic growth. Although the operation of Japan's trains has been privatized since 1987, the government owns the tracks, leases them to private companies, and reinvests the revenues into research to make the trains even faster, safer, more energy efficient, and—along with Europe's railways—the envy of the world.

In contrast, U.S. transportation priorities have heavily favored the automobile over the last half-century, particularly under the Bush administration.

Amtrak received about $1 billion in federal funds in 2003. Adjusted for inflation, this is less than two-thirds of what the rail agency received twenty years earlier. Compare that with federal spending on highways and aviation, which has more than doubled in the same time period. Congress earmarked more than $49 billion for the Federal Highway and Federal Aviation Administrations in 2007. Total federal budget outlays for high-speed rail in 2006 and 2007 combined: $0.

Pass It On

Budgets matter. Passenger rail funding in 2003 was just two-thirds the amount spent in 1983. In the same time period, federal outlays for planes and automobiles doubled. Federal investments in high-speed rail were eliminated completely in 2006 and 2007.

We have to be smart about how we incorporate trains into our transportation mix. My enthusiasm for high-speed trains doesn't mean they're appropriate everywhere, though they certainly make for a wise investment in many high-traffic transportation corridors. But Amtrak opponents argue that the government has no business running a railroad at all. They say that all subsidies should be cut, the system handed over to corporations, and unprofitable runs shut down. They even point to Japan, arguing that after its railways were privatized, ridership continued to increase, earning corporate profits approaching $2 billion annually.

This argument ignores an important truth, however. Japanese taxpayers and those of other countries with advanced systems, such as France, Switzerland, Germany, and others, set a goal of having world-class railway systems. Each country made significant investments into their systems over several decades and are now enjoying the dividends. Even after privatization, Japan continues to invest billions each year into railway infrastructure and safety and design improvements.

America's big investments in infrastructure have historically provided a foundation for economic growth. We still enjoy the benefits of public works projects in the 1930s, 1940s, 1950s, and 1960s that gave us hundreds of buildings, public pools, trails in our national parks—and, yes, our interstate highway system and nearly every airport in the country. A similar investment in a national rail system today would reconnect and revitalize American cities. Today, China invests $16 to $20 billion annually in passenger rail. France and Germany each devote 20 percent of their entire transportation budget to rail. Amtrak's $1.3 billion is less than 2 percent of our annual transportation budget.

Trains can be an elegant way to travel and reduce gridlock, but they're also a climate-friendly mode of transport. A study commissioned for the Department of Energy by the Oak Ridge National Laboratory shows that domestic airlines consumed on average 20.5 percent more energy per passenger mile than Amtrak, while cars consumed 27.2 percent more energy. To the extent that we succeed in reducing our dependence on coal and greening our electricity grid, Amtrak's trains will become an even more efficient way to travel. Meanwhile, detailed proposals have been made to establish regional high-speed train networks in Florida, the upper Midwest, and California, and expanded service on the eastern seaboard, but the plans are mostly stalled in state and federal bureaucracies.

In the end, it's a question of values and priorities. America deserves better than a third-rate rail system with technology several decades out of date. An ambitious public works program to rejuvenate the nation's passenger rail system and bring state-of-the-art high-speed rail to the United States could be one of the more effective long-term strategies to fight climate change. The alternative is to penny-pinch Amtrak, sustain its meager $1.3 billion budget, and continue to devote billions more in taxpayer funds to build more highways, airports, parking lots, and traffic cops.

If we choose that path, however, we might choke ourselves, literally. In the summer of 2007, 49 of the country's largest 137 metropolitan areas were in violation of federal Clean Air Act regulations. As the U.S. population grows and pollution levels increase, our roads will continue to be more and more crowded. According to the Texas Transportation Institute's 2007 Urban Mobility Report, traffic congestion is worsening in all of the nation's 437 urban areas. Heavy traffic caused 4.2 billion hours of travel delay in 2005 (the most recent year for which complete data was available).

Pass It On

Traffic congestion caused 4.2 billion hours of travel delay in 2005, wasting more than 2.9 billion gallons of gas and costing the economy $78 billion each year. The average driver spends a full work week stuck in traffic each year.

The typical commuter spent nearly a full work week—thirty-eight hours—suffering through traffic congestion. Nationwide, this lost productivity costs the economy $78 billion annually. Put another way, 2.9 billion gallons of gas were wasted, enough to fill fifty-eight supertankers.

Ask yourself, isn't there a better way to get where we need to go? If Japan, France, Germany, Switzerland, and other countries can have modern, comfortable, and super-fast trains, why can't we? China is investing in high-speed trains. So is Mexico, with a planned 360-mile route from Guadalajara to Mexico City. Trains of all types can help America to decrease its oil consumption, relieve gridlock, and travel in a more relaxed and convenient style. By reinvesting in a beleaguered transportation sector, we can create new jobs and once again unleash the power of American ingenuity.

Transit-Oriented Development

The secret sauce for sustainable transportation is diversity. "There is no 'magic' technology or solution on the horizon because there is no single cause of congestion," notes Tim Lomax, a research engineer at the Texas Transportation Institute. "The good news is that there are multiple strategies involving traffic operations and public transit available right now that if applied together, can lessen this problem." In the United States, 4.7 percent of commuters use buses, streetcars, or rail to get to work each day, according to the 2000 census.

Promoting transit use begins with the design and layout of our cities and towns. For much of the past seventy-five years, cheap gas and the rise of the automobile have made it possible for more Americans to move farther away from their jobs, resulting in the segregation of homes from offices and shopping, making the automobile central to daily existence. In many communities the corner store no longer exists, replaced by a strip mall supermarket with plenty of parking. Streetcar lines in hundreds of cities were ripped up long ago, with the encouragement of tire manufacturers and automobile companies. Commute distances to work lengthen for more Americans every year. Bike paths are few and far between. Sprawl continues to devour agricultural land and open space. This growth in suburban development is dramatically but rightly characterized by author and vocal critic of American development James Howard Kunstler as "the greatest misallocation of resources in the history of the world."

A reformist philosophy of traditional neighborhood design known as the New Urbanist movement has emerged in the past few decades, primarily in response to sprawl and related trends. The movement seeks to "reestablish the relationship between the art of building and the making of community," according to the Congress for the New Urbanism. Its intention is to restore urban centers and towns as the true hubs of commercial and residential life and to foster a shared sense of community. New Urbanist planners favor compact, mixed-use neighborhoods, reducing dependence on the automobile by slowing down traffic, creating more local parks and public spaces, and making it easy to run errands on foot or by bike.

I asked Shelley Poticha how this approach could help to promote greater transit use. Poticha, formerly director of the Congress for the New Urbanism, is now president and CEO of Reconnecting America, a national organization working to integrate transportation systems and the communities they serve. "It starts by making streets walkable," she answered. "Basically, unless a place is walkable, it's never going to be transit-friendly."

The idea is catching on. The state of Maryland has adopted New Urbanist principles as a core element of its town planning. Towns such as Kentlands, Maryland; Seaside, Florida; and Austin, Texas, all have examples of New Urbanist design. Although New Urbanism has its critics—many argue that its standards are too prescriptive and its designs too homogenous—planners are increasingly designing more compact urban and town centers.

Making a town or city friendly to pedestrians is just the beginning. Urban planners increasingly favor "transit-oriented development," or TOD, around streetcars and light-rail systems as a way to increase transit ridership, decrease traffic, and generally improve the quality of life in urban areas. TOD has been shown to increase property values around high-quality train systems, leading to a U.S. renaissance in light-rail systems, and particularly streetcars, in recent years: more than a hundred cities around the country have recently installed or are planning new streetcar lines, which are "a very low-cost way of developing high-quality transit," Poticha says.

One metropolitan area making great progress in promoting TOD is Denver. In 2004 its voters passed a $4.7 billion "FasTracks" ballot measure that will fund six new transit lines with 119 miles of track and seventy new transit stations in the next fifteen years. The Mile High city will also develop transit villages around these stations to provide a variety of housing and shopping choices within easy walking distance. "We're really focused on getting each stop to become a little village so there's not a sea of parking spaces," says Denver mayor John Hickenlooper. "People will actually be able to walk right from their home to the light rail and take [it] to work. . . . More families will be able to be a one-car family, instead of being a two- or even a three-car family."

In addition to states and municipalities, federal policymakers can play an important role in establishing priorities that will help reduce gridlock and emissions at the same time. The government funnels hundreds of billions of dollars each year to a range of transportation projects, from highways, bridges, and airports to bike paths and light rail. How those dollars are apportioned determines how efficient our transit systems can become. All too often, however, lawmakers have forgotten a key purpose of transportation funding: to make our towns and cities livelier, healthier, and more affordable. "We ought to be evaluating all our transportation investments against better standards: are those investments going to help us reduce our dependence on foreign oil, or reduce greenhouse gas emissions?" Poticha says. "Will they give people greater choice about how to get around? Will the investments stimulate local economic development?"

Congress is due to reauthorize the national transportation bill in early 2009. The bill will determine how federal transportation dollars are spent. It's also an opportunity to answer Poticha's questions and develop a national transportation vision that addresses the twin threats of climate change and oil dependency.

Pedal Power

Remember when you first learned how to ride a bike? Close your eyes, and you can probably remember the combination of nervousness and delight, wind blowing your hair, someone shouting encouragement behind you, handlebars shaking erratically. Learning to ride a bicycle is exhilarating and evokes strong feelings of autonomy and freedom. Making it easier for people of all ages to ride more frequently could also help bring us freedom from oil.

Getting into gear are some of America's largest cities, which see a win-win in reducing greenhouse gas emissions and other pollutants, as well as relieving gridlock. Mayor Michael Bloomberg has committed to have two hundred miles of bike trails in New York City by 2010. This total includes bike paths that are separate from road traffic, as well as bike lanes painted onto city streets. Similarly, Chicago is planning to have five hundred miles of bike trails by 2015. "We want to make Chicago the most bicycle-friendly city in the United States," says Chicago mayor and avid rider Richard M. Daley. Austin, Texas, will spend $250 million for new bike trails, including thirty-two miles through the town center. Also in Texas, Dallas/Fort Worth has $900 million in bicycle paths planned. "Texas is reaching out to embrace biking like never before," says Robin Stallins of the Texas Bicycle Coalition. "That says a lot about a shift of cultural values."

Pass It On

New York and Chicago are planning two hundred and five hundred miles of bike trails, respectively. Austin is investing $250 million in bike transit; Dallas/Fort Worth $900 million.

It also says a lot about the effectiveness of organizing by local citizens who seek to promote safe and clean transit. "The most important thing you can do to promote clean transit is to be an advocate," says Kristen Steele, outreach director for the Thunderhead Alliance, an organization that supports local bicycle-advocacy groups nationwide. Many of these groups, along with the AARP (formerly the American Association of Retired Persons) and others, are coordinating a "complete the streets" campaign, advocating more walkable and bicycle-friendly communities.

If you don't ride a bike, you can still help. One of the most effective ways to support both public transit use and cycling is to advocate for making them better integrated. Most people will walk to public transit if there is a bus or train stop within a half-mile radius—basically a ten-minute walk. Cyclists riding at a safe, easy speed can cover three to four times that distance in the same amount of time, increasing by up to ten times the total area in which commuters can conveniently take advantage of mass transit. An obvious solution, then, is to make it easier for people to ride their bikes to the bus or train.

Cyclists need to be able to either bring aboard or store their bikes securely at the train stop, or to rack them on a bus. It costs $10,000 to $12,000 to construct each auto parking space at a transit facility, compared with a few hundred for a rack or bike locker. Knowing this, some cities have made aggressive investments in racks and lockers, and are enjoying the dividends of increased ridership. In Vancouver, for example, bicycle commuting increased by 30 percent following the installation of bike storage lockers at bus and train stops. In 1994, Seattle put bike racks on every bus, helping transit use to increase by 17 percent. But only a third of all buses in North America currently have bike racks installed.

Storage is important, but safety is imperative. While in most American cities less than 4 percent of residents bike to work each day, in Copenhagen 35 percent do so. In Beijing, it's a shade over 30 percent; in Amsterdam, 40 percent. In the United States, Boulder leads with 21 percent. These cities promote cyclist- and pedestrian-first policies, with hundreds of miles of bike lanes—lanes that are raised, colored, or otherwise removed from oncoming traffic to separate motorists and cyclists. Other advantages include bike-only bridges, bicycle parking facilities, and special mirrors to avoid accidents at dangerous intersections.

In another move to reduce vehicle traffic and greenhouse gas emissions, cities in Europe, including Brussels, Lyon, Vienna, and Paris, make bicycles available for free or at a very low cost to tourists and residents alike. Paris has more than twenty thousand bikes available at nearly fifteen hundred locations across the city, or approximately one bike station every 250 yards. The first half-hour of usage is free. Parisians use them like cars to run errands around town. The city estimates that each bicycle will be used about twelve times a day, for a total of about 250,000 daily trips across the city, or 91 million per year.

Cycling keeps you healthy, saves money, and means less grit and grime in the air. It also helps make cities quieter, more peaceful, and to many, more beautiful. "Look, I know that promoting bike use is good for the climate and reduces pollution and all that," says Leah Shahum, director of the San Francisco

Bicycle Coalition. "But I just love my city, and I know that getting more cars off the road makes San Francisco a more beautiful and civilized place to live."

Get on the Bus

Let's face it: there aren't many bus groupies out there. Some people visit Japan, Germany, or France and remark about the beauty and sophistication of the country's trains. Others wax poetic about the elegant simplicity of the biking cultures of the Netherlands and China. But how frequently do you hear people purr with delight about a city's bus system? Buses are the workhorse of transportation networks. They don't get the glory, but they do get the job done—and help those who need transit options the most. For millions of Americans, buses are the most convenient form of transportation. And for millions of others who are disabled, elderly nondrivers, or too poor to own a car, bus transportation provides vital access to food, medical care, and the outside world. Since they don't require an airport or rail lines, buses are also the most flexible. All you need are passengers and roads (and a bus, of course).

OK, so you might not regularly subscribe to *Bus Transit Quarterly,* and *Innovations in Public Transportation* rarely finds itself on your bedside nightstand. That's alright. Just remember this: BRT. The increasing utilization of Bus Rapid Transit systems (BRT) is easily the most promising innovation in the world of inner city transit.

What BRT does is revolutionize the bus-riding experience. Gone are the days of slow, bumpy, lurching rides in buses belching smoke. BRT has low-riding, comfortable coaches (many, like the bus I ride, with wireless technology). They are cleaner-burning and make fewer stops; many run in lanes designated for buses only; some also have the ability to switch stoplights from red to

Pass It On

Four U.S. cities recently ordered more than seventeen hundred hybrid buses from General Motors, one of two major manufacturers of hybrid bus systems—including 950 for Washington, DC, 480 for Philadelphia, and 300 for Minneapolis and St. Paul. New York City's Metropolitan Transportation Authority began experimenting with the buses in 1998 and in 2007 ordered 850 with systems from GM competitor BAE Systems.

green as they approach. BRT lines typically cut trip times in half, and have increased ridership by more than 50 percent in many areas, enticing ever more commuters out of their cars. Further, many mass transit systems are purchasing hybrid-electric buses, which reduce gas consumption and cut down on soot by as much as 90 percent. According to a 2007 survey by the American Public Transportation Association, about 22 percent of all buses on order were hybrids at the time the survey was conducted.

When you add it all up, public transportation currently saves 1.4 billion gallons of gasoline each year, or enough to fill a supertanker leaving the Persian Gulf every eleven days. Yet highways and roads continue to get the lion's share of transportation dollars. That could change in early 2009, however, when the federal transportation bill comes up for renewal. You'll find ways to help modernize America's transportation systems in the "Take Action" section at the end of this chapter.

One Car, Many Drivers

Redesigning mobility isn't just limited to public transportation; it also includes, yes, cars. Cyclists might teach us to share the road, but we can also share our cars.

If you live in a major city, you've probably seen gas stations and corner parking lots become home to small cohorts of snazzily marked cars. A "car share" is a membership club that gives people access to a fleet of vehicles located throughout a city or region. They're different from rental agencies in that the cars are often used for just a few hours and are located in the middle of city neighborhoods, rather than in airports or other, often remote, locations. "We are trying to replace car ownership," said Scott Griffith, Zipcar's chief executive. "It's a business model that locates cars in neighborhoods and uses twenty-four-hour technology to locate the car."

Car shares are easy and cheap, for short trips. Members can reserve a car online for a couple hours, a day or weekend, or longer. They can rent a truck for moving, a convertible for the weekend, or a hybrid just because. Most members join a car share because they realize that they can walk, bike, or take transit for work and most errands, and then get the car for weekend trips, grocery shopping, or whatever. There's no hassle: the company cleans the car and takes care of oil changes, repairs, car insurance, and all maintenance. Even the gas is included in the fee.

Car shares can be an important way to reduce reliance on the automobile. Think of them as a kind of halfway house for auto addicts. There are more than a dozen nonprofit car-share organizations located throughout the United States, as well as at least one for-profit business, Zipcar. Car sharing has helped more than 40 percent of Zipcar members to either sell their car or forgo buying one altogether. Research by the company shows that each Zipcar takes twenty other vehicles off the road, and that gasoline usage by new members drops as much as 50 percent. The company estimates that its nearly two hundred thousand members sharing a total of five thousand vehicles saved a total of 32 million gallons of crude oil in 2007.

Pass It On

Public transportation currently saves 1.4 billion gallons of gasoline each year, or enough to fill a supertanker leaving the Persian Gulf every eleven days, even though highways and roads continue to get the lion's share of transportation dollars.

Individuals joining car-share programs report a 47 percent increase in public transit trips, a 10 percent increase in bicycling trips, and a 26 percent increase in walking trips. The cars are currently available in six hundred places worldwide, including New York, Chicago, San Francisco, Seattle, Portland, Los Angeles, Atlanta, and dozens of smaller towns from Rutledge, Missouri, to Fort Collins, Colorado. If you live on a farm, or out in the country, car shares probably aren't for you. But if you live in a city or town that has one, then you might have the best of all worlds by saving money and hassle, while having access to a car when you need it.

Essentially, car shares can help fill in the gaps as America shifts to a more sustainable transportation system. Although we have a long way to go in building such a system, we'll know we're getting close when getting in the car starts to seem less convenient than other options. We'll no longer be solely dependent on personal vehicles to shop, work, and play. We'll have more choices that are efficient and that work well together, so that we can pick the best form of transportation for a particular task, whether it's walking to a nearby store or place of work; taking a bullet train to a city a few hundred miles away; hopping on a bus, subway, or ferry; riding a bike; or using car share. The genius will be in cultivating an easy complexity. It may be a long journey, but it'll be a great ride along the way.

Take Action

Take it personally

1. Each of us decides where we live and work. Some have fewer options; others have more flexibility. If you do have a choice, make it a conscious one. By living near mass transit or close to where you work, you'll spend less time in traffic and less money on gas, use less oil, and create fewer emissions.

2. Once you're settled, resolve to walk, bike, or take transit when you can, drive when you must. Dust off your bike, inflate the tires, and hit the road. Join a car share. Grab your iPod or a book and hop on the bus. Even one day a week makes a difference.

3. Get involved. Your town's planning commission makes important decisions about whether we have more strip malls or walkable communities. Our federal, state, and local tax dollars are spent on a long list of transit projects. Should we invest more public dollars in trains, bike paths, and rapid-transit systems? Explore the groups listed in the resources section later in this book, follow the news, and share your opinions with officials and candidates for office.

Express yourself

1. *At your workplace.* Some states and cities allow employers to offer incentives to take mass transit, such as pretax vouchers. Does yours? Is there space available for employees to store bicycles? Make sure that your company is part of the solution.

2. *At your school.* Help create walkable communities by signing up your school for the International Walk to School Day. In 2007, more than twenty-seven hundred schools from all fifty states participated. You can also initiate a Safe Routes to School program—see www.saferoutesinfo.org.

3. *Take the train.* We can start by fully funding Amtrak, and then make significant and strategic investments to modernize and update our train systems. Lobby your local politicians until they get on board. The earliest opportunity to bring bullet trains to the United States may be in California; check out the Web site of CALPIRG (www.calpirg.org) for updates on a planned bullet train between Sacramento and

San Diego. Or join groups such as the Midwest High Speed Rail Association and the National Association of Railroad Passengers, which support high-speed rail lines across the country.

4. **Get on the bus.** Join a local bus riders' union and lobby for affordable, efficient, and environmentally smart mass transit. The Los Angeles Bus Riders Union (www. busridersunion.org) works to reduce fares and increase service to promote sustainable transit for all. Help bus systems in other cities secure a greater share of state and federal financing. Don't have a union in your area? Start one, or at least ask friends to join you in writing to local officials for more balanced financing.

5. **Hop on a bike.** Use your own bike, but don't stop there. You can support local cycling organizations and lobby officials for more bike-friendly transit, safe bike trails and lanes, and storage at train stations and on buses. An effective national group is the League of American Bicyclists (www.bikeleague.org).

Stay engaged

Adopt a project. What do you care about most? If you're inspired by the idea of a modern train system in the United States, then make that an effort in which you stay active for the long haul. Have fire in your belly about buses or bikes? Lobby for better service, a street path, bike lane, bike racks, or other project; find a local group or start your own. In 2009, the national transportation bill will be reauthorized. It will direct billions of dollars to a wide variety of projects—don't let it be stuffed with more pork for the auto and highway lobbies. The bill is as yet unnamed, but join one of the organizations listed in the resources section to stay involved.

CHAPTER 6

Jump-Start Detroit

How Automakers Can Save Themselves, and the Planet

If we are going to create jobs—good, family-sustaining
manufacturing jobs—we are going to do it with clean
vehicles, mass transportation, and renewable power.
There are no other markets with this potential.

— LYNN HINKLE, UNITED AUTO WORKERS,
LOCAL 879, MINNESOTA

The woman's voice on the voicemail at Rainforest Action Network was anxious but determined.

"Jennifer, this is Heather. Ford wants its truck back—and the representative is getting pretty insistent. I think we need to do something."

Heather Bernikoff-Raboy and her husband, Dave Bernikoff-Raboy, live on a 160-acre ranch in the foothills of the Sierra Nevada. Dave is a software engineer turned rancher, and Heather a former healthcare professional. They're both passionate about electric vehicles and how they help reduce American oil consumption.

"We use the Ranger for just about everything on the ranch—we've even towed a forklift out of the mud with it," says Dave. "It's all-electric, and with our solar panels, the cost to run the truck is almost nothing. It requires hardly any maintenance, no oil, and no gas. Nothing. People stop me on the street all the time and ask me how they can get one of these trucks for themselves."

The Bernikoff-Raboys acquired their electric Ford Ranger in April 2001 through Ford Motor Company's GreenLease program. In January 2004, the company sent the Bernikoff-Raboys a letter giving them the option "to make arrangements to purchase the leased vehicle," adding, "Ford Credit can finance the purchase." Dave sent a certified letter to Ford accepting its offer of sale, and after the lease expired he continued to send payments, which the company deposited.

Then they were told that a mistake had been made. On November 18, 2004, Ford sent another letter to the Bernikoff-Raboys, this time reneging on its sales agreement: "Unfortunately, there is no possibility to extend your lease or for you to purchase your vehicle."

The Bernikoff-Raboys had driven the Ranger on the ranch for three and a half years, and didn't want to go back to another gas guzzler. They thought it was strange that Ford was refusing to sell them the Ranger EV, but they weren't surprised. The company wasn't quite pulling out all the stops to market these vehicles. "We had to search online to find this truck, and when we went to lease it, the salesman was not enthusiastic," Heather recalls. "The truck was practically hidden at the back of the lot. And they couldn't even find the key! We had to wait an hour while the dealership got a locksmith to come out and make us a new one."

The Bernikoff-Raboys' experience was not unique. Some research revealed that other Ranger EV owners were also being asked to turn in their trucks, as were the owners of Ford's electric Th!nk vehicles. At the same time, Toyota, Honda, and Nissan were reclaiming their electric vehicles, and GM was taking back its EV1, as depicted in the movie *Who Killed the Electric Car*. The automakers' plan was to take all the electric vehicles off the road, crush them, and turn them into scrap.

Here's a little background on this story. In 1990, the California Air Resources Board, in an attempt to reduce smog and other pollutants, mandated that 5 percent of all vehicles made for California produce zero emissions by 2001. The auto industry vigorously opposed the rule, arguing that (a) the technology for zero-emission vehicles wasn't ready, (b) even if it was ready, the vehicles would be too expensive, and (c) there wasn't enough demand for pollution-free vehicles anyway. Reluctantly, however, automakers began manufacturing thousands of electric cars and trucks to meet the mandate, all the while arguing that the burden of producing them was too onerous. The vehicles were a hit with customers, but the automakers weren't interested in expanding their electric-vehicle programs. Once the Air Resources Board rescinded the zero-emission-vehicle mandate, the auto industry moved quickly to pull its electric cars off the road.

"It didn't make sense to us," says Heather. "Electric vehicles don't have a tailpipe and don't emit any smog or greenhouse gases. The central valley of California has some of the highest asthma rates in the state. We thought it was criminal that Ford and everyone else would forcibly take these vehicles off the road."

The Bernikoff-Raboys were ready to take action. They contacted Jennifer Krill and Jason Mark, program directors at Rainforest Action Network and Global Exchange. Krill and Mark had recently helped to prevent several dozen all-electric Th!nk vehicles from being crushed and would later help protect more than a thousand Toyota electric RAV4s from the same fate—all part of a national campaign to compel Ford and other automakers to build zero-emission vehicles nationwide.

Dave and Heather didn't consider themselves protesters, but they wanted to do something to keep their truck on the road. Together with Krill and Mark, they hatched a plot to stage a literal auto "sit-in." Think of it as a Charlton Heston–inspired demonstration: they'd drive to the Ford dealership, alert the media, and dare the company to pry the truck from their cold, well . . . maybe not dead, fingers. The gamble was that Ford would blink—that the company couldn't possibly be so determined to crush these vehicles that they'd risk such negative publicity. When Heather received a call from Ford in January 2005 that their truck would soon be seized, the plan went into motion.

Joined by Bill Korthoff, who brought his own Ranger EV, and some other supporters, the Bernikoff-Raboys staged a round-the-clock vigil in their truck outside the Downtown Ford dealership in Sacramento. "That first night was pretty cold and lonely," Heather said, recalling how they shivered in the foggy, freezing winter weather. But the media coverage made the sacrifice worthwhile. An article in the *Los Angeles Times* quoted Dave: "If this truck was good enough that Bill Ford drove it to work every day, how come it's not good enough for me to buy? How come they're not going back and getting all the Pintos? How about the Excursion—it's being discontinued. It gets 12 miles per gallon. Why not go back and crush all of those?"

News reports on television soon made the group minor celebrities. As the days passed, local residents came to share a drink, deliver hot coffee and home-cooked meals, and take pictures with their kids under the "Declare Independence from Oil" banner that hung from the trucks.

On the seventh day, Ford relented, offering to sell Ranger EVs back to their lessees for $1. The Bernkikoff-Raboys and other EV owners were happy to purchase their vehicles but amazed that Ford needed to be pressured at all. "It's unfortunate it took this level of effort to get them to do the right thing," Dave told a reporter.

By the time Ford reconsidered, only a few hundred electric Rangers were still on the road. More than a thousand electric Ford Th!nk, Toyota RAV4s, and other electric vehicles were also saved, but thousands of others were crushed. "I wish every single one of our products generated as much customer passion," said Niel Golightly, Ford's director of environmental strategies. If Ford produced more electric vehicles, maybe that would be the case.

In the end, Ford and other automakers had made a big mistake: they had infuriated loyal customers and inspired them to get organized. The former drivers of those vehicles know what it's like to have cars and trucks that don't run on gas. They've continued to pressure the automotive industry, and are beginning to have an impact. With any luck, soon you'll be driving an electric car, too.

Internally Combusting

It's exasperating. One of the best opportunities to fight climate change and beat America's addiction to oil is being largely ignored by federal policymakers and major automakers.

Here's the reality that we face. In the United States, more than 40 percent of our oil is burned in passenger cars, trucks, and SUVs. One out of every seven barrels of the world's oil is consumed on American highways. When you factor in trucking, shipping, and airlines, about two-thirds of American oil consumption is used for transportation. The vehicles made by the Big Three automakers in Detroit—GM, Ford, and Chrysler—emit more greenhouse gases than every country in the world except China, the United States, Russia, and Japan. But automakers are stuck in neutral: the average fuel economy for passenger vehicles in the United States is less than twenty-five miles per gallon—or almost exactly the same level it was at twenty-five years ago.

The problem will get worse before it gets better. In 1950, there were 50 million cars and trucks on the planet. Today, there are about 650 million. Within twenty years, there will be more than one billion.

Here's the kicker. Technology available today could make a huge dent in this problem, but it's barely being utilized by automakers. An analysis done by the Union of Concerned Scientists and the Center for Auto Safety in 2001 showed that a national fleet average of fifty-five miles per gallon was achievable using technologies in existence back in 2001, including hybrid-electric engines. Hitting this average would save more oil each year than the United States uses from the entire Persian Gulf and California coast, as well as the oil believed to be in the Arctic National Wildlife Refuge.

The report was released seven years ago. Since then, hybrid and electric battery technologies have advanced considerably. Plug-in hybrid electric vehicles—where no gas is used for the majority of trips—can boost fuel efficiency to more than a hundred miles per gallon. That's utilizing existing technology—no new inventions required. Using lightweight materials as recommended by the Rocky Mountain Institute can yield even greater increases, while not sacrificing safety or performance. And the rebirth of electric vehicles might change the automotive industry completely.

"Clearly, the entire industry could build nothing but zero emission cars today if it wanted to," said Ford's Niel Golightly in 2004. But besides a handful of electric and plug-in hybrid electric vehicles that exist now, or that the major automakers promise are just around the corner, the industry continues to churn out gas-guzzling cars and SUVs by the millions. What's preventing change? The same list of reasons that the industry used in California: that the technology isn't ready, it's too expensive, and customers don't really want fuel-efficient cars (even though they say they do).

Pass It On

There are 650 million cars on the road globally, up from 50 million in 1950. By 2025, there will be more than one billion. Transportation accounts for two-thirds of U.S. oil consumption, and today's automobiles are 97 percent reliant on oil as a fuel.

Let's put the objections of automakers into perspective. This is the same industry that fought taking lead out of gasoline and using catalytic converters to reduce toxic emissions in the 1970s. America's automakers also fought mandatory seat-belt laws, resisted making air bags standard in all vehicles, and insist on using manual typewriters instead of computers in all their offices.

OK, that last part isn't true. But seriously, domestic automakers are rarely accused of being enthusiastic innovators when it comes to safety or fuel economy. Some automakers—and President Bush—have attempted to deflect criticism with the promise of hydrogen-fueled vehicles. But those vehicles are more than a decade away and would require retrofitting every gas station in the country.

Pass It On

The average fuel economy for passenger vehicles has hovered around twenty-five miles per gallon for more than twenty years. The Ford F-150, America's best-selling truck, gets less gas mileage today than did the Model T from early in the twentieth century.

We deserve better. Remember, the top-selling truck in America, the Ford F-150, gets lower gas mileage today than did the Model T in the beginning of the twentieth century. When automakers came to Washington in June 2007 to discourage senators from raising fuel-economy standards, they met a cool reception from some. "I think the issue is over. I think you've lost that issue," said Senator Byron Dorgan of North Dakota. "I think your position is 'yesterday forever.'"

The industry's stubbornness is compounded by the unwillingness of federal regulators to give it tough love. Led by the congressional delegation from Michigan, lawmakers have routinely blocked legislation that would boost mileage standards significantly. The energy bill passed by Congress in late 2007 will only increase fuel economy to thirty-five miles per gallon by 2020—the standard of the EU and Japan today—and even that bill has loopholes large enough for a Hummer.

Meanwhile the American auto industry is hemorrhaging money and workers. GM lost $2 billion in 2006; Ford lost $12.6 billion, or the cost of a $25,000 Mustang nearly every minute. In the late 1990s, GM had 225,000 workers; by 2007 there were only 73,000. Ford has also laid off tens of thousands of workers; among those slated to lose their jobs are the nearly two thousand employees at Ford's Twin Cities Automotive Plant, in St. Paul, Minnesota. The plant, which operates on clean energy from the eighteen-megawatt hydroelectric plant on the Mississippi River, made Ranger pickups and EVs like the one the Raboys drive today. In late 2005, Ford revealed that the plant was to be shut down, part of the company's massive layoff and restructuring plan, which management perversely named "The Way Forward."

One of the Twin Cities plant workers, Lynn Hinkle, flew with others to Ford's headquarters in Dearborn, Michigan, to propose converting the plant to produce hybrid or other fuel-efficient vehicles, or trucks that would run on biofuels (so-called "flexible-fuel vehicles," discussed in the next chapter). Given the strong demand for Toyota's hybrids, Hinkle was optimistic. "We felt that if Ford would capitalize on this market, it would be a win-win for everybody. A green plant producing green cars . . . the impact on Ford's brand would have been enormous," he told me. However, the plan was quickly rejected. On April 13, 2006, Ford announced that it would shut the plant down in mid-2008.

American autoworkers used to be the backbone of the U.S. economy, part of a proud and prosperous working class. They could be so again. One study calculated that reaching an average fuel efficiency of just forty miles per gallon by 2015 would lead to 161,000 more jobs, including 40,800 in the auto industry, and save consumers an annual $23 billion to boot. Minor progress was made in the 2007 energy bill, but federal lawmakers continue to resist strong attempts to modernize the industry, a pattern that *New York Times* columnist Thomas Friedman is fond of calling an "assisted suicide."

It's time to stop playing small ball over tiny increases in fuel economy when a complete automotive revolution is not only required but achievable. We don't need dramatic breakthroughs or new inventions to rescue the United States from its oil dependence. Game-changing solutions are available today. Our country has the technology, the resources, and the know-how to build clean cars and to dramatically reduce our use of dirty oil. The only thing we lack is the political courage to make the profound changes that the industry needs to thrive in a world with climate change.

In the sections to come, I'll discuss the innovators and advocates who will soon take plug-in hybrid vehicles to the mainstream, and the Silicon Valley entrepreneurs who are making some of the fastest—and cleanest—cars on the planet. I'll also describe the policies that could help kick-start an automotive revolution, and suggest ways to make sure that revolution actually happens. First let's meet the godfather of the plug-in hybrid engine: a professor from California's Central Valley.

Plug It In!

It's said there are two ways of teaching people to swim: give them lessons or just throw them in the water. Professor Andrew Frank learned about automobiles the harder way.

"My father bought a car for me in 1948 for about $25," Frank recalls. "It was a '29 Nash, but it didn't run. My dad said, 'Well, son, you're kinda interested in cars. Why don't you fix it? Make it run, and it's yours.'"

Frank chuckles. "I was up for the challenge. I not only fixed it but turned it into a hot rod. Chopped the engine out, replaced it, took the top off, the whole thing."

Having first taught himself, Frank has been teaching others for more than forty years, first electrical engineering at the University of Wisconsin, then mechanical engineering at the University of California at Davis. He's also been watching—and trying to work with—the auto industry. "I remember that when Toyota first introduced the Prius in 1997, American carmakers were ecstatic. They said that if Toyota really pushed their hybrid program, they'd go out of business!" Frank laughed.

In April 2007, Toyota overtook General Motors as the world's largest, and most profitable, automaker. The next month, the company announced it had sold its millionth hybrid vehicle.

Frank is working to promote the next generation of efficient vehicles, plug-in hybrids. Hybrid engines like those used in the Toyota Prius, Honda Civic, or Ford Escape use a combination of gas and electric power. Plug-in hybrids, by contrast, use electric power for a range of thirty to sixty miles and rely on a combination of gas and electric power for longer trips. Moreover, a study from the U.S. Department of Energy showed that plug-in hybrids reduced greenhouse gas emissions in forty-nine states across the country—even in states that were heavily dependent on coal to generate power. States that use large amounts of hydroelectric power, such as Washington and Idaho, produce emission savings of more than 80 percent with plug-in hybrids. North Dakota, which relies upon coal that is particularly low in energy output, won't enjoy any savings from plug-ins until it cleans its electricity grid.

Chelsea Sexton, a former GM employee featured in *Who Killed the Electric Car?* who promoted the electric EV1 until it was discontinued, says that plug-in hybrids are "the best of both worlds" between hybrids and electric cars. "Maybe your first forty miles of the day are all electric," Sexton says. "Monday through Friday you may never use gasoline. But if you want to drive to Vegas on the weekend, you have gasoline in the tank as a backup. We call plug-in hybrids 'electric cars with a safety net!'"

A typical hybrid gets twice the gas mileage of your average gas-powered car, and plug-ins get about twice the mileage of a typical hybrid. Since 78 percent of all commuters live within twenty miles of their employers, plug-in hybrids would produce zero emissions and use not a single drop of gasoline for most trips. Most of the plug-in hybrids on the road today exceed a hundred miles per gallon. On longer voyages, to go camping or to visit grandma for the weekend, a combination of gas and electric power gives plug-in hybrids a range of four to five hundred miles. After that, drivers can just pull into any gas station, fill up, and go. Frank estimates that a plug-in vehicle would cost about $4,000 to $6,000 more than a conventional car. "That's what some people pay for a sunroof, leather seats and a fancy navigation system," he says.

Pass It On

Plug-in hybrid vehicles can travel more than a hundred miles per gallon of gas. Vehicles can drive up to forty or fifty miles on a single charge, and can recharge the electrical battery at the equivalent of $0.75 to $1.00 per gallon.

Frank has been advancing plug-in hybrid automotive technology for years. He built his first plug-in hybrid in 1971, as part of a Department of Transportation contest on the future of urban driving. In the mid-1990s Frank and his UC Davis students designed a series of improved plug-in hybrid vehicles that achieved far better mileage than anything Detroit was putting on the road. Frank offered the technology to major automakers, but everyone passed.

Several years ago, Frank and his team made further advancements. They modernized a 2002 Ford Explorer, producing a 325 horsepower vehicle that could go fifty miles on a single electric charge and get twice the gas mileage of a hybrid vehicle. Once again, Frank offered the technology to major automakers. Once again, everyone passed—except Toyota. The automaker sent a team to Davis, California, that packed up the entire vehicle, shipped it to Japan, put it through a battery of tests, and returned it a few months later.

On a hot summer day in late June 2007, Frank told me he had recently formed his own company, Efficient Designs. He had spent the morning with an official from India, and much of the afternoon with officials from China. He was planning a presentation on plug-in hybrid technology for the Chinese government later that year. "We're talking about a mandate to increase production volumes for plug-in hybrids in the near future," he said. "China could do it, and do it quickly, and if a 'low-tech' country such as India or China leapt ahead of the United States, then maybe then U.S. car companies would pay attention."

It could be a Sputnik moment.

Taking Plug-Ins Mainstream

If we wait for Detroit to voluntarily mass-produce vehicles that sip rather than chug gasoline, we'll be waiting a long time. However, a constellation of individuals, entrepreneurs, and organizations has emerged to pressure automakers and regulators to get moving. They span the political spectrum and boast support from Hollywood celebrities and businesses alike. "I call this a coalition of the tree huggers, do-gooders, sod-busters, cheap hawks, evangelicals, utility shareholders, mom and pop drivers . . . and Willie Nelson," says R. James Woolsey, former CIA director, conservative war hawk, and plug-in hybrid enthusiast.

Plug In America is one organization leading the way. Founded by ex–GM employee Sexton and other electric-vehicle enthusiasts, it held one of its first meetings in Dave Raboy's living room. The organization lists ways for its members to take action to accelerate the transition to zero-emission vehicles. "I think it is important for government to set standards making cleaner cars because what we know for sure is that Detroit doesn't have a history of wanting to do it on their own," Sexton observes.

Plug-In Partners, an organization founded by the city of Austin, Texas, has organized hundreds of cities, states, and businesses to push for the rapid production of plug-in hybrid vehicles. The coalition—which includes the cities of Anchorage, Chicago, Miami, Chapel Hill, and Salt Lake City, organizations such as Rainforest Action Network, and companies such as Google and Auto Nation (the country's largest auto dealership)—is collecting vehicle orders to demonstrate the growing demand for plug-ins. "We believe that the 50 largest cities in the United States, united in purpose, can build a groundswell in demand sufficient enough to entice automakers to mass produce" these vehicles, says Will Wynn, Austin's mayor.

Unwilling to wait for the automakers, several groups have begun helping people to convert existing hybrids into plug-in ones. Felix Kramer founded CalCars in 2004, soon after buying his Toyota Prius. Like many Prius owners, he wondered about the purpose of the nonfunctioning, unmarked button just to the right of the steering wheel. A little online research revealed that in Japanese and European models, pressing the button allowed the car to run exclusively on electric power. However, since the U.S. Prius batteries were so small, the car could only drive one to two miles on the electrical charge.

An engineer in Texas had figured out how to program U.S. vehicles to use the electric power in a way similar to the Japanese and European models. CalCars soon published a manual on how to convert the Prius into a plug-in hybrid that travels a hundred miles per gallon or more. Other than devoting a small portion of the trunk's space to a pack of batteries, the car looks and rides like a typical car, only one that gets four times the mileage of your everyday sedan. The biggest challenge is to convince Detroit to bring these vehicles to market quickly, says Kramer. "How do you take an idea that makes sense into something real? Plug-ins are cleaner, cheaper, and domestic. We can electrify transportation, and then clean the grid. This will do more than anything to solve global warming."

Lithium ion battery manufacturer A123 Systems will begin marketing battery packs and training third-party mechanics to perform plug-in hybrid conversions in 2008. The company's CEO, David Vries, estimates that a typical conversion will take two hours. The cost is significant, $10,000, but for an average commuter driving a vehicle eleven thousand miles per year, the time needed to realize that amount in savings would be 5.5 years (with gas at $3 per gallon). A federal tax credit for plug-in hybrid conversions would cut the payback time considerably. Most important, the costs are expected to drop significantly as economies of scale are achieved. "We estimate a fivefold increase in demand from an increasingly responsive American public," Vries said. The Silicon Valley Leadership Group announced in September 2007 that a hundred of its CEOs pledged to buy converted plug-ins in 2008.

Another company that isn't waiting for Washington or Detroit to show the way is California-based startup Tesla Motor Company. It's a small firm with some big goals. "Whether it's because of high oil prices or climate change, we essentially have to retool the entire automotive industry," says J.B. Straubel, Tesla's chief technical officer. Tesla is off to a good start. The company's first vehicle, the Tesla Roadster, is an electric vehicle that can travel about 220 miles on a single charge. It beats the Lamborghini Murcielago and is quicker than any Porsche currently in production, traveling from zero to sixty in under four seconds—without a drop of gas. The price is a cool $92,000, yet the company's first edition of one hundred Roadsters sold out in weeks.

Pass It On

The Tesla Roadster is an electric car that can go from zero to sixty in four seconds and travel 220 miles on a single electrical charge.

I went for a test ride at the company's headquarters in San Carlos one bright February morning. As we cruised through the hills above Silicon Valley, the company's strategy became perfectly clear: Tesla wanted to help "retool" the auto industry by getting people excited about cars again. Because this car was fast. I felt like a pilot on *Battlestar Galactica* as the car accelerated, pushing me back in my seat. Tesla employees have a favorite trick to pull on passengers taking their first rides: he or she is asked to turn on the radio—and simultaneously the driver hits the accelerator. The passenger can't sit forward enough to reach the dials.

Backed by deep-pocketed investors such as Google founders Larry Page and Sergey Brin, PayPal founder Elon Musk, and eBay founder Jeffrey Skoll, Tesla plans to hit the family car market in 2010 or 2011. "We've always envisioned the company to be more than a high-end niche sports-car manufacturer," says Straubel. "It's a great way to change the world's perceptions of EVs and to show what electric cars can do, but we want to make affordable vehicles in much greater quantities." Adds Musk, Tesla's chairman, "Climate change is the biggest challenge that mankind has ever faced. If we can't change such a simple thing as the cars we drive, we're going to be in trouble."

Mobile Power Plants

On a sunny California afternoon in June 2007, about two hundred staff, guests, and media stood in the parking lot of Google's headquarters. Google's nonprofit division, Google.org, had just finished a press conference to announce several new climate-change projects as part of its new RechargeIT program. The search-engine giant had recently made plug-ins from four Toyota Priuses and two Ford Escape hybrids, and had committed to converting up to a hundred more cars. They also had installed the country's largest commercial solar array, 1.6 megawatts, so that the new plug-in cars—and a substantial portion of Google's headquarters—could be powered by renewable energy.

But perhaps the most visionary demonstration that day was to showcase a technology called vehicle-to-grid power, or V2G. Envisioned by Dr. Willett Kempton at the University of Delaware, this technology helps plug-ins and electric vehicles address a fundamental problem with the power grid: "The electrical system has no way of storing energy. When you turn on a light switch, somebody has to turn on a power plant somewhere to create the power," describes Frank.

There are various ways to store electricity for the power grid. One is with batteries, which are limited by high costs and relatively short life spans (although experimental sodium-sulfur batteries hold some promise). There are also mechanical processes, such as compressing air or pumping water up a hill when excess electricity is available. These methods are also expensive, however, and lose at least 25 percent of the stored energy. Instead, the grid often uses "peaker plants," some of the oldest and most inefficient power facilities in the country. Peaker plants are fired up only to meet excess demand, typically on hot summer days and evenings.

If they were produced on a large scale, plug-in hybrid and electric cars could offer an excellent alternative. The development of large, rechargeable batteries in these vehicles offers a way to extend the power of solar and wind by storing, at high efficiency, the excess electricity that they produce. "The sun doesn't always shine, and the wind doesn't always blow," says Frank. "To help out solar and wind, you need electricity storage, and that's where plug-in hybrids come in. They provide batteries to store energy, whether it's to drive your car or power your home."

"For alternative energy sources like wind and solar, where you might not necessarily be generating the power exactly when you need it, you can store this power and delay when it's used by holding it in the battery," says Alec Proudfoot, a mechanical engineer at Google. The batteries in plug-in hybrid and electric vehicles become short-term energy banks. They can plug in at night, when demand is lowest, and then put some of the energy back into the grid during the daytime, when demand typically hits its peak.

I don't want to sugar-coat this: there are some significant obstacles to wide adoption of vehicle-to-grid technology. First, automakers need to build hybrids and electric vehicles in significant quantities. GM has announced plans to produce up to sixty thousand plug-in hybrid Chevy Volts by 2010 or 2011. Toyota's first plug-in hybrids are due in 2010. Mitsubishi says it will sell small quantities of an electric car, the Colt, also in 2010. Subaru plans to release an electric minicar, the R1E, in 2009, and Dodge is testing a commercial van, the Sprinter, for commercial release by 2010. Given the industry's poor track record on zero-emission vehicles, one might be skeptical that the automakers will make good on these plans. The challenge will be to make sure that automakers move as quickly as possible to scale up production.

Further, some new infrastructure would be required. Although plug-in hybrids or electric vehicles need only a standard 120-volt plug to charge up their batteries, plugging electricity back into the grid is more complicated. Drivers would need to estimate how much electricity they needed before the next recharge. To sell the rest back to the grid, they'd park in lots or garages outfitted with computer technology to monitor the energy drained from each battery and credit the vehicles' owners. Although this technology currently exists and can be installed cost-effectively, it's a bit complicated and would require voluntary participation from drivers.

All things considered, it's best to think of plug-ins and electric vehicles primarily as an excellent way to reduce emissions and win freedom from oil. Any future use of these vehicles to supplement the electricity grid would be a bonus.

And some of the world's best engineers are working to turn that promise into a reality. At Google's headquarters, the crowd gathered to watch a car act as a mobile power station. Larry Brilliant, Google.org's executive director, flipped the switch and . . . nothing. A few seconds passed as Brilliant grinned mischievously and Proudfoot's brow furrowed in anticipation. Suddenly, the monitor came alive and there was a vehicle-to-grid transmission. The plug-in hybrid car in front of us had just become California's newest power source. Brilliant said, "You can recharge the car from the sun, you can recharge the grid from the car, and you can recharge our enthusiasm for trying to tackle the problems of global warming all at once."

Rescuing Detroit

Engineering innovators and passionate consumers are playing key roles in helping to create a sustainable future for the automobile, but they need much more help on the policy side. Rather than assisting the auto industry's suicide, the federal government should be playing the role of life coach. Lawmakers should regulate the industry and hold it to much higher standards for fuel efficiency.

Other policy measures that could be implemented by Congress and the White House include the following:

- An immediate purchase order for thirty thousand plug-in hybrid and electric vehicles. The federal government buys sixty-five thousand new vehicles each year. Dedicating approximately half of these purchases to advanced automotive technology such as plug-in hybrid or electric vehicles would offer a powerful incentive for change.

- Tax credits of up to $6,000 for buyers of the first million plug-in hybrid and electric vehicles; reduced credits of $4,000 for buyers of the second million vehicles. It is estimated that the extra cost of a plug-in hybrid vehicle could be $6,000 to start, declining as economies of scale are developed. This tax credit would cost $10 billion over several years, but could be paid for several times over by eliminating subsidies to the oil industry.

- Allow owners of plug-in hybrids and electric vehicles to use carpool and high-occupancy-vehicle lanes at all times. A similar law in California for traditional hybrid vehicles helped to jump-start the hybrid market several years ago.

- Send a strong price signal to automakers and car buyers alike that the days of cheap oil are gone forever by enacting a gas tax. Gas taxes are regressive, so the revenues would need to be rebated to low-income taxpayers.

There's plenty more that federal and state policymakers could do, such as enacting "feebate" legislation: adding one-time fees to the purchase price of inefficient vehicles while reducing by a similar amount the cost of the cars earning the best fuel economy. At some point, though, the auto industry will need to become a willing partner in its resurrection. Industry executives would be wise to hire fewer lawyers and lobbyists and more engineers. Cars will need to play a smaller role in our transportation mix, but that doesn't mean we can't get excited about them again. Major automakers have a powerful new opportunity to respond to Americans like the Raboys, who know that cars can be part of the solution. In doing so, they can also meet the challenge of innovators like Tesla who understand that we still want to love our cars as well.

Take Action

Take it personally

1. It's important that automakers build more fuel-efficient vehicles, but it's also important that we drive less. Join a carpool if you can. Hop on a bus or a bicycle, or telecommute. There are plenty of ways to reduce your dependence on the automobile.

2. Even so, most American households will still need a car. Some 17 million new cars and trucks are made in the United States each year. Your responsibility couldn't be clearer: vote with your dollars. Don't buy gas guzzlers and enable America's oil addiction. If you can put off a purchase, let the automakers know that you won't buy a new vehicle until they produce plug-in hybrid or electric vehicles. Otherwise, buy the most fuel-efficient model for the size and class that you need. And when you rent a vehicle, ask for a hybrid.

3. If you already own a hybrid, convert it to a plug-in if you can afford to. Your car could travel thirty to sixty miles without using a drop of gas, and earn up to a hundred miles per gallon or more. Contact CalCars or A123 Systems to find an auto shop near you that does conversions.

Express yourself

1. California regulators often set the standard for the rest of the country. Ask the California Air Resources Board to reinstate the zero-emission mandate and bring more plug-in hybrid and electric vehicles to the road. Visit www.pluginamerica.org for more information.

2. Jump-start Detroit! Ford and GM used to be symbols of American ingenuity and automotive know-how, but now they're stuck in neutral. Urge automakers to build plug-in hybrid and electric vehicles and revitalize our manufacturing base. You'll find a description of other organizations working on this issue in the resources section.

3. Contact your representatives in Congress and urge them to get real on oil and climate. Recent legislation that pushes automakers to thirty-five miles per gallon within ten to twenty years is a nice first step but doesn't solve the problem, given the added vehicles that will soon be on the road. It's time for Congress to offer incentives—and set standards—to convert the entire U.S. fleet to plug-ins and electric vehicles as soon as possible.

4. Join Plug-In Partners. Make a pledge to buy a plug-in hybrid if or when automakers manufacture them at www.pluginpartners.org. Pressure your city or state to use its automotive purchasing power to demand change. It can join New York, Minnesota,

San Francisco, Los Angeles, and others to commit to buy plug-in hybrid cars once they're manufactured. Convince your employer to do the same. Together, we can create demand for hundreds of thousands of plug-in hybrids, and let automakers compete for this growing market.

Stay engaged

Explore other effective, creative ways to help automakers stay viable in an era of climate change and volatile oil prices. Join Global Exchange and visit your local dealership and ask that it become part of the effort to push the industry to provide cars that don't pollute. If you own stock in any of the major automakers, contact the Interfaith Center on Corporate Responsibility or other shareholder advocacy organizations to use your leverage as an owner of the company. Review the resources section at the end of this book for other ways to take effective action.

CHAPTER 7

Growing Gas

Are Biofuels Fueling or Fooling America?

*The only way to reap the benefits of biofuels
without squeezing the food supply is to take food
out of the picture.*

—JOEL K. BOURNE, JR.

Imagine the wonder of seeing an orangutan in the wild for the first time," Dr. Birute Galdikas told me. "You're walking on the forest floor, you can hear and feel an orangutan's presence, and then you spot one moving in a shaft of sunlight in the rainforest canopy. Orangutans are very gentle and quite large—adult males weigh over three hundred pounds. When you see these animals move with such grace, it takes your breath away."

I had the chance to speak with Galdikas as she traveled in the United States to raise awareness about the threat to orangutans posed by the expansion of the palm oil industry. Galdikas has been an advocate for orangutans for decades. She arrived on the remote island of Borneo at the age of twenty-five to study wild orangutans in Indonesia's tropical rainforests. With Jane Goodall and Dian Fossey, who studied and lobbied for the protection of chimpanzees and mountain gorillas in Africa, Galdikas was a fellow protégé of the famed paleontologist Dr. Louis Leakey. She established a research facility—Camp Leakey—near Indonesia's Tanjung Puting National Park, and has maintained a presence there for more than thirty-five years, tirelessly defending orangutans and other endangered species in Indonesia's lush forests.

"Orangutans really are our cousins," Galdikas says. "They share approximately 97 percent of their genetic material with human beings. In their emotions and perceptions—even in their cognitive abilities—they're very much like humans." Indeed, the name *orangutan* comes from the local Malay, meaning "person of the forest." And it's a "person" with a big brain on its shoulders: a recent study led by Harvard University psychologist James Lee identified orangutans as the most intelligent animal (other than humans, presumably). Of the twenty-five primate species, orangutans have the greatest ability to learn and solve problems. They've been observed weaving leaves together to make hats to shelter themselves from the rain, building roofs, and teaching each other how to build simple tools to get food. Orangutans are also noted for their intense maternal instincts; mothers typically are inseparable from their offspring for the first eight to ten years.

Yet the biggest problem orangutans face is outside their control. Indonesia and Malaysia produced 87 percent of the world's palm oil in 2006. To achieve this production, more than 6.5 million acres of irreplaceable tropical forests have been cleared for massive palm oil plantations. "Palm oil is the worst enemy of orangutans," declares Galdikas.

How does the fate of orangutans relate to America's fossil-fuel addiction? Just this: although it has typically been used in processed foods and for soaps and cosmetics, palm oil has recently become a lucrative feedstock for the exploding biofuels market. Each year, plantation owners set huge fires to clear forests and expand their holdings, often directly in orangutan habitat. While the forests burn, airline flights are routinely canceled or delayed, and smoke from the region can often be seen from outer space. The fires in Borneo in 1997–98 alone destroyed 5 million acres of rainforest and led to the deaths of an estimated one-third of the world's remaining orangutan population.

Without a dramatic turnaround, orangutans face a brutal fate. Millions more acres of palm plantations are planned to meet the booming biofuel demand. Sadly, orangutans are threatened not only by habitat destruction. Since they eat the young palms that produce oil, many plantation owners offer a bounty on them. "We find orangutans burned, or their heads cut off. Hunters are paid 150,000 rupiah (about 20 bucks) for the right hand of an orangutan to prove they've killed them," says Dr. Willie Smits, founder and chair of the Borneo Orangutan Survival Foundation.

Biodiversity throughout the region suffers from the destruction of Indonesia's rainforests, nearly 75 percent of which has already been laid waste—mostly within the past four decades. As the world's demand for "green" biofuels grows, the pace of destruction is rapidly increasing. The United Nations Environment Program estimates that up to 98 percent of orangutan habitat may be lost by 2022, threatening not only these primates but also the Sumatran tiger, Asian elephant, and countless other species in this wondrous and diverse rainforest.

"It would be a much lonelier planet if orangutans disappeared," Galdikas says. Clearly, that is a very real risk, and the world's growing demand for biofuels will only make it worse.

Dead-End "Solutions"

The lure of biofuels is seductive. Rather than bankrolling terrorists and cooking the planet by burning gas in our cars, trucks, and SUVs, America can grow its way to energy independence, or so the thinking goes. Some crops, such as corn, sugar beets, and sugar cane, can be converted into ethanol, while the oil from palm, rapeseed (known as canola in this country), soy, and other plants can be transformed into biodiesel. Both are either added to gas or used to replace gasoline entirely. Plant-based fuels can be domestically grown, have the potential to clean up our air and water, and require no changes in driving habits.

Sounds good, doesn't it? The reality is more complex and a lot less sunny. This country's most popular fuel alternative is ethanol from corn, which might produce less energy than is used to grow and process it. Corn is also one of the most resource-intensive and environmentally damaging industrial crops; it exacerbates soil depletion and creates "dead zones" in waterways, due to fertilizer runoff. And if dead orangutans aren't gruesome enough, consider that biodiesel from palm oil in tropical rainforests can produce up to ten times as much greenhouse gases as conventional oil.

Pass It On

Palm oil from tropical regions such as Indonesia and Malaysia creates up to ten times more greenhouse gas emissions than oil, and causes the displacement of millions of Indigenous people.

It gets worse. Demand for plant-based fuels is growing so fast that many industrial farmers find it more profitable to grow fuel than food crops. This is causing the prices of corn, wheat, meat, and other products to rise significantly, with devastating consequences for the world's poorest people, who find they are competing with automobiles for food. All for dubious benefits: even if every ear of corn in the United States were devoted to ethanol, only 12 percent of the gasoline we now use would be replaced.

But don't go crying in your cornmeal just yet. International experts distinguish "agrofuels"—the product of highly mechanized factory farms with significant social and environmental downsides—from "biofuels," which can offer some benefits to both people and the planet. The difference is similar to that between giant industrial farms—let's call them "food factories"—and small family farmers who can grow food in a sustainable way. Our country can ill afford any further subsidies or growth in the agrofuel economy, but biofuels *may* have a small yet useful role to play, as long as strict environmental and humanitarian rules are established and enforced. We'll sort through these different approaches in the following sections.

Biofuels 101

The largest producers of ethanol in the world today are the United States, which uses corn to produce 95 percent of its ethanol, and Brazil, which relies mostly on sugar cane. Most biodiesel crops are grown either in Europe or in Southeast Asia; in 2005, Germany produced more than half of the world's biodiesel from rapeseed. However, palm oil is growing rapidly as a feedstock. Giant palm plantations are appearing throughout the tropics, from Indonesia, Malaysia, and Papua New Guinea to the African countries of Ghana, Kenya, Senegal, Nigeria, and Uganda, as well as throughout Latin America, particularly in Colombia, Venezuela, and Bolivia.

How can a plant make your car move? Let's talk about conventional ethanol first. As you might guess, sugar cane and sugar beets contain sugar. Other crops such as corn, barley, sunflower, and wheat contain starches, which can easily be converted into sugar. Once this is done, the sugar is fermented with yeast to produce the same product long used to spike the punch at college parties:

grain alcohol. This alcohol is purified to produce ethanol, which is then mixed with gasoline.

Henry Ford originally designed his Model T to run on alcohol. He called it "the fuel of the future." (Oil companies had a different idea.) When you see E-5, E-10, or E-85 at the gas pump, the numbers refer to the percentage of ethanol that has been blended with conventional gasoline. If your car was manufactured since the early 1980s, you can use up to 10 percent ethanol without any modifications needed. To use fuel containing larger percentages requires driving a "flexible fuel vehicle," which automakers are manufacturing in increasing quantities each year.

Biodiesel production is also straightforward. The process is called trans-esterification, in which chemicals are mixed with vegetable oils or animal fats to separate glycerine from methyl esters. Glycerine is often used for soaps and cosmetics; methyl esters is the scientific name for biodiesel. Biodiesel can be made from almost any fat or oil, from palm, soy, rapeseed, jatropha (a leafy bush found in dry regions near the equator), or even recycled cooking grease.

Finally, fuel can be generated from the cellulosic matter in grasses, agricultural waste, and even trees and algae. Researchers working on this experimental process believe that significant energy savings and reductions in greenhouse gas emissions can be achieved. Other experts doubt that this fuel will be available commercially any time soon, and point out different, but significant, environmental drawbacks. We're talking about "cellulosic ethanol" here, the stuff of prairie switchgrass and State of the Union speeches. We'll examine the issue more closely later in this chapter.

Here's what the availability of biofuels means for you and me. If you own a diesel-powered vehicle that has been manufactured since 1993, you can drive on 100 percent pure veggie oil. If you have a flexible-fuel vehicle, you can power up on at least 85 percent corn. The burning question (pardon the pun) is: should you really want to?

Driving Food Insecurity

Agriculture's rapid shift from food to fuels is sending shockwaves throughout the globalized food system. Ethanol production in the United States totaled nearly 5 billion gallons in 2006, an increase of almost 300 percent from 2000. The construction of new ethanol refineries will add an additional 6 billion gallons of capacity by 2009, still a small amount compared with the 140 billion gallons of gas the United States consumes each year. The energy bill signed in 2007 mandates that 36 billion gallons of fuel come from biofuels by 2030.

Worldwide total production of ethanol and biodiesel has more than tripled since 2000, reaching 16 billion gallons, which is still less than 3 percent of the global transportation supply. In the European Union, agrofuels comprised just one percent of transportation fuel in 2005; the EU has committed to increase biofuel consumption to meet 10 percent of their transportation fuel needs by 2020.

Pass It On

U.S. ethanol production grew from about 1.6 billion gallons in 2000 to nearly 5 billion gallons in 2006. By 2009, it is projected to total 11 billion gallons. By 2030, 36 billion.

An in-depth study released by Iowa State University revealed that current levels of agrofuel production in the United States have already raised retail food prices for basic staples, including cereals, eggs, milk, meat, and other essentials, by more than $14 billion. The study showed that if the United States hit projected levels of ethanol production by 2020, the U.S. acreage devoted to corn would increase significantly, further crowding out soy, wheat, and other crops. The U.S. Department of Agriculture has released advisories about rising food prices; the United Nations Food and Agriculture Organization (FAO) has issued similar warnings, citing the demand for agrofuels as a main cause.

The food and energy sectors of the economy, once separate, are thus converging. The world's poor will be hurt the most, as a rush to agrofuels will increase food shortages and drive up prices. Nearly 2.5 billion people in the world live on less than $2 per day, according to the World Bank. Increases in the prices of their food—whether grown in-country, imported for sale, or distributed as aid—could be devastating. "The stage is now set for direct competition for grain between the 800 million people who own automobiles, and the world's 2 billion poorest people," writes Lester Brown of the Earth Policy Institute. "The risk is that millions of those on the lower rungs of the global economic ladder will start falling off as higher food prices drop their consumption below the survival level."

Filling the gas tank of a typical SUV with 100 percent ethanol just once requires more than 450 pounds of corn, or enough calories to feed one person for an entire year. The United Nations World Food Program estimates that 850 million people in thirty-four countries are facing urgent and persistent food shortages. The program can afford to feed just 90 million of those people, and warns that food-price increases due to the booming agrofuels market might further cut the number of people it can serve. In December 2007, Jean Ziegler, the U.N. special rapporteur on the right to food, called agrofuels a "crime against humanity" and demanded a five-year moratorium on the expansion of the industry.

More than eighteen thousand children die every day around the world due to lack of food and malnutrition. Continued growth in agrofuel production could make this tragedy even worse. If strong action isn't taken, the decision about whether food goes into children's bellies or into automobiles will be made by some of the world's largest corporations.

The ABCs of Agrofuels

The industrial powerhouses behind agrofuels are an alphabet soup of corporate plunderers. In the United States we have mainly Archer Daniels Midland Company (ADM) to thank for the development of the corn-based ethanol market. ADM's former CEO Dwayne Andreas was infamous for cutting the $25,000 check to pay for Nixon's hacks to break into the Watergate in 1972. He began peddling ethanol back in the 1970s to diversify the company's market for corn. ADM now leads the country in ethanol production, supplying more than 25 percent of the market here in the United States. A large donor to both Republicans and Democrats, ADM receives billions of dollars in federal and state ethanol subsidies. The conservative Cato Institute in 1995 called the company "the most prominent recipient of corporate welfare in recent U.S. history."

In expanding the global trade in agrofuels, ADM is joined by its agribusiness competitors Cargill and Bunge. All three companies are expanding massive soy plantations in South America's Cerrado, a vast forested savannah encompassing parts of Brazil, Paraguay, and Bolivia that is inhabited by thousands of Indigenous peoples and an extraordinary diversity of plant and animal life, including jaguars and maned wolves. Deforestation rates in the Cerrado rival that of the Amazon, where more than 15 million acres were cleared by entrenched and often corrupt businesses to feed mills operated by Cargill and Brazilian companies. Under pressure from Greenpeace and other environmental and human rights organizations, Brazilian companies and their international counterparts agreed to a moratorium of several years to prevent further deforestation in the Amazon.

No such agreement exists in the Cerrado, however, or in any of the other regions where Cargill, ADM, and Bunge operate. Furthermore, human rights abuses such as forced labor are rampant on these plantations. "Agribusiness is having a party but not inviting the rest of us," says Hiparidi Toptiro, president of the Mobilization of the Indigenous People of the Cerrado (MOPIC). When ADM, under pressure, came to RAN headquarters for a meeting in September 2007, it was the only company that had declined to sign an antislavery pact to prevent forced labor on plantations in Brazil. An ADM executive told us that the issue was "highly complex," and it would take time for the company to determine the "appropriate" response. Incredulous, I asked, "How many more meetings will it take before you decide slavery is bad?" A month later, ADM informed us that it would sign the pact.

Cargill and ADM are also profiting from palm oil throughout the tropics. Plantations owned by Cargill contribute to extensive deforestation in Papua New Guinea and Indonesia, including prime orangutan habitat near Indonesia's Gunung Palung National Park. ADM is a major investor in Wilmar, a Malaysian-owned firm that operates palm plantations to the east and west of Indonesia's Tanjun Puting National Park as well as in Malaysia, Uganda, and elsewhere.

Land Grab

The explosion of agrofuel production in many tropical countries has all the makings of a human rights disaster: weak and corrupt governments, powerful corporations seeking land from poor and marginalized farmers, and the potential for enormous profits.

In Colombia, the threat of agrofuel plantations and attendant human rights violations has been added to the terror of a decades-long civil war. There are more displaced citizens in Colombia than in any other country except Sudan. Many palm plantations in the country have been established illegally, using force and without any consultation with local landowners. It's likely to get worse, as Colombian authorities try to double production of palm oil by 2011.

Milvia Días lost her land and her father, Innocence Días. Several years ago, Innocence was threatened by paramilitaries who wanted the family's land. One afternoon he went out to fix a small hole in a fence. "We stayed up all night waiting for him," Milvia recalls. The family sent out a search party early the next morning, to find that Innocence had been murdered. "He was in the field where he had been mending the fence. He had seven stab wounds and his throat was cut from ear to ear. And they ripped his throat out." The family fled, and Milvia now resides in the western Choco region of Colombia. The farm they were forced to abandon is now covered with palm trees.

It is a sad irony that, in the rush to find alternatives to oil, corporations and nations are allowing the same abuses to occur that once characterized the oil boom. "If you don't negotiate with us, we'll negotiate with your widow" is a common line used by thugs in Colombia to pressure peasants to sell their land, according to an advocate with Christian Aid.

In a globalized world, however, the rights and dignity of people can no longer be violated in secrecy. Organizations such as Food First, Christian Aid, Sawit Watch, and Via Campesina document and publicize these violations, amplifying the voices of poor and marginalized communities that are being violently displaced in Paraguay, Indonesia, Brazil, Uganda, and around the world.

Few studies exist that document how many people worldwide are being forced off their land to feed the agrofuel craze. The United Nations estimates that in the province of West Kalimantan, Indonesia, alone, up to 5 million indigenous people are likely to be displaced by palm oil expansion. "Indigenous people are being pushed off their land to make way for the expansion of biofuel crops around the world, threatening to destroy their cultures," says Victoria Tauli Corpuz, chair of the U.N. Permanent Forum on Indigenous Issues.

One villager in West Kalimantan lost his farm in 2006. "I went to my land one morning and found it had been cleared. All my rubber trees, my plants, had been destroyed," he told a BBC reporter. "Now I have to work as a builder in Malaysia, so I can feed my three children."

Runoff Pollution at Home

It's like something you'd watch on television on a lazy Saturday afternoon: the Dead Zone. Here's what's happening. As ethanol booms here in the United States, corn prices are increasing, leading more farmers to plant more corn more frequently. Most farmers used to rotate soybeans and corn crops annually to maintain soil quality and reduce the need for fertilizers and pesticides. Now, however, many are extending the time between rotations, often planting corn for several straight seasons.

As a result, many farmers are increasing their use of chemical fertilizers, causing increased soil runoff and water contamination. Corn production consumes 40 percent of all commercial fertilizers used in the United States, including nitrogen and phosphate. These nutrients flow straight into our waterways, causing algae blooms, which in turn deplete the water of oxygen.

No oxygen means no fish. One of the largest "dead zones" can be found in the Gulf of Mexico, where the Mississippi River dumps fertilizer runoff from the Midwest. The Gulf dead zone in 2007 swelled to seventy-nine hundred square miles, about the size of Delaware and Connecticut combined. The Ecological Society of America calls it "the most widespread water quality problem in the United States and many other nations."

Pass It On

The dead zone in the Gulf of Mexico has grown to seventy-nine hundred square miles—about the size of Delaware and Connecticut combined—in large part due to fertilizer runoff from increased corn production.

If these nutrients are damaging aquatic ecosystems and killing fish, you can imagine that they are threatening human health as well. Fertilizers wash off farms and contaminate underground water supplies. High levels of nitrates in drinking water cause a wide range of health effects, from spontaneous miscarriages and birth defects to ovarian, uterine, and bladder cancers.

More Hot Air?

Another controversy is whether agrofuels actually save energy—in other words, does it take more fossil fuels to produce them than they can put in the gas tank? This "net energy balance" is calculated by subtracting the energy required to grow and harvest the fuels (fertilizers, tractor diesel, transport, etc.) from the stored energy those fuels contain.

Until recently, many studies showed that corn-based ethanol had a negative net energy balance. The calculation is complicated by the fact that ethanol contains 33 percent less energy than gasoline, meaning that you need more fuel to go the same distance. The industry has become more efficient in recent years, however, leading some (though not all) researchers to believe that corn-based ethanol has achieved a positive energy balance. Other agrofuel sources require much lower inputs of fuel. Biodiesel from soy, for example, produces five times as much fuel as it consumes, while ethanol from sugar cane produces eight times as much.

Unfortunately for most agrofuels, that's the easy part. The next challenge is to determine whether the fuel will decrease greenhouse gas emissions. To calculate this, we must remember the role that forests and soils play in mitigating climate change, because carbon is stored in trees, plants, and soil. The Intergovernmental Panel on Climate Change estimates that, on average, 20 percent of annual greenhouse gas emissions come from agriculture, deforestation, and other "land use changes." The worst of these is the clearing of tropical rainforests, which, because of their ability to absorb carbon, are critical to moderating the effects of climate change.

Most agrofuels do not pass the test of lowering greenhouse gas emissions. In February 2008, two articles in the prestigious journal *Science* examined the life-cycle impacts of many agrofuel sources. They found that almost all agrofuels actually caused *more* greenhouse gas emissions than conventional fuels, in large part due to the conversion of wild lands—whether rainforests or grasslands—to plantations. Other factors, including which crops were grown, how they were cultivated, and how much fossil fuel was used to fertilize them and process the fuel, caused further increases in emissions, to varying degrees. Only ethanol from sugar in Brazil was believed to reduce greenhouse gas emissions.

Without strict controls, the agrofuels industry could create a climate disaster. Nowhere is this problem worse than in Indonesia. A study by Wetlands International reveals that the draining and burning of peat forests to produce palm oil in Indonesia results in the release of up to thirty-three tons of carbon dioxide for each ton of palm oil produced, or as much as ten times the emissions that come from petroleum! It's crazy, but true: when we clear tropical forests to grow agrofuels, we're destroying one of the best tools that we have to protect our climate in an ill-fated attempt to . . . protect our climate.

Fueling Responsibly

Biofuels may have an important role to play in replacing some oil use—provided that at least five conditions are met. They must reduce greenhouse gas emissions substantially; not displace food crops and threaten food security for the world's poor; uphold the integrity of critical ecosystems, particularly in tropical forests; and strengthen the human rights of community farmers and Indigenous people. Most importantly, biofuels should be developed only as part of a broader strategy to reduce fuel consumption and redesign mobility. If these standards can be enacted and strictly enforced, then biofuels can be one element in a sustainable transportation system.

Fortunately, there is a small but growing movement of individuals and organizations showing how it can be done. Organic Valley Family of Farms is one example. It's North America's largest organic-farming cooperative, with more than eleven hundred farmers in twenty-nine states and one Canadian province, and more than $334 million in sales in 2006. "We were formed by just seven farmers in 1988," says Cecil Wright, its director of local operations. "Our aim is to provide safe and healthy organic food to American families, and to sustain family farms and rural communities while doing so."

Organic Valley recently decided to provide locally grown, 100 percent biodiesel fuel for its distribution fleet. Local Organic Valley farmers will alternate between fuel and food crops. They'll use fuel crops that have short growing seasons, such as camelina (another flowering plant in the same family as rapeseed), so that they can grow their own fuel without limiting food production or increasing prices. Since most organic farms must maintain buffer areas of twenty-five to fifty feet around conventional farms (to stay clear of pesticide spraying), Organic Valley farmers can also grow fuel crops in those areas, where organic food can't be grown. "We're just experimenting now," says Wright. "But our farmers know that there's a way to reduce oil dependence, help the climate, and support family farms at the same time. We're determined to make this work."

One form of biofuels with a passionate following is biodiesel made from recycled oil, grease, and animal fat. This waste oil can be collected from restaurants, hotels, and other places where food is prepared, and converted into a fuel. While it's an excellent alternative, waste oil is available in limited quantities, currently providing less than 5 percent of all agrofuel production in an industry that provides less than 5 percent of the nation's gasoline.

An early waste-oil pioneer is a former diesel mechanic, Robert King. Back in the mid-1990s, workers at a Maui landfill were concerned that restaurant grease brought to the site was not only creating a fire hazard but also could contaminate local groundwater. King did a little homework, discovered that the waste oil could be made into a fuel, and set up his new company, Pacific Biodiesel, Inc., within months. Four years later, his company had built a small biodiesel plant in Honolulu, with a capacity of fifteen hundred gallons per day, and today operates similar plants in Oregon, California, Texas, Nevada, and Nagano, Japan.

Who Makes the Rules?

Between exacerbating world hunger, degrading endangered ecosystems, violating human rights, and increasing greenhouse gas emissions, there are too many ways in which agrofuels can create more problems than they may solve. The rapid growth of the industry only increases these risks further. But the absence of any strong, binding national or international standards for responsible production is what makes the growth of the agrofuels industry a recipe for disaster. It would be wise to put a global moratorium on the expansion of the industry until we can get it right, seeking input from the stakeholders that would be most affected by agrofuels development.

In the meantime, there are some nascent efforts to develop voluntary standards. For the small but growing U.S. biodiesel market, a strict code of ethics is being developed by the Sustainable Biodiesel Alliance (SBA). This group represents biodiesel producers, farmers, distributors, consumers, and even a few celebrity biodiesel enthusiasts such as Willie Nelson and Daryl Hannah. The SBA requires that biofuels not degrade or damage soils nor contaminate or deplete water supplies, and that they produce significantly lower greenhouse gas emissions than fossil fuels over their life cycle.

Internationally, several voluntary initiatives are underway. The Roundtable on Sustainable Biofuels (RSB) has brought together corporations, nonprofits, farmers, scientists, governments, and intergovernmental agencies to develop guidelines for improved production. Utilizing a "bioenergy wiki" (based on the online user-generated encyclopedia Wikipedia), participants share their perspectives on sustainable biofuels. There's also the Roundtable on Sustainable Palm Oil in Southeast Asia and the Roundtable on Responsible Soy in South America—both of which seek to bring together diverse stakeholders. On the one hand, it's good that these discussions are taking place. But the processes have no enforcement mechanisms and little accountability, and certainly are not yet pushing the agribusiness giants to reform their practices.

The European Union may offer the first sign of real hope. In March 2007, the EU made its commitment to produce 10 percent of its vehicles' fuels from biofuels by 2020. Almost immediately, there was an outcry from European citizens about the dangers of unregulated agrofuels. The EU quickly pledged to develop sustainability standards. It is establishing guidelines that would prohibit imports of agrofuels that do not meet minimum standards for greenhouse gas reduction and endangered ecosystem protection. As of this writing, those standards were still being developed.

As for the United States, the only policy seems to be to increase agrofuels production as fast as possible. So far, agribusiness and its supporters have resisted developing any social or environmental standards. But pressure is mounting.

The Way Forward

Let's remember, above all, that biofuels can only make a small dent in fuel consumption. Even though the yield per acre for different crops varies, there's not enough arable land in the United States to replace all—or even most—of the gasoline we use. Biofuels will need to be combined with other solutions.

The first three steps to promote sustainable transport don't involve biofuels at all. They are: (1) prioritize mass transit so that more people can drive less, (2) switch to plug-in hybrid or electric vehicles as quickly as possible, and (3) "green the grid" by producing electricity with renewable energy. When we get serious about fighting climate change and reducing oil consumption, those steps come first.

Let's call biofuels step 4. "Simply replacing one fuel with another won't work," says Heidi Quante, former director of the Sustainable Biodiesel Alliance. "In the end, it's not about volume; it's about finding a sustainable way to produce energy. Focusing on a single cheap and abundant source is what got us into trouble the last time. Biofuel is a solution, but it's only one part."

On the horizon are the development of cellulosic ethanol and the use of algae to produce biodiesel. At present this sector is mainly a parking lot for excess cash from billionaire investors: Richard Branson is a believer. So are Microsoft founder Bill Gates and Sun Microsystems cofounder and venture capitalist Vinod Khosla. These moguls, along with the U.S. Department of Energy and others, are investing millions in a race to convert native plants into low-cost fuels. What they're counting on is the ability of scientists—often using genetic engineering—to find an efficient and cost-effective way to break down the cellulose in fast-growing plants and grasses that have very high yields but comparatively low energy requirements.

Don't bet the farm on it, though. Production costs for these greener biofuels are still prohibitively high. The Department of Energy estimates that cellulosic ethanol costs twice as much as corn-based ethanol, which itself is one of the more costly and heavily subsidized agrofuels on the planet. The biggest technical hurdle is that the cellular bonds in the tissues of these plants are much more "recalcitrant," as the experts say, to being broken down into simple sugars.

Khosla isn't worried. "Today there are companies willing to invest around $60 million to $70 million of their own money [to commercialize cellulosic ethanol]. That is serious private money," observes Khosla (who stands to profit handsomely if this prediction comes true): "So, my guess is, if we're lucky, we'll have commercial-scale plants in three years. If we're very unlucky, it will be six."

I have to admit that it all sounds a little too much like boosterism to me. Perhaps there may be some breakthrough that doesn't cause unintended negative consequences, but in the meantime, let's push ahead with the sustainable transportation solutions that are available right now.

And let's set some simple rules, for cellulosic ethanol and all agrofuels. The true "fuels for the future" shouldn't poison our bodies or our waterways. They shouldn't degrade priceless ecosystems or kick people off their land. They certainly shouldn't cause people to go hungry.

If allowing our country to get hooked on oil and coal was America's biggest energy mistake in its recent past, then fostering dependence on ethanol and other agrofuels might be the worst blunder we could make in the near future. We'd be solving one set of problems by creating new ones. If we see ethanol, palm oil, and other agrofuels as a silver bullet, we'll be more likely to use that bullet to shoot ourselves in the foot.

Take Action

Take it personally

1. There are plenty of ways you can help promote sustainable fuel use. Do you drive a diesel car? Go veggie, but only if the fuel is from recycled waste oil or from local sources that don't degrade ecosystems and displace food crops. Visit the Sustainable Biodiesel Alliance at www.sustainablebiodieselalliance.org for a list of distributors in your region.

2. If you don't drive a diesel, hold off on buying your next new car until automakers provide "tribrids": plug-in hybrid, flexible-fuel vehicles. This choice lets you plug in and use electrical power for most trips, and then switch to biofuels (if they're sustainable) and some gasoline for longer trips.

Express yourself

1. You can start to encourage responsible fuel production by holding corporations accountable. Archer Daniels Midland (ADM) is the largest promoter of agrofuels in the United States. Write to ADM CEO Patricia Woertz (or her replacement). Let her know that you don't support agrofuel production that violates human rights, degrades pristine ecosystems, and threatens our climate. Write to the CEOs of Bunge and Cargill, too.

2. Contact your congressional representatives and urge them to put a moratorium on agrofuel expansion by cutting all agrofuel subsidies to ADM and other companies. Remind them that America can't grow its way out of our oil addiction, and pressure them to support legislation ensuring that all biofuels meet standards as strong as those established by the Sustainable Biodiesel Alliance.

3. Besides cutting subsidies, we must have strong standards to ensure that agrofuel production does not add to global-warming problems, nor contribute to hunger, deforestation, poverty, and human rights abuses. Please join one of many organizations, listed under this topic in the resources section of this book, that can help your city, state, or the federal government put a moratorium on agrofuel consumption until those standards can be developed.

Stay engaged

Join Rainforest Action Network, Indonesia-based Sawit Watch, and Birute Galdikas's Orangutan Foundation International's campaign to protect rainforests in Indonesia and throughout Southeast Asia from the expanding biofuels industry, a long-term effort. Be part of an international movement that challenges the agribusiness practice of establishing giant food and fuel factory plantations that push communities off their lands and destroy ecosystems. Organizations listed in the resources section can help you make a positive difference.

CHAPTER 8

Greening the Grid

How Sun and Wind Can Generate Power and Prosperity

The best time to have taken action on energy
issues would have been thirty years ago.
The second best time is right now.

— REPUBLICAN GOVERNOR TIM PAWLENTY
OF MINNESOTA, MAY 2007

P*rice. It all comes down to price. Renewable energy may sound exciting, and it will probably grow a little over the next twenty years or so, but it just won't be able to replace coal, oil, nuclear power, or natural gas in any real way. There might be some room for the occasional rooftop solar system here, or even the odd wind farm there, but both solar and wind will be playing on the margins for at least the next several decades.*

"Why? Because coal is cheap, and America has lots of it. Designing and installing a photovoltaic (PV) solar system on a rooftop, building a wind farm, or even siting a utility-scale solar array in the desert is far more expensive than power from coal or even natural gas, in almost every location around the country. We owe it to ratepayers to get our energy as cheaply as we can.

"But let's say for argument's sake that somehow prices drop and renewable energy becomes competitive. There's still no way that renewable power can produce electricity on the scale America needs. And what do you do when the wind doesn't blow or the sun doesn't shine? Face it, solar and wind just can't be relied on to do the job. Renewable energy will remain only a bit player for the foreseeable future."

That sales pitch, my friends, is exactly what the coal, oil, nuclear, and natural-gas industries want you to believe. These interests (which energy expert Harvey

Wasserman collectively dubs King CONG) will work to convince you that America's energy needs are too great to rely upon solar, wind, or any other renewable form of energy. They want you to believe that electricity demand is growing so quickly that we'll risk widespread blackouts if we try to change course. Most of all, they say that coal is abundant, and cheap, cheap, cheap.

And if you believe all this, those industries have more than a hundred new power plants they'd like to sell you, a legacy of the infamous Bush-Cheney energy plan. But not only are the costs of dirty energy much higher than King CONG would have us believe, the advantages of switching to renewable power are much greater. Embracing clean energy is not an obligation, it is an opportunity. Coming clean has never felt so good.

For the past three chapters we've been talking about transportation, where oil still rules. Now we move into a different realm of energy use: the electricity that powers other sectors of our economy. Here, coal is king, generating about half of the electricity in the United States. Coal's dominance produces a common misunderstanding about our future energy choices: that we don't have many options, and that utilities must continue to build coal plants or risk pulling the plug on the American economy.

Fortunately, neither is true. Since it's not possible to eliminate all coal use completely and immediately, the transition from coal to renewables will occur in two stages. Our first challenge is to avoid locking in our coal addiction for decades to come. As of this writing, more than a hundred new coal plants are still on the drawing board. Over the next few years, policymakers must choose between building those plants and finding a better solution. If business-as-usual sentiments prevail and the proposed plants are built, hundreds of billions of public and private investment dollars will be sunk into expanding coal industry infrastructure, and we'll be stuck with a new generation of inefficient plants, each belching millions of tons of greenhouse gases, plus heavy metals and other pollutants, into the air year after year.

But there are increasing signs that policymakers are embracing a cleaner energy pathway. One report released in January 2008 documented fifty-nine proposed coal plants that were rejected or withdrawn in 2007 alone. As these plants are rejected one by one, we can begin to set our sights on the second stage of the clean-energy transition: identifying the oldest and dirtiest coal-fired plants, shutting them down, and replacing them with the efficient use of clean power.

Detailed energy analyses by a wide range of research groups show how the U.S. economy can be carbon-free and nuclear-free within the next thirty to fifty years. Many claim that a full transition to clean power sources will require a massive public investment on the scale of fighting World War II, or at least comparable to the Apollo Project, which put a man on the moon in the 1960s. In some ways, this is accurate, but it's also misleading. We'll be making vast investments in our future energy supply anyway. The question is whether we devote billions of dollars to the same fossil-fuel sources we've exploited since the industrial revolution, or whether we can break from our past.

Green-Collar Jobs

Persuading America to buy into a future of power without pollution will take pragmatism as well as idealism. Yes, it's a good thing that moving to renewables will lower our greenhouse gas emissions, thus preventing seas from rising and storms from intensifying. And of course, limiting the likelihood of oil spills and coal-mining catastrophes is a smart thing to do. But a rapid transition to renewable energy—solar, wind, geothermal, biomass, tidal energy, and some hydro projects—will help our economy as much as the planet. We'll focus on solar and wind in this book because they have the potential to grow most quickly and provide "energy security" for farmers and families. They'll also serve as an economic stimulant, creating new, well-paying jobs and saving taxpayer dollars.

In 2006, the most recent year for which figures are available, 2.4 percent of the United States' electricity was generated by renewables. The Union of Concerned Scientists estimates that increasing renewable energy's contribution to our power supply to 20 percent by 2020 will create 185,000 new jobs and save consumers a total of more than $10 billion in lower electricity bills. The Apollo Alliance, a coalition of unions, churches, elected officials, and environmental, farm, and business groups, in 2004 conducted a broader analysis of the impact of a major clean-energy initiative that would include transportation, electricity, and energy efficiency. Its report, "New Energy for

America," showed that a $300 billion, ten-year investment in clean energy would create 3.3 million new jobs, add $1.4 trillion to the U.S. gross domestic product, and save $284 billion in energy costs over that period.

The prospect for new jobs from a major commitment to renewables is especially strong. While fossil-fuel development is capital intensive (a typical coal plant costs at least $1 billion to build), renewable energy is more labor intensive. University of California researchers found that wind power could produce nearly three times as many jobs per unit of power produced as coal. Rooftop solar could generate seven to ten times as many jobs.

Whether it's installing solar panels on rooftops; manufacturing, repairing, or maintaining utility-scale solar and wind farms; or weatherizing and improving the efficiency of millions of homes, there's plenty of work to be had in a postcarbon economy. On the 2008 campaign trail, Senators Edwards, Obama, and Clinton all announced proposals for increased funding for green-jobs training. "We can turn the crisis of climate change into an opportunity for a new energy economy, right here in America," said Edwards.

Pass It On

Clean energy equals good jobs. An analysis of thirteen independent reports studying the effects of clean energy on employment found that wind power could produce up to nearly three times as many jobs as coal per unit of power produced. Solar photovoltaics were found to generate seven to ten times as many jobs.

Such jobs may also offer economic self-sufficiency for those who need it most. Green-collar jobs "can do more than just save the planet or help avoid oil wars in the future," explains Van Jones, cofounder of Green for All, a project to secure $1 billion in government funding for job training in green businesses. "For the tens of thousands of Americans who are falling behind in the global job market, these work opportunities can also create green pathways out of poverty."

One woman making a direct and positive impact in her community is Michelle McGeoy. A successful computer entrepreneur in the 1980s and 1990s, she grew increasingly concerned about the growing digital divide and gave up her lucrative career to form a nonprofit social enterprise to teach disadvantaged youth computer skills, from data entry to creating Web pages to running their own Web development businesses.

Also a passionate environmentalist, McGeoy a decade later started a new career as a solar-design technician, climbing up on rooftops to determine where best to install solar panels and assisting customers with installations. But she soon noticed that the solar industry lacked diversity and wasn't fulfilling its potential to lift low-income workers out of poverty. McGeoy saw an opportunity to improve the economy of her hometown of Richmond, California—which has some of the state's highest homicide rates—reduce violence, and protect the environment all at once. "Solar power is a great antidote to pollution, but jobs are also a wonderful antidote to violence," she says.

McGeoy founded Solar Richmond, a nonprofit designed to train residents in the new-energy economy. Operating in the shadow of the city's giant, toxic Chevron refinery, Solar Richmond in August 2007 began a jobs program that teaches community members to install solar panels, places trainees into jobs with local installers, and advocates with municipalities to enhance economic development with smart-energy policies. It's working. McGeoy recalls the day when one of her early trainees came back to announce that he had just got a job installing solar. "I did everything I could not to break down in tears in front of everyone," she says.

It's an exciting opportunity. If the first industrial revolution established the modern economy, bringing great convenience to many and great wealth to a few, the clean-energy revolution can restore a balance between economy and ecology, and bring jobs to a broad spectrum of Americans. But is renewable power ready for prime time? Can we foresee the day when solar and wind and other clean-energy sources begin to displace "King CONG"? Judge for yourself.

Watt's That?

For background, let's look at how the United States produces and consumes electricity today. Our power is measured in watts: a thousand watts is a kilowatt, a million watts is a megawatt. We also measure power use over periods of time. So if your lamp has a hundred-watt bulb and you read this book for ten hours in bed this week (glad you're enjoying it!), you'll use a hundred watts times ten hours, or one kilowatt hour of electricity. The average American home uses 938 kilowatt hours on a monthly basis. About two-thirds of that is for appliances (14 percent for refrigerators, 9 percent for lighting, 6 percent for clothes dryers).

A great many of these kilowatt hours used to come from burning oil, but oil is no longer a major player. In the autumn of 1973, before the Arab oil embargo, the United States derived nearly 25 percent of its electricity from burning oil. The subsequent oil shock raised prices, cooled the economy, and motivated many Americans both to buy more fuel-efficient vehicles and to lobby their legislators for policies aimed at reducing dependence on foreign oil. Fifteen years later, oil produced only 10 percent of the nation's electricity, and today the figure is less than 2 percent. America's success at eliminating oil as a source of electricity demonstrates that smart public policies joined to individual action can make a big difference.

Coal remains the largest source of electricity, providing nearly 50 percent of U.S. power in 2006. In the same year natural gas generated 20 percent and nuclear 19.4 percent. The rest is split between hydroelectric (7 percent), renewable power sources (2.4 percent), and oil (1.6 percent). Nationwide demand has been increasing by about 1 to 2 percent per year. To meet it, natural-gas usage has grown at an average annual rate of 4.6 percent in the last decade, while coal has declined slightly. Renewable energy enjoyed a surge in 2006, led by wind, which increased its generating capacity by 49 percent in one year alone.

A typical coal-fired power plant is often described in terms of the maximum number of megawatts it can generate at any one time: a "400 megawatt plant" or a "750 megawatt plant." In contrast, the numbers for renewable power are typically much smaller. A typical photovoltaic (PV) solar installation on a rooftop produces 3 kilowatts of electricity. Utility-scale solar farms (which I'll discuss later in this chapter) can be much larger, generating 100 to 500 megawatts per site. A modern wind turbine is often 1.5 megawatts or so. Wind farms can generate 50 to 3,000 megawatts of power.

To track progress in reducing our dependence on coal, here's the number to remember: the total generating capacity of U.S. coal plants is about 313,000 megawatts. And with the goal in mind of breaking with our dirty energy past to create a clean-energy future, here are two other numbers: there are about 500 coal-fired power plants in this country, with 1,493 individual generators using coal as a predominant fuel source. That many and no more. With enough vision, innovation, and commitment, we can start rolling those numbers back, as more and more megawatts are saved through efficiency and others are generated by solar and wind.

Every Rooftop Matters

It was my fault that the meeting got off track.

We were in the studio office attached to the sunny Palo Alto, California, home of Herman Gyr and Lisa Friedman. They are consultants who have worked with an impressive list of Fortune 500 CEOs and management teams, and were eager to help Rainforest Action Network (RAN) catalyze a shift toward sustainability in corporate America. Just as we sat down after a short break, I happened to ask Gyr about the solar panels on the roof of their home.

His face brightened. "Do you want to see them?" he asked. "You bet." Everyone jumped out of their chairs and followed Gyr as he gave us a tour.

The remarkable thing about solar-powered homes is how thrillingly un-remarkable they are. The lights work, the refrigerator hums, everything is normal. Throw a few dozen photovoltaic (PV) cells on your roof and you can achieve energy independence. "I care deeply about climate change, but I also want to support sustainable business," Gyr explained. "By putting solar panels on my home, I can do both."

"Here's the best part," Gyr said, leading us to the side of the house to look at the electricity meter. In a typical home powered by coal, nuclear, or gas, the meter spins day and night, counting the watts used by each DVD player, clock, light, radio, and other appliance. But as we gathered in the sunshine in Gyr's yard and bent to look at the meter, we could see that it was spinning backward. The solar panels were producing not only enough electricity to power the home and office, but also excess power that could be sold back to the utility for another home or business to use.

"Most solar homes are connected to the grid these days," Gyr explained. "Imagine if there were a million of these homes in California. Or five million. We could start shutting down polluting power plants one by one."

What's not to like about solar power? The fuel source doesn't have to be mined, refined, gasified, or blown out of a mountain. The power doesn't have to be shipped long distances, and it doesn't pollute our water, bake the planet, or give our kids asthma. Solar energy bypasses the long fossil-fuel supply chain. Whereas a single coal plant is fed daily by a train of coal cars up to a mile long, solar power can be delivered straight to the user, every day, for free.

Solar power began to ascend in response to the first oil crisis and rising energy prices in the mid- to late 1970s. That's when solar houses started to be built, and PV panels were installed on the roof of the White House. Then Reagan was elected president, the panels were torn down, oil prices tanked, and the dream of solar power was put on hold. Those dreams were delayed again in the 1990s when natural-gas prices collapsed, leading to a national stampede to add gas-fired power plant capacity. But now solar (and wind) are growing much faster than dirty-energy sources, and are the target of a major boom in clean-energy investment.

In 1997, global solar PV production totaled 126 megawatts. By 2007, production reached 3,800 megawatts. Installation of PV cells and modules around the world has been growing at an average annual rate of greater than 35 percent since 1998. "This level of growth is more akin to the PC, wireless, and Web industries during their heyday than the usually staid and slow-moving energy sector," notes Clean Edge, a market research firm.

As part of its commitment to photovoltaics, California in October 2006 passed SB1, the "Million Solar Roofs" legislation, setting aside $3.2 billion in rebates over a ten-year period for homeowners who install solar panels on their roofs. "Every rooftop matters," says Danny Kennedy, cofounder and president of Sungevity, a California-based solar provider. "Our goal is to make clean energy available to everyone. Every time we install a new solar rooftop system, we're cutting away at the market for coal and nukes."

Commercial use of solar is also growing quickly. In June 2007, Google completed a 1.6 megawatt PV system (enough to power a thousand homes), installed by union workers at its corporate headquarters. At the time it was announced, the solar installation was the largest by any corporation in the United States. Wal-Mart announced in early 2007 that it would install twenty megawatts of solar power at twenty-two stores in California and Hawaii, and the company has set a goal of ultimately sourcing 100 percent of its power from renewable energy.

Other firms, such as Staples, Whole Foods, and Walgreens, have installed solar arrays on dozens of their stores across the country. "The solar revolution does not require new breakthroughs in technology," says Travis Bradford, author of *Solar Revolution: The Economic Transformation of the Global Energy Industry.* "You could do it with the technology we have, scaling it up and learning how to do it incrementally better every year—which is what naturally happens with scale."

Achieving large-scale installation of rooftop solar systems would have a profound impact on the U.S. energy landscape. For starters, individual home-owners and business owners could achieve energy security, controlling their own energy supply right where they live or work. In a time of volatile energy prices and climate destabilization, the value of a reliable and consistent supply of energy should not be underestimated.

Furthermore, rather than predominantly producing electricity at central coal, nuclear, or natural-gas plants, our future energy grid would feature power that has been generated from literally millions of rooftops, wind farms, and other locations. This decentralized, consumer-oriented power network is similar to the revamped media and telecommunications industries, which have undergone sweeping changes in how they distribute information. Gone are the days when three broadcast networks controlled most television news and entertainment programming. Today, consumers not only customize how they want to receive information but generate and distribute it to others. In a similar way, distributed energy generation can empower individuals and communities.

But if you're like me, you still have that number—313,000 megawatts of coal-fired power capacity—branded in your head. You're probably feeling a little skeptical right now, realizing that if we had just a hundred megawatts of rooftop solar in 2006, then we have a long way to go to replace coal. We do. Then you might add a few dozen megawatts for Wal-Mart here and some more from Starbucks there, and think . . . we still have a long way to go.

Here's the good news. The solar industry grew at a 55 percent annual rate globally in 2005, and at a rate of nearly 40 percent in 2006, according to Clean Edge. State policies will accelerate this growth further. For example, California's SB1 went into effect on January 1, 2007. By the end of September that same year, new solar installations nearly matched the total amount of solar the state had installed in the previous twenty-six years.

That's just the beginning. As this book is being written, "renewable portfolio standards" have been enacted in more than twenty-five states. Arizona has committed to generate 15 percent of its energy from renewable resources by 2025. Montana pledged to reach the same goal ten years earlier. New Hampshire and Montana have both committed to use renewable power for 25 percent of their electricity by 2025. Meanwhile, California mandated a 20 percent renewables standard by 2010, and is beginning to set rules to ensure that at least 33 percent of its energy will come from renewables by 2020.

Pass It On

More than twenty-five states have made commitments to increase their purchases of renewable power.

The potential for solar energy to meet America's electricity needs is enormous. Enough energy from the sun hits the earth's surface in forty minutes to meet the world's total energy consumption for an entire year. A 1999 report in *Science* magazine showed that the United States could meet its entire electricity needs with a single hundred-square-mile solar array in the Nevada desert. Taking notice are investors and utilities in California and throughout the Southwest, who are beginning to build some of the largest solar power plants on the planet.

The Promise of Big Solar

In ten to twenty years, the U.S. energy mix is likely to include large amounts of power from solar rooftop systems. To accelerate the transition away from coal, however, we need to install massive quantities of clean power as quickly as possible. Enter Big Solar. Industrial-strength solar facilities are being constructed in the sun-drenched deserts of California and other parts of the West. These facilities are orders of magnitude larger than the PV arrays on residential and commercial rooftops and thus produce much larger volumes of solar energy at a greatly reduced cost. One by one, these solar farms will soon cut into the market for coal-fired power.

There are several different technologies, including "parabolic troughs" and other technologies that focus the sun's rays, as well as solar-dish engines, thin-film solar panels, and concentrating photovoltaics. The first large solar facility in the United States was built in the Mojave Desert in the 1980s and early 1990s. The Solar Energy Generating Systems, or SEGS, is a solar thermal power plant that uses parabolic troughs, or curved mirrors, that track the sun and concentrate its rays to heat a liquid and make steam. The steam moves a turbine, producing electricity. SEGS was built in thirty- and fifty-megawatt installments over a period of seven years, and is a good indication of how costs decline with scale and experience. The first fifty megawatts of power cost 28 cents per kilowatt hour. The last installment of fifty megawatts cost less than 16 cents.

Pass It On

Every forty minutes, enough sun hits the earth's surface to meet the entire world's energy needs for a year.

SEGS has a capacity of 354 megawatts, and has been reliably producing solar power from the strong desert sun for more than twenty years. The promise of a rapidly growing solar thermal industry was thwarted in the 1990s, as natural-gas prices plummeted, flooding the market with cheap fossil fuels. SEGS was the largest solar plant in the world when it was completed, and it's still the largest facility today. But that will soon change. Solar thermal technology has improved, and concerns about climate change are driving demand for clean energy.

Solel Energy Systems signed a contract in July 2007 to produce 550 mega-watts of solar power (about as much as a coal-fired power plant) for Pacific Gas and Electric (PG&E). Another company, Ausra, Inc., which is using similar solar thermal technology but with less expensive, nearly flat mirrors, has an agreement with PG&E to produce 177 megawatts of solar power. Both facilities are expected to be online by 2011 or 2012. "What I find attractive about Ausra is that it's taking approaches used in the past and driving the price down, making it cheap," says PG&E CEO Peter A. Darbee. "It's lower risk and environmentally friendly. I'm very enthusiastic about the technology."

Another way to concentrate solar power is the solar-dish engine, popular-ized by Stirling Energy Systems of Phoenix, Arizona. Whereas the parabolic troughs use steam to drive a turbine, dish engines use steam to move pistons.

Although this technology has not yet produced electricity at large scale, some believe a breakthrough can be achieved. Stirling Energy has signed contracts to deliver 900 and 850 megawatts of solar energy to San Diego Gas and Electric and Southern California Edison. Other technologies also hold promise. At Nellis Air Force Base in Nevada, construction was completed in December 2007 on a field of seventy thousand photovoltaic cells—the largest PV solar array in North America.

Meanwhile, New Mexico utility Public Service of New Mexico (PNM), in partnership with Sandia National Laboratories and others, is seeking bids for concentrated solar power. In September 2007, PG&E announced that it would double the amount of solar thermal power it would purchase, pledging to add an additional thousand megawatts of solar power within five years. It's boom times for the solar industry, and with every 100-, 250-, or 500-megawatt solar installation, we move closer to being able to shut dirty-coal plants down.

But taking coal plants offline isn't as simple as replacing one five hundred megawatt coal plant with a single five hundred megawatt concentrated solar plant and calling it even—or even with a few thousand rooftop solar arrays generating an equivalent amount of power. Because a coal plant, unless it's down for maintenance or has a supply disruption, can generate five hundred megawatts of electricity twenty-four hours a day. Solar power, of course, can be generated only during the daytime. One way to extend the reach of solar power into nighttime hours is through energy storage, which I'll discuss later. But solar power can also be complemented by other clean-energy solutions, including biomass, geothermal, tidal energy, and most importantly for now, wind.

Wind at Our Backs

I still remember the first time I saw a wind farm. It was 1985, I was thirteen years old, and my family was about to complete a great adventure through California and the desert Southwest. Growing up on the New Jersey shore, I had never been west of the Appalachians before, and had experienced a near-religious introduction to the Grand Canyon two weeks earlier. On this day, we were driving from Yosemite National Park to San Francisco. I had dozed off with my legs stretched across my younger brother's lap, much to his dismay.

I woke up just as we were winding through the golden hills of Altamont Pass near Livermore, California. I rubbed my eyes and saw hundreds of turbines on the hilltops, turning gracefully in the wind. I thought they were beautiful. My father told us that the former governor, Jerry Brown, had pushed to have them installed, and that this wind farm alone produced enough power to light up most of San Francisco. As a teenager, I had seen how California skateboards and, earlier, surfboards had swept across the country, and I wondered how long it would take before these wind farms would do the same.

Wind power hasn't taken over the country yet, but much has happened in the last twenty years. Total installed wind power exceeded thirteen thousand megawatts in 2007, enough for 3 million homes. Moreover, wind power has been the fastest-growing source of energy in the past twenty years, as its costs have dropped by more than 90 percent. Many of today's larger wind farms can compete on a price basis with coal, even if coal's water- and air-pollution costs are not included in its price.

The cost of wind power has dropped as knowledge in the field has grown. Bob Dylan famously sang, "You don't need a weatherman to know which way the wind blows," but if you're designing a wind farm, a slight variance in wind speed makes all the difference. The energy the wind contains is a calculation of the cube of the speed of the wind. This means that a site with an average wind speed of sixteen miles per hour can create nearly 50 percent more wind energy than a wind farm with an average speed of just fourteen miles an hour, and costs about half as much. Choosing the best sites for wind farms is critical to optimizing their power output.

Also, bigger is better. A modern wind turbine with fifty-meter blades can generate up to fifty-five times more electricity annually than a typical model installed in the early 1980s, which had blades just ten meters long. The new turbines take advantage of an increase in the swept area and a substantial increase in wind speeds at greater heights. There are also significant advantages of scale for an entire wind farm. The American Wind Energy Association estimates that a fifty-one-megawatt wind project delivers electricity 40 percent more cheaply than does a three-megawatt project, mostly because the administrative costs to finance, operate, and maintain larger farms can be spread out over more kilowatt hours.

As advancements in wind-energy technology have lowered the price, it's becoming more profitable to expand the size and generating capacity of wind farms. And the potential for wind power to meet a substantial portion of U.S. electricity needs is real. The amount of wind energy available in twelve Midwestern and Rocky Mountain states is about two and a half times the electricity production of the entire country. Six of those states—North Dakota, Texas, Kansas, South Dakota, Montana, and Nebraska—could each supply more than 20 percent of America's electricity needs. Put another way, just three of those states could create more power than all of the country's coal plants combined.

Pass It On

The wind energy available in twelve Midwestern and Rocky Mountain states is equal to two and a half times the total electricity consumption in the United States today.

Wind power has its detractors, however. Some environmentalists and bird enthusiasts have raised concerns about the threats that the rotating blades pose to birds and bats, as well as their risk of electrocution from power lines. One study estimated that an average of two to five birds is killed per wind turbine, per year. However, bird mortality can be significantly reduced through proper location of wind farms and other best management practices. The American Bird Conservatory recommends conducting detailed studies on the potential impact of a wind farm on local birds and bats before the wind farm is constructed. Kansas, Washington, and the U.S. Fish and Wildlife Service have all adopted standards for siting and operating wind farms to minimize bird mortalities. Wind-power providers would be wise to adopt these guidelines.

Then there's the question of aesthetics. Although some find wind turbines to be sleek and attractive, others (and not just coal executives, mind you) find them ugly and intrusive. A bitter fight has erupted over a proposed 420-megawatt wind farm to be built in Nantucket Sound off the Massachusetts coast. The farm would produce up to three-quarters of the electricity needs of residents of Cape Cod, Nantucket, and Martha's Vineyard but has provoked fierce opposition from such celebrities as Walter Cronkite, Senator Ted Kennedy, and others who have homes on the islands. They've been criticized for this stance. As Greenpeace's Kert Davies told the *New York Times,* "It's sad for me to be arguing against the Kennedys . . . and Cronkite, who is everybody's grandfather. But we, as environmental advocates, have to be consistent. . . . It's not fair to stump about how scary global warming is one week, then oppose this the next. It's not fair, in terms of environmental justice, for communities with cash to demand that projects they don't want be built somewhere else."

Aside from the occasional local skirmish, producing energy from wind enjoys broad-based support. The advantages of the technology are obvious. Even a small, 750-kilowatt turbine will prevent twelve hundred tons of carbon dioxide from being released into the atmosphere annually. That same turbine will prevent 6.9 tons of sulfur dioxide and more than 4 tons of nitrogen oxide from being emitted each year, in addition to other pollutants. Moreover, wind farms can help rural communities diversify their income sources and keep their homes and farms intact, through a process called community-based energy development. Leading the way is Dan Juhl in Minnesota.

Rescuing Rural Economies

Fortune Small Business magazine says, "When the history of wind power is written, Dan Juhl will rate a chapter." A Vietnam vet, Juhl has more than thirty years' experience in the wind-power industry. He installed windmills up in Fairbanks, Alaska, then came home to Minnesota and plowed his life's savings into setting up his own wind farm in the southwestern part of the state, signing a contract to sell the power to Xcel Energy. Juhl also worked for Aerostar, a Danish wind turbine manufacturer, creating wind farms in India and China.

"When we started, we were so committed to renewable energy, but the technology for wind was barely ready," says Juhl. "We've spent years refining the technology, getting everything to work right, and it's like night and day compared to the beginning. Now everybody's jumping on the bandwagon because we can compete with coal, even though so many of the costs of coal are hidden." Juhl soon turned a profit and began consulting on the side, helping farmers in the region install wind turbines on their land.

Besides operating his own wind farm, Juhl works to promote community-based energy development, or C-BED, in Minnesota and elsewhere. C-BED promotes local ownership of wind energy and other clean power sources, which helps rural people diversify and stabilize their income and ensures that the financial benefits of renewable energy stay within the community. A September 2004 General Accounting Office study showed that local ownership of wind generates 2.3 times more jobs and has 3.1 times the economic impact in a region when compared with out-of-town ownership. In May 2005, a Department of Energy study for Arizona, Colorado, and Michigan showed that wind energy would bring the "highest direct economic benefit to the state," compared with coal and natural gas. Minnesota passed C-BED legislation later that year. Nebraska followed in May 2007 with similar legislation that exempts C-BED projects from sales and other taxes.

"C-BED is so good for so many people, it's hard to beat down," says Juhl. He estimates that a farmer who owns his own wind turbines can generate $25,000 to $30,000 in profits for the first ten years, and then $100,000 annually after the capital costs are fully paid. "I started doing this work because I cared about the environment," says Juhl. "Learning about climate change made it even more important. But the social aspect is the most important to me now. C-BED can give a life-changing economic boost to so many farmers. That's why this is so important."

From Here to There

If you've purchased this book and read this far, you're probably not opposed to renewable power. You might like solar because of the energy security it can give your family or business. You may be a fan of renewables in general because of the jobs they'll create, or the greenhouse gases, air pollution, and smog they'll prevent. Perhaps you're just a sucker for new technology and think that mining and burning coal to keep the lights on is so ... nineteenth century. If so, you'll undoubtedly want clean energy to be the dominant source of power as soon as possible. The question is how we get from here to there—from an economy that's mostly powered by coal, oil, nuclear, and gas to one that is smart, secure, and sustainable.

One common concern is "intermittency"—the term used to describe the unsteady supply of renewable power. Although wind speed is variable, and the sun doesn't always shine, the intermittent capabilities of these and other clean power sources, such as geothermal energy, can offset each other. Advances in energy storage will increase renewables' potential even more. In late February 2008, Arizona Public Service, the state's largest utility, announced plans to build a 280-megawatt solar array in the desert seventy miles southwest of Phoenix. Notably, the plant will produce power for up to six hours after sunset, using molten salt to store solar energy. "When the suns sets, this plant keeps on ticking," says Arizona Public Service president Don Brandt. "We'll have solar energy in the dark."

Making a full transition to a clean energy economy will take determination and commitment at all levels of society. We'll need individual homeowners, farmers, and businesses to become distributed suppliers of solar and wind as they are able. We'll need city, state, and regional policies to strengthen the market for clean energy and solidify long-term demand. And we'll need all levels of government to end all subsidies of dirty power.

But to complete the transition to clean power, we'll need strategic public policies that support large-scale investments in clean energy. Here are four ways in which local, state, and federal policies can give us the clean electricity that we deserve.

Encourage Long-Term Investments

Germany receives as much sunshine annually as Nome, Alaska, yet it's become the world's top producer of solar energy. Germany collects a small fee from electricity users, about $1.80 per month per household, and then reinvests that money to provide solar tax and investment incentives and, most importantly, a "feed-in tariff." Feed-in tariffs, sometimes called advanced renewable tariffs in the United States, are a price support system that commits utilities to buy renewable power at a price that will ensure profitability for clean-power providers. In California, a smaller but similar charge of about $0.50 per month per household has put the state far above any other in solar-power generation.

Such public policies can assure investors and entrepreneurs alike that clean energy is a long-term priority, which in turn stimulates more renewable energy development. In the United States, rather than providing tax breaks to oil and coal companies, we should provide them to the purveyors and purchasers of renewable power.

Another innovative approach was recently launched by Berkeley, California, which approved a policy in November 2007 enabling homeowners to install rooftop solar with no money down. The city pays for installation and is repaid through an assessment added to property taxes over twenty years. There's very little risk for homeowners or the city: the monthly payment for property owners is set at a level equal to or less than the savings on each month's electricity bill.

Create Significant Demand Incentives

Twenty-five states have already issued standards to increase the percentage of clean power that is produced. On top of that, more than five hundred local organizations in more than fifty states and Canadian provinces have undertaken the "Campus Climate Challenge" to help inspire colleges and universities to reduce greenhouse gas emissions and increase their utilization of renewable energy. Meanwhile, the Sierra Club's "Cool Cities" program has signed up more than nine hundred towns and cities to join the clean-energy revolution. Evanston, Illinois, committed to add wind farms to its electrical grid; Seattle, Boulder, Salt Lake City, and many others have climate-action plans.

A major reason the solar and wind industries are growing so rapidly is that grassroots activists have been building consumer demand for clean power. As more schools, cities, and states join this effort—and as the renewable-power standards increase over time—the industry will continue to grow. Is your campus pushing utilities to provide more green power? How about your city or state? Or your church?

Share Power Fairly

When the sun is shining, many homes or businesses with rooftop solar panels generate more electricity than they need. And when the wind is blowing, the same may be true for small wind-farm owners. In many states, regulations allow homeowners or businesses to sell the excess power to the grid and then buy it back at night or on calm or rainy days. These so-called "net metering" laws allow small renewable energy providers to pay for the "net" charge on their electricity meter by subtracting the amount of power produced by solar or wind from the total amount of electricity consumed in the home or business.

It sounds simple, but although forty states have net-metering laws, many of those laws are rigged to favor large corporate utilities. For instance, some regulations force homeowners to sell clean power to the utility at wholesale prices, then compel them to buy power back at a higher retail charge. Other rules limit the size of solar installations that are eligible for net-metering provisions. For example, New York limits the maximum size to which net-metering laws apply to just ten kilowatts, which limits the profitability of large commercial systems. New Jersey has the best standard, giving net-metering rights to all systems up to two megawatts in size. By copying the best elements of policies in each state, we can help more homeowners and businesses to provide their own clean power on site.

Build a Clean Energy Infrastructure

For the past hundred years, our country has created and expanded a fossil-fuel infrastructure, including the sites where coal is mined and oil is extracted, railroad lines and pipelines to ship materials, power plants, and then lines to transmit power over long distances. We'll need to modernize parts of this infrastructure to transmit clean power across the country. For instance, in many regions, wind resources are underutilized or neglected entirely due to the lack of high-voltage transmission lines. Similarly, large areas of the desert Southwest are unsuitable sites for utility-scale solar because there's no way to deliver the electricity to towns and cities that will use it.

At each point in the clean-energy infrastructure, we'll want to avoid the mistakes of the past. Wind farms and solar stations will need to be cited in an environmentally responsible way. Transmission lines, if they're estab-lished, must also be built with minimal impact on communities, wildlife, and wilderness values. And distributed power will play an important role in the electricity grid of the future, by reducing the number of miles our energy must travel.

• • •

While just 2.4 percent of our electricity is derived from renewable sources, we can reach 20–30 percent within a decade and create an economy that is carbon-free by midcentury. What we need most is strong leadership. "The greatest obstacle to implementing a renewable U.S. energy system is not technology or money," observe Ken Zweibel, James Mason, and Vasilis Fthenakis in a *Scientific American* article entitled "A Grand Solar Plan." "It is the lack of public awareness that solar power is a practical alternative."

The researchers show how the United States would be able to derive 69 percent of its electricity from solar alone by 2050—including enough power for 350 million plug-in hybrid electric vehicles. The price tag? A public investment of $10 billion per year from 2011 to 2050. Compare that to annual U.S. fossil-fuel subsidies of about $49 billion, as discussed in chapter 3.

Shifting public investments toward clean energy will hasten the phase-out of dirty coal. With each passing year the price of renewable power drops and the economics of clean energy versus coal become more favorable. To illustrate, in May 2008 the California Energy Commission evaluated the cost of generating new capacity from different sources. Wind was cheapest, at $8.91 per kilowatt-hour. Pulverized coal with unregulated greenhouse gas emissions came in at $10.55, and concentrated solar power at $12.65. However, solar was far less expensive than "clean coal." When attempts to store emissions are factored in, power from coal would cost $17.32 per kilowatt-hour.

Future trends don't look good for Big Coal, either. Coal prices, like those of oil, have increased significantly in recent years as demand from China and India strains the industry's capacity. And as coal prices climb, so too do the costs of building new power plants. Cambridge Energy Research Associates released a report in February 2008 showing that the cost of building U.S. power plants has increased 130 percent since 2000, and 27 percent from October 2006 to October 2007 alone. And let's not forget that the cost of financing risky coal plants will also increase as banks become more cautious of accepting the carbon risk associated with coal plants.

With strategic public policies and corporate pressure, we can make coal more obsolete with each passing year. As investor Vinod Khosla puts it, we can reverse the common question "How soon will solar be competitive?" and instead ask, "How long will coal be competitive?"

Take Action

Take it personally

1. Every rooftop matters. Installing solar on the roof of your home, school, church, or office will save money, help create well-paying jobs, and reduce our country's reliance on dirty coal. Financing is sometimes available so that each month's payment for the system is less than the savings you'll enjoy in your electricity bill. More information is available in the resources section to help get you started.

2. If you live in a rural area, consider wind power and community-based energy development to put money in your pocket and keep coal in the ground.

Express yourself

1. *Local.* Organize in your community to make clean energy a priority. Does your employer have solar panels installed? How about municipal buildings? Your school or church? Not only can your town or city utilize clean power for its own buildings, but it also can provide financial incentives and tax credits to help area businesses and homeowners to do the same.

2. *State.* Help make your state a leader in clean energy. Urge state leaders to enact strong net-metering laws, establish a renewable portfolio standard to rapidly advance wind and solar, and give tax and other financial incentives to encourage homeowners and businesses to switch to clean power.

3. *Federal.* Let Congress and the White House know that they should provide stable, long-term investment and production tax credits that reward investments in clean energy. Support a carbon tax or other means of putting a price on greenhouse gas emissions, which would begin to make the price of coal reflect its cost to society.

Stay engaged

In every household, city, and state across the country, there are ways to accelerate the development of renewable power. If you're passionate about climate change and clean-energy issues, join the Vote Solar Initiative and visit the Web sites of some of the other organizations listed in the resources section. Attend meetings of your local and state public utility commission meetings, and urge them to adopt strong policies on the issues discussed in this chapter. Your voice matters, so please use it.

CHAPTER 9

Less Is More

Fighting Climate Change while Living the Good Life

That's not a free lunch—it's a lunch you're paid to eat.

— AMORY LOVINS, SPEAKING OF
ENERGY-EFFICIENT DESIGN

As far as I know, no universities or concert halls are named after Amory Lovins. Nor are there any bridges, parks, or city centers named after Ed Mazria or Art Rosenfeld. In truth, most Americans probably don't know who these men are or what they've accomplished. Yet they are leaders of a movement that is reshaping how Americans live, work, and play. Their ethos—doing more with less—offers some of the best ideas for fighting climate change and breaking our addiction to dirty energy.

A hundred years ago, leading industrialists like John D. Rockefeller, Andrew Carnegie, and J. P. Morgan were lauded for creating vast empires in the oil, steel, railroad, and banking industries. Called "captains of industry" by some and "robber barons" by others, these men built much of the industrial foundation of this country and were usually regarded as heroes in their day.

As America faces the challenges of climate change and fossil-fuel dependence early in the twenty-first century, it's time to pick some new heroes—the visionaries who show how proper planning, design, and construction can reduce energy use and greenhouse gas emissions and improve the quality of our lives at the same time. Another innovator, Michael Corbett, helped design a Davis, California, development that set a standard for residential efficiency in the late 1970s. He says, "You know you're on the right track when you notice that your solution for one problem accidentally solves several other problems."

A refreshing optimism permeates the pronouncements of many leaders in the efficiency field. In a 2005 *Scientific American* article, "More Profit with Less Carbon," Lovins wrote: "A basic misunderstanding skews the entire climate debate. Experts on both sides claim that protecting Earth's climate will force a trade-off between the environment and the economy. According to these experts, burning less fossil fuel to slow or prevent global warming will increase the cost of meeting society's needs for energy services. . . . Yet both sides are wrong. If properly done, climate protection would actually reduce costs, not raise them. Using energy more efficiently offers an economic bonanza—not because of the benefits of stopping global warming but because saving fossil fuel is a lot cheaper than buying it."

Aggressive investments in efficiency offer immediate opportunities for businesses and municipalities alike. McKinsey and Company estimates that 85 percent of the projected growth in electricity demand through 2030 can be met through better efficiency in our buildings, appliances, and factories alone. Implementing these technologies will bring some up-front costs, but they would pay back those costs and more over time.

Gone are the days when utility companies handed out free hair dryers to encourage more energy consumption. Nobody wants to increase waste. Yet many regulators, lawmakers, and corporate executives still find it easier to call for more power plants than to figure out the best ways to use energy more effectively. With a few rule changes and some tough love for these decision makers, however, we can put efficiency at the top of the list of energy choices. And watch the leaders of the new energy economy continue to shine.

Cold Beer, Hot Ideas

Using energy efficiently is different from conserving energy. Conservation can be described as making do with less—shutting off lights and turning down the heat for the good of the planet. Energy efficiency, on the other hand, entails finding clever ways to use energy more effectively while enjoying the same level of comfort. Conservation can involve sacrifice, while efficiency does not; the latter is so sensible and appealing that it should be a no-brainer.

Here's how the Center of the American West and the Southwest Energy

Efficiency project describe what it would be like to take "energy efficiency" out on a date: "On your first outing, you will need to remember to bring your wallet. Energy efficiency is not a cheap date; you will have to make an investment to get this relationship off the ground. But, in short order, after you have paid for the first dinner or two, and maybe for theatre or concert tickets, the terms will shift and energy efficiency will begin treating you. Each time you reach for your wallet, energy efficiency will snatch the check and say, 'No, really, this one's on me!' In no time at all, energy efficiency will pay you back—and more!—for the investment you made at the start of your relationship."

Indeed, there are some barriers to entry in the field of efficiency. Some money must be invested: perhaps by a family stocking up on compact fluorescent light bulbs that cost more at the register but pay back over time, or a business seeking to install more efficient motors and pumps in its factories. Planning and research are also required. There are as many ways to be wise with energy consumption as there are ways to consume energy. Keeping up with the latest technologies and techniques can be a tall order.

But opportunities abound. In consumer electronics or home appliances, a little research will turn up energy-efficient options for everything from televisions to dishwashers to floor lamps, often at a comparable cost. For home, office, and commercial buildings, advanced materials and good design principles can cut energy use in half, then in half again. Nearly everywhere energy is being used, consumption can be reduced.

Even so, the rules are stacked against energy efficiency in most states. Guidelines force regulators to add generating capacity to match increases in population, regardless of whether energy demands can be met another way. Meanwhile, regulators allow utility companies to earn a far greater profit by selling power than by saving it, in most cases. As a result, the energy policy for much of the United States has been consistent: if you build them (more power plants), demand will come.

But we can't continue to build our way out of this problem. The biggest remaining energy source won't be found in a deep coal seam in the northern Rockies, nor in a newly discovered oil field in the Amazon. The largest "new" source is the energy we can save in our lights, homes, appliances, computers, and office buildings. Dozens of examples show that investing in energy-efficient systems is cheaper than extracting, processing, transporting, and burning fossil fuels. And it will create far more well-paying and safe jobs than we'll find in a coal mine or oil field.

Using energy efficiently is a winner on every front; it creates sustainable jobs, cleans the air, protects the climate, and saves money for consumers, businesses, and governments alike. Setting high efficiency standards will not only prevent new power plants from being built; it will help shut the dirtiest ones down. Best of all, our lifestyles will improve. We can indeed have cold beer, hot water, loud music, bright lights—and use far less energy. To show how this can be done, we need look no further than California—and not just the state's recent leadership on energy but a decades-old history of innovation.

California Dreaming

On a Friday night in late November 1973, physicist Art Rosenfeld was still at work at Lawrence Berkeley National Laboratory. He had received his bachelor of science degree at the young age of eighteen, joined the Navy toward the end of World War II, and then, in 1954, earned his PhD under the acclaimed physicist Enrico Fermi at the University of Chicago. In the late 1960s, Rosenfeld led a team of researchers that helped UC Berkeley professor Luis Alvarez win the Nobel Prize for Physics. By 1973, Rosenfeld was in the midst of a stellar career. But, though he didn't know it at the time, he was about to begin an entirely different one.

The country was experiencing its first oil shock. In October, Arab nations had announced an oil embargo against the United States and other Western countries in retaliation for their support of Israel in the Yom Kippur War. Within a year, the price of oil in the United States soared by a factor of four. Inflation increased, and the economy dipped into recession. Gas was rationed; vehicles with license plates ending in an odd number could buy gas on odd-numbered dates, the others on even-numbered dates. Hour-long lines at gas stations were common.

As Rosenfeld was preparing to leave work that Friday evening, he thought of the long gas line awaiting him the next day. He looked around the building and noted that nearly every office had been vacated with the lights still blazing. Rosenfeld quickly calculated that his twenty-floor building would consume energy equivalent to a hundred gallons of gas between Friday night and Monday morning. Never a fan of waste, Rosenfeld spent the next half-hour turning off the lights and vowing to get UC Berkeley and its laboratories to do something about conservation.

Rosenfeld suspected, as did many of his colleagues, that the United States wasted far more energy each year than it imported from OPEC countries. A crisis soon became an opportunity: by identifying and implementing ways to use energy more efficiently, the country could shrug off the oil embargo and save money at the same time. In the summer of 1974, with Robert Socolow at Princeton University (who with Stephen Pacala in 2005 developed the famous "wedge" theory of fighting climate change), Rosenfeld organized a month-long strategy session with the country's top scientists, engineers, and policy experts. As he recounted in his autobiography, "By the end of the first week, we realized that we were discovering (or had blundered into) a huge oil and gas field buried in our buildings, factories, and cars, which could be 'extracted' at pennies per gallon of gas equivalent. . . . Many of us became aware that our new knowledge would soon change our lives."

Rosenfeld gave up his career in particle physics and devoted himself to the new field of energy efficiency, cofounding the Energy Efficient Buildings program, which later became the Center for Building Science at Lawrence Berkeley Lab. The center has played a vital role in helping the state develop efficiency standards for appliances, buildings, and lighting systems.

Other efficiency programs took root across the country, focusing primarily, though not exclusively, on reducing oil consumption. The results were impressive. From 1977 to 1985, total oil consumption dropped by 17 percent, even as the economy grew by 27 percent. In that same period, American dependence on oil from the Persian Gulf declined by 87 percent.

Beginning under the leadership of former Governor Jerry Brown, California initiated a multitude of programs to increase efficiency in lights, appliances, buildings, and more. Many of these programs save a kilowatt of power more cheaply than coal can generate it, and the standards are continually updated as technology improves. From 1977 to 2005, California produced savings of more than forty thousand gigawatt hours of electricity each year, eliminating the need to build twenty-four coal- or gas-fired power plants. There's good news in all directions: consumers and businesses have saved billions of dollars, greenhouse gas emissions have been reduced by millions of tons, and the competitive position of the state's businesses has been strengthened.

Pass It On

From 1977 to 2005, California's energy efficiency program saved forty thousand gigawatt hours of electricity, avoiding the need to build twenty-four large coal plants. The state's per capita energy use has remained constant since the late 1970s, while demand in the rest of the country has risen by more than 50 percent.

Recently, more ambitious targets have been established. Rather than continuing to build more power plants to meet ever-increasing demand, California has a new "Energy Action Plan" mandating that energy efficiency must be the top priority in all energy investment and policy decisions. This means that electric utilities in the state must maximize gains in efficiency before they can consider adding any new generating capacity. After efficiency measures, expanding renewable power comes next, according to the California plan. Fossil-fuel plants can be built in the state only after investments in efficiency and renewable power are made. Even then, the only power plants permitted are those at least as efficient as a modern natural-gas plant, effectively banning new coal-fired plants in the state.

From 2006 to 2008, California invested at least $2 billion in efficiency projects and educational programs run by the state's investor-owned utilities—Pacific Gas and Electric, Southern California Edison, San Diego Gas and Electric, and Southern California Gas. "This is the most important thing we can do for long-term energy reliability in the state," said Susan P. Kennedy, a California energy commissioner. "What this plan does is help us meet our growing needs, first and foremost, with the cleanest, most cost-effective energy of all—greater efficiency."

Funded by ratepayers through a charge of about one percent of a typical electricity bill, the efficiency program was expected to produce savings of more than fifteen hundred megawatts over three years, or enough to avoid the construction of another three large power plants. After paying back the initial investment costs, California's efficiency program will produce net ratepayer savings of $2.7 billion and prevent 3.4 million tons of greenhouse gas emissions, equivalent to taking 650,000 cars off the road.

Since the mid-1970s, California's per capita electricity consumption has remained constant, whereas per capita consumption for the rest of the United States has surged by more than 50 percent. It's an impressive feat. The state boasts the largest economy among the fifty, and the seventh largest economy in the world. Culturally, California can hardly be called a place of restraint and self-denial. Yet with foresight and wise long-term investments in efficiency, California gets far more in savings than it spends, year after year.

Obstacles and Opportunities

There's a disconnect here. If California is making such substantial gains, why wouldn't businesses and governments everywhere sink all the resources they could into increasing efficiency, so long as they could do so cost-effectively? In fact, many states, cities, and businesses are making at least small investments in efficiency. But few of them pursue efficiency opportunities with much tenacity, instead wasting energy and leaving money on the table. How can this be?

One explanation is that inertia is difficult to overcome. Not everyone acts in their own best interest, at least not right away. Think about it from your own perspective. You've probably read about the benefits to wallet and planet of buying compact fluorescent light bulbs, but be honest: have you changed the bulbs in your home and office yet? If so, how long did it take you to act on this? If it takes time and initiative to be energy efficient at home, imagine the difficulty of doing the same for an entire school or building or factory.

Another reason is the widespread misconception that saving energy in significant amounts demands austerity, discomfort, a rejection of the good life—essentially, a lifestyle of "less with less." Yet another obstacle is the difficulty of keeping up with new technologies and practices to conserve energy. Energy is used in thousands of ways, and just as many techniques can be employed to save it. Even the most dutiful energy planners and efficiency experts update their guidelines only every two to three years, so their policies become dated only months after being finalized.

But perhaps the biggest challenge is a lack of clarity regarding the economic benefits of using energy more wisely. Without conducting an energy audit and devoting resources to the issue, most companies and public officials remain in the dark about efficiency's potential. "Everyone knows that there's money out there (in energy efficiency)," explains Matt Arnold, co-director of Sustainable Finance, Ltd., a consultancy that helps Fortune 500 companies manage sustainability issues. "The difficulty is finding out just how much. Are there $100 bills lying on the floor, or just piles of dimes and quarters here and there?"

One metric used to determine if substantial investments make sense is to evaluate the cost to save energy. If the cost of saving energy is less than the cost of generating it, then it's a good deal for governments and businesses alike. One reason California is making such robust investments in energy efficiency is that its cost of saving energy to date is less than half what the state otherwise spends to produce it. Many other municipalities and companies are capitalizing on similar opportunities.

The state of Vermont adds a small charge to ratepayers' utility bills each month to fund the nation's first energy-efficiency utility—one that doesn't create new power but is devoted solely to reducing demand. Efficiency Vermont is operated by a nonprofit that works directly with state households and businesses to help reduce energy costs. The program offers free technical advice for residents seeking to make their home or business more efficient, gives rebates on purchases of efficient lamps and bulbs, and provides free or subsidized home-weatherization services to low-income homeowners. These programs have cut residents' energy bills by $31 million from 2000 to 2006. In 2006 alone, Efficiency Vermont helped 38,655 residents—more than 10 percent of state residents—make energy investments that will produce annual savings of 56 million kilowatt hours.

Connecticut has a similar system of rebates and incentives. The state subsidizes the cost of making new homes more efficient by reimbursing new homeowners for the average incremental costs incurred with energy-efficiency investments. Connecticut offers free energy audits to many businesses, as well as rebates for purchases of efficient lighting, heating, cooling, and other equipment. The American Council for an Energy-Efficient Economy ranked

California, Vermont, and Connecticut tied for first in its annual state-efficiency scorecard in 2007.

In the private sector, some leading businesses are lowering emissions and expenses in tandem. Bayer cut its overall greenhouse gas emissions 60 percent from 1990 levels by 2004, even though production increased 16 percent in that period. Dupont increased its production by 35 percent while reducing greenhouse gas emissions by 67 percent between 1990 and 2005, saving more than $2 billion in the process. At Johnson and Johnson sales have increased 372 percent since 1990, but greenhouse gas emissions dropped 16.8 percent from 1990 to 2006. The company's investments in greenhouse gas reductions create positive cash flows and "internal public relations benefits," meaning that employees like it. As of this writing, Johnson and Johnson the second largest nonutility user of solar cells in the country.

Pass It On

States such as Vermont, Connecticut, and California are leading the way forward. From 2006 to 2008, California is investing an additional $2 billion in efficiency programs, which will save another 2.5 gigawatt hours of power and cut energy costs for residents by $5 billion.

Creating a Climate for Efficiency

Amory Lovins calls it a "negawatt revolution," estimating that electricity consumption can be cut by radically by increasing standards in appliances such as refrigerators, dryers, and consumer electronics; installing more efficient industrial pumps and motors, and investing in advanced lighting fixtures and efficient bulbs. William McDonough—a pioneer of the sustainable-design movement whose imaginative designs for factories, office buildings, and homes have earned him a bevy of honors, including three U.S. presidential awards and a "Hero of the Planet" recognition by *Time*—prefers the term "abundance by design," believing that we can not just minimize waste but eliminate it altogether. Both emphasize that growth can be achieved by using less resources, not more—addition through subtraction. Joining them in making this vision real are hundreds of other designers, planners, builders, and a growing list of companies and municipalities.

Smart public policies that accelerate energy-efficiency efforts can have a profound effect on the American energy landscape. They could allow us to retire the country's dirtiest coal plants, replace those plants with efficiently utilized renewable energy, and rejuvenate our economy in the process. Here's how we can cover ground quickly.

Getting Priorities Straight

All fifty states could adopt a "loading order" for energy, similar to California's, mandating that energy efficiency is the first choice for energy development in the state. In practical terms this means that energy planners must endeavor to match incremental growth in energy consumption by saving energy elsewhere. In a December 2007 report suggesting greenhouse gas abatement strategies, the international consulting firm McKinsey and Company identified energy efficiency as a significant "negative cost option," meaning that investments in energy efficiency would pay off. The report's authors warn that time is running short: "Many of the most economically attractive abatement options we analyzed are 'time perishable': every year we delay producing energy-efficient commercial buildings, houses, motor vehicles, and so forth, the more negative cost-options we lose. The cost of building energy efficiency into an asset when it is created is typically a fraction of the cost of retrofitting it later, or retiring an asset before its useful life is over. In addition, an aggressive energy-efficiency program would reduce the demand for fossil fuels and the need for new power plants."

A loading order that puts efficiency and renewable energy at the front of the line for policymakers would give us our best chance to create an energy U-turn: stopping the expansion of fossil-fuel consumption, and advancing efficiency and renewables rapidly enough that they can begin to replace the dirtiest power plants as quickly as possible.

Decoupling Profits from Sales

In many parts of the country, utilities can still make more money by producing power than by saving it. This creates a powerful incentive for waste.

One solution is "decoupling," in which regulators offer utilities a chance to increase profits by being more efficient. "Decoupling breaks the link between a utility's financial health and their gas or electricity sales," says Ralph Cavanagh, senior attorney for the National Resources Defense Council. "Until you do that, it's very hard to get a utility to make significant efficiency investments."

Here's how it works. First, regulators determine how much revenue a utility needs to cover its costs and bring a return to shareholders. They then establish electricity rates based on demand forecasts so that utilities can meet their revenue targets. If utilities collect too much from ratepayers—or too little—adjustments are made in the next period's rate structure. All of this provides different profit incentives for utilities, including rewards if they achieve certain efficiency goals. When those goals are met, everyone wins: customers save money, the utility earns a higher rate of return, and greenhouse gas emissions and other pollutants are reduced. "The most environmentally benign . . . power plant I can build is the one I don't build," says Duke Energy CEO Jim Rogers.

The California Public Utilities Commission (CPUC) first enacted decoupling legislation for gas in 1978 and for electricity in 1982. These moves were an integral part of the state's efficiency success story. As this book was being written, however, only five states—California, Idaho, New York, Vermont, and Connecticut—had enacted decoupling legislation for electricity. Others, including New Jersey, Maryland, Virginia, and Hawaii, were considering it. Twenty-five states have either adopted or were considering decoupling legislation for gas.

Pass It On

Decoupling legislation creates efficiency incentives by allowing utilities to make money by selling less power. As this book was written, only five states had adopted decoupling legislation.

Pulling the Plug on Incandescents

This has to be the simplest and most cost-effective way to save energy: switch to more modern light bulbs. Producing light from a typical incandescent light bulb lit up by a coal-fired power plant is only 3 percent efficient, according to the Rocky Mountain Institute. The efficiency of light bulbs is typically measured in lumens per watt, which is a function of how much brightness is produced (lumens), relative to how much power (watts) is consumed. An average incandescent light bulb emits twelve to fifteen lumens per watt, whereas compact fluorescent light bulbs (CFLs) produce around sixty lumens per watt (and last up to ten times longer). Some CFLs were criticized for producing a cold, harsh light when they were first introduced, but new designs make the light much softer, comparable to most other lighting available on the market.

With one policy shift, an entire nation's energy consumption can be painlessly reduced. Australia was the first, adopting legislation in February 2007 to ban incandescent bulbs by 2010, which will save an estimated 4 million tons of CO_2 by 2012. "If the whole world switches to these (compact fluorescent) bulbs today, we would reduce our consumption of electricity by an amount equal to five times Australia's annual consumption of electricity," said Malcom Turnbull, Australian environment minister. Canada followed one month later with a similar ban.

Some U.S. lawmakers are trying a different approach, choosing not to ban a particular technology (like incandescent bulbs), but to set higher efficiency standards and allow any technology to compete to meet that standard. This seems fair enough. The only danger is that the standards will be set too low. Here's what I mean: In June 2007, Nevada became the first state to adopt higher lighting efficiency guidelines. The Nevada law prohibits the sale of any bulbs that produce less than twenty-five lumens per watt by 2012. By all accounts, this is genuine progress. The bill is expected to save consumers $1.3 billion by 2020 and about three hundred megawatts of peak power, or the equivalent of about 40 percent of one of Nevada's proposed new coal-fired power plants. The trouble is that a compact fluorescent bulb is already more than twice as efficient as what Nevada will require in 2012. In December 2007, as part of the energy bill, President Bush signed into law a similar measure, requiring that all bulbs use 25 to 30 percent less energy by 2014. It's progress, but not much to get excited about when bulbs available today could reduce consumption by a factor of four or more.

Developing technologies of so-called solid-state lighting, such as light-emitting diodes (LEDs), are even more efficient. Some LED lamps in the marketplace are already producing up to ninety lumens per watt, and industry experts believe greater gains and cost savings will be realized in the next few years as the market expands and prices drop. "The efficiencies of LEDs keep increasing, and there's no reason to think that they won't continue to do so," says Dr. Robert Steele of Strategies Unlimited, a market research firm.

In October 2007, Ann Arbor, Michigan, became the first U.S. city to commit to converting 100 percent of its downtown streetlights to LED technology. These streetlights will last five times as long as the bulbs they'll replace, using half the energy. The switch will save the city at least $100,000 annually. In November 2006, Wal-Mart announced that it would install LED lighting in refrigerated display cases in five hundred stores. "You're saving energy, and in the case of Wal-Mart, reducing the heat," says Steele. "In a commercial setting, those benefits are quantifiable." The company estimates that it will save $2.6 million annually.

In 2007 Congresswoman Jane Harman (D-CA) introduced a bill in the U.S. House of Representatives that would require all bulbs to produce 60 lumens per watt by 2012, 90 lumens per watt by 2016, and 120 lumens per watt by 2020. This is the current gold standard for lawmakers at the local and national level. Responsible elected officials and concerned citizens will push for guidelines that meet or exceed the standard in Harman's bill.

Slaying the Vampires

Have you noticed that more and more cell phones, printers, and even computers don't have an "off" switch? Take a walk around your home at night, after all the lights are turned off. You'll notice that the clocks on the microwave and coffee maker continue to keep time, the iPod and cell phone are charging, and the computer, television, cable box, and DVD player are all plugged in.

You have "vampires" in your house. That's the term energy experts use to describe consumer electronics that suck electricity from the grid even when they're turned off. A microwave might draw three watts per hour, a DVD player six. Computers can draw fifty watts an hour or more while in standby mode. It adds up. The Department of Energy estimates that 5 percent of U.S. electricity used is for electronics in the "off" or "standby" mode, or the output of about twenty-four midsize coal plants, wasting $5 billion every year. Globally, the International Energy Agency estimates that electronics in "standby" mode waste two hundred to four hundred terawatt hours (one trillion megawatt

Pass It On

Approximately 5 percent of the electricity used in American households is consumed by "vampire" appliances, which continue to suck energy even when turned off. These appliances consume the energy equivalent of twenty-four midsize coal plants each year and waste $4 billion. .

hours) annually. How much is that? About as much as the entire country of Italy uses in a year.

There are two ways to deal with this. One is for a couple hundred million Americans to unplug their chargers, computers, DVD players, and other devices each night—or, to make it easier, consolidate many of these onto power strips (without blowing a fuse!) so they can be all turned off with one switch. That will help, but there's a surer way: set government standards for manufacturers so that products use a minimum—or zero—electricity when not in use. Dell voluntarily introduced a computer in 2004 that used 1.4 watts per hour (compared to 50) while on standby, and just one watt when turned off. Why not make that the standard, and set similar guidelines for all products?

Establishing New Building Efficiency Standards

Ed Mazria is a partner in Mazria Odems Dzurec, a design firm based in Santa Fe, New Mexico. Mazria authored *The Passive Solar Energy Book,* a guide to fully utilizing the sun's energy to heat and cool homes. Reading about his work, Mazria seems like a nice enough guy, but he may not be too popular at industry get-togethers. That's because he goes around saying that architects are responsible for nearly 50 percent of all greenhouse gas emissions.

We tend to think in terms of big SUVs or polluting power plants when considering how to limit climate change, Mazria notes. But 76 percent of all coal-fired electricity is consumed by residential, commercial, and industrial buildings, which are responsible for 48 percent of all greenhouse gas emissions. "Over the next twenty years, we'll add 22 million homes and other buildings in this country," Mazria says. "When did you ever hear someone say, 'Hey, we're going to put in 22 million little power plants . . . in the next twenty years'?" he asks.

It is a design axiom that all the really important design errors are made on the first day, when the purpose of a project is defined. Architects determine what a building looks like, how it functions, what materials will be used, and how efficiently energy will be utilized—decisions that will affect a building's energy performance for the next fifty to a hundred years. So they must be encouraged and trained to make smart energy choices.

In 2005, Mazria founded an organization called Architecture 2030 to help lead his profession in the fight against climate change. One objective is to train new designers and planners for a clean-energy economy by requiring students to design buildings that consume little or no fossil fuel. Another priority is the Architecture 2030 Challenge, whose goal is to make all new buildings—and a substantial number of existing buildings—carbon-neutral by 2030. The challenge urges all architects and builders to pledge to design buildings using 50 percent less fossil fuel than the regional average for the particular building type. Structures built in 2010 would use 60 percent less energy; in 2015, 70 percent; and so on.

The goals are ambitious, but the project is gaining momentum. The U.S. Conference of Mayors has signed the Architecture 2030 pledge. So have the U.S. Green Building Council, the American Institute for Architects, the World Business Council on Sustainable Development, the cities of Santa Fe, Albuquerque, Plano (Texas), and many others. Up next is to make these goals not voluntary but mandatory. Architecture 2030 advocates national building codes that would require 50 percent reductions in fossil-fuel use immediately. As Winston Churchill once said, "We shape our buildings, and afterwards our buildings shape our lives."

• • •

This is only a sampling of public policies that can foster investments in efficiency, from standards for bulbs and buildings to state decoupling legislation or loading orders. Federal policymakers can also accelerate efficiency investments by enacting legislation to put a price on carbon, but individuals and companies alike can pursue their enlightened self-interest and cut costs and carbon at the same time. Over the next few decades, fighting climate change will present some tough challenges. Saving energy through efficiency isn't one of them. Let's not squander any easy victories.

Take Action

Take it personally

1. Do you know how much energy you consume in your home or apartment each month? How much does your office consume? Your school or church? Look closely at your energy bill and keep track of your progress. If you like gadgets, consider buying a home energy monitor at www.diykyoto.com, or elsewhere.

2. Want to know how much of your electricity comes from coal, nuclear, gas, or renewable power? Visit the U.S. Environmental Protection Agency's Energy and You page, www.epa.gov/cleanenergy/energy-and-you/how-clean.html.

3. Reduce your own consumption. Visit www.greenmadesimple.com and enter your zip code to find out the rebates, incentives, and financing programs available for energy efficiency and renewable power in your area. Consult the organizations in the resources section to learn how to cut your energy bills and greenhouse gas emissions.

Express yourself

1. Write to your governor, utility commission, and state representatives urging that your state pass decoupling legislation and prioritize efficiency and clean power.

2. Another bright idea: write to your state and congressional representatives to press for policies that either ban inefficient incandescent bulbs outright or set a standard of sixty lumens per watt or more. Encourage your city's leaders to follow Ann Arbor's example and install energy and budget-saving LED lights for municipal lighting.

3. Slay vampires—call on your state and congressional representatives to enact electronic "vampire" legislation that minimizes or eliminates the amount of electricity appliances use when turned off.

4. If you're an architect, designer, or planner, take the Architecture 2030 challenge to begin designing buildings to use at least 50 percent less energy. The rest of us can lobby officials to change building codes so that this efficiency level becomes the norm.

Stay engaged

Efficiency is not a one-time effort. As Earth's population increases and new technology develops, there will be constant pressure to use even more energy, not less. Organizations such as Natural Resources Defense Council, Rocky Mountain Institute, and the Union of Concerned Scientists publish extensive information online on how to cut energy bills. Finally, many important decisions affecting our energy systems are made at state and local public utilities commissions. Learn more about your local PUC, and get involved.

power. An aggressive, national program with these goals not only would create hundreds of thousands of well-paying, "green-collar" jobs, but would also remind Americans that we can meet our toughest challenges.

When we do, life gets better. Twenty years ago, it was perfectly legal to dump highly radioactive nuclear waste directly into the ocean, but citizens rallied globally and now the practice is banned. People of all colors couldn't drink from the same water fountain or sit at the same lunch counter, until Americans of good conscience taught the rest of the country to try to live as brothers and sisters. Until recently, a planeload of passengers would be trapped for hours breathing unhealthy air anytime a fellow traveler decided to light up and smoke—but health advocates enabled us all to breathe more easily in flight.

Bullies in the Schoolyard

But it won't be easy. Too many of our corporate and political leaders are play-acting when they talk of energy independence. If we're to believe the petroleum industry, there simply aren't any practical alternatives to oil on which we can depend in the near future, and forget about those pesky electric cars and plug-in hybrids. Most politicians are clever enough to introduce or at least vote for patriotic-sounding legislation that claims to help achieve American energy independence. If you look closely at the fine print, however, those bills barely make a dent in the problem; typically they're an excuse for more corporate welfare for clean coal, corn-based ethanol, or other misguided adventures. Coal companies, for their part, don't see much of a problem: coal can be "clean," climate change is a hoax, mining is safe, and pigs can fly.

What's missing from this whole debate is an honest conversation about power—but not the electric kind. There's one predominant reason we're hooked on dirty energy. It isn't because Americans are gluttonous and wasteful, although acknowledging our personal responsibility is important. It isn't because of a lack of solutions. It isn't even because of fears about high energy costs. We're addicted to oil and coal because most politicians and their power-wielding appointees lack the courage, determination, and grit to take these industries on. It's also because the business and banking communities traditionally have been in bed with the extraction industries, or lack the incentive to take risks on cleaner innovations.

We're taught on the playground in grade school to stand up for ourselves and not be pushed around by bullies. As children we learn about fairness, respect, and how to be kind to each other. But as adults, we find ourselves in a world where too many businesses are exempt from rules of fairness and decency and are able to pollute our environment and threaten our rights with impunity. Just like in the schoolyard, we have to stand our ground.

To be successful, we'll need to turn the might and power of these corporations to our own advantage. It will always be useful to confront oil and coal companies directly and expose their mistakes and untruths, but it will be even more important to dry up their government subsidies, cut off their corporate financing from Wall Street, challenge them in the courtroom, refuse their products in the marketplace, and put every ounce of consumer, political, and financial power behind clean and beneficial energy solutions.

They'll resist. Oil and coal companies will do whatever they can to distract attention from their misdeeds and deflect any criticisms. They'll distort the political and scientific debate by fomenting doubt about factual matters. And when the situation gets dire, they'll depress prices in order to defend their turf. Like all bullies, they may fight mean, but they also have their weaknesses. Rather than adjust to a changing world, many of these companies cling to outdated technologies and assume that politicians will always maintain the status quo. They've misjudged the values of Americans who don't believe we should have to sacrifice our health, climate, or freedoms to keep the lights on and the economy healthy. We can learn to fight back, and because we have a better vision, we'll prevail.

Brilliant Distractions

Here's one trick that some corporations are turning into an art form: greenwashing. It's a popular trend in corporate PR. If you're a big polluter and find yourself battling with regulators, citizens groups, and angry customers, don't accept the role of villain. Reinvent yourself as a sensitive, helpful, multinational corporation that cares. Here's one example. The world's largest tobacco company, Philip Morris, has fought legal, regulatory, and public relations battles for years because its products kill people. In an attempt to put a positive spin on this inconvenient fact, Philip Morris in 2000 commissioned a report in the Czech Republic extolling some unexpected "positive effects" of smoking deaths on the country's finances: smokers' early mortality would save the country money by reducing pension and housing costs for the elderly. That didn't go over so well, as you might imagine.

In 2003, the company changed its name to Altria and began a vigorous new ad campaign touting the company's human-centered values. Altria's Web site warned people of the dangers of smoking the company's products, hoping to buy time and curry favor with lawmakers negotiating a settlement with the tobacco industry. Health advocates weren't fooled, and the industry remains on the defensive.

British Petroleum gave corporate reinvention a try in 2000, when it bought Solarex Corporation for $45 million and rebranded itself as BP—Beyond Petroleum. We got a chuckle out of this at Rainforest Action Network because we had been running our "Beyond Oil" campaign throughout the late 1990s, targeting BP among others. BP's new ads adopted a concerned but friendly tone. One asserted, "It's time to think outside the barrel," and discussed the dangers of, and alternatives to, oil dependency. That's ironic, since the company continues to invest far more money in new oil exploration than in renewable energy. After many of its feel-good advertisements, BP adds the tagline, "It's a start." There hasn't been much of a finish.

Chevron launched a new Web site and ad campaign in the summer of 2005. Chevron urges visitors to the site to "join the discussion" with this rhetoric: "We can wait until a crisis forces us to do something. Or we can commit to working together and start by asking the tough questions: How do we meet the energy needs of the developing world and those of industrialized nations? What role will renewables and alternative energies play? What is the best way to protect our environment? How do we accelerate our conservation efforts? Whatever actions we take, we must look not just to next year, but to the next 50 years."

One Chevron ad says, "A 5 percent reduction in global energy use would power Australia, Mexico, and the entire U.K. So what are we waiting for?"

Another billboard proclaims, "Over half the world's oil lies in five countries. So where do you live?"

"Chevron's ads are brilliant distractions," notes Peter Walbridge, creative director for Big Think Studios. "They're provocative because they appeal to the reader or viewer's better self. They attempt to remove the consumer's guilt in buying their gasoline, and throw into question what is really happening in regard to Chevron's environmental record. Like a good card trick, the goal is to distract. And in Chevron's case to make it seem as though the company itself bears no responsibility."

When you notice companies or politicians lying about their records on human rights or the environment, don't despair. Rejoice: it's another opportunity to tell the truth.

Paralysis by Analysis

Here's another trick that's even more common: the independent review. Let's say that there's a U.S. president under intense criticism for—oh, I don't know, a costly and seemingly endless war. Pressure is mounting, voters are impatient. Politicians from the president's party are starting to worry about the upcoming election. Presto! Faster than you can say "task force," "pilot program," or "blue-ribbon panel," a bipartisan group of unassailable experts is appointed to study the issue. Everything is on hold until that study is released. It's a double victory for cowardly decision makers: they avoid taking responsibility and undermine their critics at the same time.

In some cases, a pilot project or in-depth analysis may be appropriate. More often it's just a smokescreen. During a campaign to protect British Columbia's Great Bear Rainforest, we used to call this tactic "talk and log." Logging companies would readily agree to extensive negotiations with environmentalists. They'd hire facilitators, rent conference rooms, sit on conference calls to develop detailed agendas, and schedule check-ins before and after the negotiations. In the meantime, clear-cut logging continued.

The best way to combat this tactic is to keep the pressure on. Rarely do task forces and committee meetings save forests, stop unjust wars, or protect the climate. Vigilant opponents should contest the legitimacy of these panels, projects, and studies when they're announced, and keep the heat on. It wasn't until profits were threatened by a boycott of the wood and paper coming from British Columbia that the industry agreed to halt all logging in pristine forests while negotiations took place.

Skeptics for Hire

The fossil-fuel industry has one quality in spades: tenacity. You won't often find its executives, lobbyists, and PR officials relaxing after a victory; rather they are racing to secure their position. In the spring of 1998, fossil-fuel companies were riding high. Most of the world's nations had recently passed the Kyoto Protocol, but the oil, coal, and utility industries had so thoroughly intimidated federal lawmakers that the U.S. Senate voted 95-0 to withhold support.

Within just a few weeks of the vote, the industries formed a new Global Climate Science Communications Team. The project's goal was to create conditions in which a "majority of the American public, including industry leadership, recognizes that significant uncertainties exist in climate science, and therefore raises questions among those (e.g., Congress) who chart the future U.S. course on global climate change." Among those developing the plan were executives from coal-burning utility Southern Company, Exxon, and Chevron; the Frontiers of Freedom, an extreme right-wing group that among other things has fought tobacco regulation, endangered species protection, and forest conservation; and Steven Milloy of the so-called Advancement of Sound Science Coalition. In his former career Milloy was a tobacco lobbyist. Today he is a regular commentator on Fox News. Meetings were held at the American Petroleum Institute headquarters. Victory would be achieved when, among other things, "media 'understands' (recognizes) uncertainties in climate science."

The Global Climate Science Communications Team achieved its goals up to a point. Strong climate legislation has escaped Congress in the decade or so since the Kyoto Protocol was first rejected. And studies have shown that elements of the mainstream media continue to profess doubt on whether climate change is human-caused.

Exxon in particular has long been the sugar daddy for climate skeptics. In a report for *Mother Jones,* journalist Chris Mooney details how Exxon has funded more than forty organizations dedicated to creating confusion and uncertainty about the science of climate change. The oil giant has given at least $155,000 to the Acton Institute for the Study of Religious Liberty, which calls CO_2 limits "a misguided attempt to solve a problem that may not even exist." Exxon has made grants of more than $960,000 to the American Enterprise Institute, which counts Dick Cheney as a former senior fellow and has fought climate change legislation at the state and federal levels for more than a decade.

Industry-funded public relations and lobbying campaigns also abound globally, many with deceptive names. You might see ads in major newspapers paid for by these groups "proving" that climate change is natural, or that it really isn't so bad. There's the New Zealand Climate Science Coalition and the Scientific Alliance in the United Kingdom. Up in Canada, the Friends of Science has recently been formed not too far from Alberta's tar sands. The Friends are "active and retired earth and atmospheric scientists, engineers, and other professionals" who believe that "the current obsession with global warming is misguided in that climate fluctuations are a natural phenomena." The group won't reveal where it gets its funding, but reporters at the *Toronto Globe and Mail* tracked down one significant source: Canada's oil companies. Are you shocked?

Climate skeptics are playing a losing game, and they know it. Their objective isn't actually to win a scientific debate, but simply to make it seem like there is a debate. In an infamous memo to Republicans in 2003, strategist Frank Luntz advised candidates, "Voters believe that there is no consensus about global warming within the scientific community. Should the public come to believe the scientific issues are settled, their views about global warming will change accordingly. Therefore, *you need to continue to make the lack of scientific certainty a primary issue in the debate.*" (The italics are Luntz's.)

Coal and oil companies are entitled to their own set of opinions and values, but not their own set of facts. The truth is there is no scientific uncertainty: climate change is real and human activities are the cause. We will also be the solution.

Twenty Years to a Clean-Energy Society

It's clear that the dinosaurs of dirty energy aren't dying out fast enough, and we can't wait for a planetary catastrophe to hasten their extinction. But we won't have to. Thanks to the work of entrepreneurs, innovative public servants, forward-thinking investors, and people like us demanding a better way, a vision of a clean-energy society has begun to emerge. And as that vision becomes manifest—in the form of high-speed rail, community-based energy development, a million-strong workforce in energy efficiency and renewable power, and more—the fossil-fuel industry will decline. When people experience the benefits of living with clean energy, we won't want to go back.

Whether deciding on a new home or car, where to work, or where to live, Americans increasingly will enjoy practical options that depart from a fossil-fuel-based economy. Gaining energy security with a solar rooftop will make the health and environmental costs of coal-fired power seem prohibitive in comparison. Zero-emission electric vehicles will render gas-guzzling cars and trucks obsolete and unpatriotic. The contrasts between old and new technologies and dirty- versus clean-energy choices will become ever more stark as public policy and consumer demand fuel further innovation.

In this and other ways, the clean-energy revolution will be self-reinforcing. Take the electricity market. Congress undoubtedly will soon pass climate legislation that will increase the price of carbon-intensive fuels, affecting coal-fired power plants the most. Meanwhile, growing demand for renewable power will continue to drive down the costs of clean energy. Solar and wind will become less expensive relative to fossil fuels, which in turn will further stimulate the demand for clean power, reducing costs even more. Similar dynamics will be at play in other industries.

Coming clean will impact every facet of our lives—our homes and offices, jobs, health, how we get around, what we eat, and even how America views itself. In some ways a clean-energy society will be very similar to the one in which we live today: we'll still enjoy much the same services and conveniences that we tend to take for granted. But in other ways, breaking the hold that fossil fuels have on our world will change almost everything. Within twenty years or so, here's what we could expect to see:

In Our Cars and Trucks

Perhaps the most dramatic evidence of the move to clean energy will be the vehicles we drive. By 2030, every new vehicle manufactured in the United States should be an electric vehicle, or at least a plug-in hybrid electric vehicle. It will take years after that to get all the older gas-powered cars and trucks off the road, but twenty years from now we should only be manufacturing the cleanest cars possible. Transportation can be fully electrified, connected to an increasingly clean grid. Cars will conveniently recharge at home, work, or public parking facilities; parking lots shaded with PV solar panels will be common.

This is eminently achievable, but it will take Congress, state legislatures, and automakers themselves to set industry standards as though the climate really mattered. Pilot projects and solitary showcase models just won't do. As discussed in chapter 6, all of the necessary technology is available today. Electric vehicles are already on the road in small quantities. Plug-in hybrids will be produced in the tens of thousands within a couple years. As the technology becomes more widespread, most plug-in owners will be able to go weeks on end without using a drop of gas. With advances in battery technology, electric-vehicle owners will travel several hundred miles or more on a single charge. By 2030, vehicle-to-grid technology will be widespread; millions of vehicles will offer extra storage capacity for clean power to help meet peak energy demand.

In Our Towns and Cities

In the next few decades, achieving energy self-sufficiency is likely to be a top priority for local communities. Volatile energy prices and the growing impacts of climate change will lead many public officials to secure access to reliable, inexpensive, and carbon-free energy resources. Communities and municipalities that take early action will be best positioned in a clean-energy economy.

The choices our towns and cities make will transform the transportation sector. Changing the cars we drive will determine how much gas we consume, but changing how our towns and cities are zoned and redeveloped will determine to what extent cars are needed in the first place. Integrating carbon-conscious urban planning with a rededication to mass transit will make our communities more walkable and our transit systems more coordinated. By 2030, urban residents—representing more than 80 percent of the U.S. population—will be able to reject the automobile as their primary way to get around. Housing, shopping, and office space will be in close proximity. Transportation will become multimodal, with residents able to choose from an array of convenient options, whether bike, bus, streetcar, light rail, or a good pair of shoes. Eventually the car will become unnecessary for most trips, and people will enjoy less time in gridlock, less pollution, and less income being diverted to the gas tank.

Communities large and small will directly determine the degree to which they become self-sufficient producers of clean power. Smart public policies will help local homeowners secure reliable access to renewable energy. State laws in California, Rhode Island, Ohio, and other states already allow communities to act as purchasing collectives, with the ability to buy clean energy and bypass utilities dependent on fossil fuels. One by one, as families, businesses, and municipalities choose renewable power, cities can break ties with dirty-power producers, so the most polluting plants can be retired and replaced.

Getting out of our cars and producing clean power also will make our towns and cities much cleaner places to live. When my wife and I lived in San Francisco, each week we'd have to wipe away a layer of city smudge that accumulated on a white table on our small deck. The clean energy revolution will stop this pollution at its source.

In Our Homes and Offices

The impacts of climate change will become clearer with each passing year, bringing greater urgency to eliminate dirty power as quickly as possible. Energy retrofits to both residential and commercial buildings will become more common as conspicuous consumption is replaced by creative conservation. Strong national efficiency standards will be consistently updated for all appliances and consumer electronics. Strategic efficiency guidelines plus continued growth in renewable power will help every new building to be carbon-neutral by 2030.

Over the years to come, millions of buildings will become sources of clean power, accelerating the process by which our electricity grid becomes decentralized and diversified. Office towers, such as the recent Condé Nast building in New York's Times Square, will use solar panels not just on roofs but integrated into the facade.

In Our Economy

Making the transition to clean energy offers an unprecedented opportunity to pioneer new development pathways for an economy that grows in wise directions. Rather than plundering endangered ecosystems for their natural resources, we'll create and expand entire new industries to produce sustainable energy, and to use it efficiently. At the local level, achieving energy self-sufficiency will mitigate against fluctuating energy prices, and will offer regional economies a buffer against recessions as well. Weatherizing homes, installing solar panels, maintaining wind turbines: many jobs in a clean-energy economy can't be outsourced and will benefit local communities.

Developing clean energy will help rejuvenate rural economies in particular. Community-based energy development will provide steady and diversified income to struggling farmers and ranchers. As the wind industry grows, more jobs will be created for wind technicians in rural areas throughout the Midwest and other regions. In Texas, the country's largest supplier of wind energy, the rapid growth of wind farms has brought much-needed new revenue to towns that once suffered the collapse of the local oil industry. "Wind has invigorated our business like you wouldn't believe," says Marty Foust, the owner of a clothing store in Sweetwater. "When you watch the news you can get depressed about the economy, but we don't get depressed. We're now in our own bubble."

Reinventing a postcarbon economy will be an engine for job growth: in the automotive sector, producing a new generation of zero-emission vehicles; in energy generation, installing and maintaining large-scale solar facilities; and in scrapping old coal plants.

In How America Views Itself

When we break our addiction to oil and coal, our country can get its mojo back. Rather than just talk about climate change, America can face it head-on and help our allies follow our lead. Rather than exploit other countries' dirty-energy sources—or use their failures as an excuse for inaction—we can set the right example, exporting energy-efficient technologies, wind turbines, solar collectors, and effective public policy solutions.

In the process, Americans will take part in literally hundreds of individual victories: to stop the construction of coal plants, resist an oil-drilling proposal, pass an efficiency standard, install a wind farm, and train or retrain tens of thousands of new workers. Each victory will build momentum for the next. As Cesar Chavez said, "Once social change begins, it cannot be reversed. You cannot uneducate the person who has learned to read. You cannot humiliate the person who feels pride. You cannot oppress the people who are not afraid anymore. We have seen the future, and the future is ours."

Join Us: It's Fun Over Here

The hardest part of standing up for your rights is to stand up the first time. In her book *Love Canal: My Story*, Lois Gibbs writes of being so nervous the first time she went to talk to neighbors about pollution in Love Canal, New York, that she went home after knocking on one door. The next day, she summoned the confidence to begin anew. Years later, Gibbs not only forced the polluters to pay for the cleanup and relocation of residents but helped inspire legislation that forced hundreds of companies elsewhere to do the same.

We don't all have to be national heroes like Gibbs. But every time one of us takes a stand for what we believe is right, it contributes to a collective impact. One letter to Home Depot didn't convince the company to change. After more than a hundred thousand letters, actions by consumers and shareholders, and public advertisements, the company overhauled its environmental policy and is now a leader in green purchasing.

We deserve to be able to drink water from a stream just like our grandparents did, or to eat fish from a river, as people have done for thousands of years. We should be free to swim at any beach without fear of getting a nasty rash or disease. And when Americans work together to reinvent our industrial way of life, we can have more of what we want, not less.

Health care costs will decrease as our air quality improves. Fewer children and adults will experience the gripping panic of an asthma attack. Less dioxin, sulfur dioxide, nitrogen oxides, and other pollutants in our bodies will result in more pregnancies carried to term, healthier babies, and reduced cancer rates. Diminished particulate matter will decrease the likelihood of heart attacks, and reduced soot and smog will produce cleaner cities and clearer skies from the Grand Canyon to the Great Smokies.

Getting serious about clean energy will also be an economic bonanza, as Amory Lovins says. Using less energy in our homes and businesses will save money for families and corporations alike, while allowing factories to increase productivity. Cutting off all government subsidies for oil and coal and related industries will save even more taxpayer money and permit reinvestment in new energy projects that offer broad social benefits.

America has the resources. Our country has been spending an estimated $4 billion each week on a war in Iraq. Imagine how that money could be better spent in mobilizing for energy independence—helping our automobile industry produce a fleet of zero-emission vehicles and resurrecting our manufacturing base in the process. We could weatherize millions of low-income homes, put solar panels on the rooftops of millions of homes and businesses, and so much more. Rather than relying on centralized power plants, our power grid would become diversified and distributed, more resistant to a terrorist attack or systemwide blackouts due to malfunctions.

When we achieve energy independence, America no longer will be sending billions of dollars in oil money overseas, but will be able to reinvest its energy dollars here at home. Our trade deficit will disappear. Our balance of payments with other countries will be restored. Our national debt and annual national deficits will also decrease as energy is conserved. As Paul Hawken points out in Leonardo DiCaprio's film *The 11th Hour*, "The great thing about the dilemma we're in is that we get to reimagine every single thing we do." We can see this as a burden, he observes, but I share his preferred view: that it's an incredibly exciting time to be alive.

Described in this book are dozens of different ways to make a difference. Dozens more can't fit between these pages. We can challenge airlines to recycle their aging fleets and utilize newer planes that burn less gas, so they become "Jet Green." Push United Airlines to stop using oil from the Alberta tar sands as a source of jet fuel. Urge plastic manufacturers to replace petroleum-based plastics with sustainably grown, plant-based alternatives. Eat less meat and buy organic food (many pesticides are oil-based)—or better yet, eat local (it takes a lot of oil to ship those blueberries from New Zealand). We can gather friends, our church group, family members, or fellow students for a conference call to a CEO; visit a congressperson; hold a house party; join a press conference; or donate to a favorite nonprofit.

In the United States, we have the right to remain silent. But we also have a responsibility to speak out and to stand up for what is right. America isn't getting the action we need from Wall Street or Washington, so we citizens need to inspire, persuade, embarrass, support, direct, and demand greater accountability. It's up to us to break our national addiction to dirty energy.

And we will. If you think it's a disgrace that we're fighting terrorists on one hand and funding them with the other, then take action. If you believe that we can meet the challenge of climate change and create a safer, healthier, and more peaceful world, then please raise your voice. If you're already involved, bless you. Don't give up.

Resources

You're not alone. Polls show that most Americans support a future in which our energy is safe, secure, and sustainable. And history has shown that there is great power in collective action.

In this section, I've listed some of the most active organizations promoting a clean government, zero-emission vehicles, renewable energy, and other issues addressed in this book. Please give them a hand. The list begins with organizations that tackle climate change and our dependence on dirty energy with multiple initiatives. You'll also find suggestions for further reading or other sources of information on particular issues, and listings of visionary companies where you can get information about retrofitting your home with renewables, learn about incentive programs, and so on.

Multiple Issues

SUPPORT THESE ORGANIZATIONS AND PROGRAMS

Natural Resources Defense Council
www.nrdc.org
> One of the nation's largest environmental groups is a strong voice in the campaign to stop expansion in Canada's tar sands. Join NRDC in its effort to seek "friendlier skies" by urging major U.S. and Canadian airlines, including United, American, and others, to swear off jet fuel from unconventional oil sources. NRDC is also a leader in promoting energy efficiency and clean, renewable power.

Rainforest Action Network
www.ran.org
> Do you think it's outrageous that your money is being used to fund coal plants and build oil pipelines? Or that American companies such as Archer Daniels Midland and Cargill destroy rainforests in the name of biofuels? RAN thinks so too. Join its Global Finance, Rainforest Agribusiness, or Freedom from Oil campaigns and get involved with a group the *Wall Street Journal* calls "some of the savviest environmental agitators in the business."

Sierra Club

www.sierraclub.org

In a saner world, we wouldn't have to fight to keep the oil industry from trampling our best parks and last wilderness areas. Nor would we have to challenge automakers and utilities to do what's right. Through its Public Lands and Resilient Habitat programs, coal campaigns, lobbying of Congress and automakers to increase fuel efficiency, and more, the Sierra Club has been doing heroic work for decades to defend the environment.

Union of Concerned Scientists

www.ucsusa.org

UCS's team of experts produce credible, timely information to help consumers and policy-makers alike improve performance and reduce emissions in American cars and trucks. UCS has also been a leading voice promoting clean-energy solutions, exposing utilities and the coal industry's impact on human health and the environment, protecting the Arctic National Wildlife Refuge and more.

LEARN MORE

DeSmogBlog

http://desmogblog.com

Highlights the most creative actions and solutions to fight climate change, while "clearing the PR pollution that clouds the science on climate change."

Grist

www.grist.org

Compiles the best in environmental journalism, delivering a daily dose of "gloom and doom with a sense of humor."

It's Getting Hot in Here

http://itsgettinghotinhere.org

This blog collects the writings of a hundred voices from the youth movement to stop climate change and is one of the best sites to visit to take action on clean energy.

Solving Climate

http://solveclimate.com

Based on the assumption that the country knows what is needed to meet our climate challenge—and can afford to implement climate solutions—this blog aims to show how it can be done.

WiserEarth

www.wiserearth.org

A community directory and networking forum that connects more than 100,000 environmental and social justice organizations around the world, enabling individuals, organizations, philanthropists, media, and others to find each other, build alliances, and share strategies and resources.

Big Oil

Amazon Watch
www.amazonwatch.org
> Tracks the operations of oil companies throughout the Amazon basin and exposes them in the boardroom and the court of public opinion. Has led the campaign to hold Chevron accountable for toxic oil spills in Ecuador, which could help establish a global precedent for the overseas operations of the world's largest energy corporations.

Communities for a Better Environment
www.cbecal.org
> Works to amplify the voice of communities of color and working-class communities to promote environmental health and justice. Fights toxic oil refineries throughout California.

EarthRights International
www.earthrights.org
> Led by Ka Hsaw Wa, a 1999 Goldman Environmental Prize recipient, and Katie Redford, a 2006 Ashoka fellow—both honored for their courageous work to defend environmental and human rights in Burma—EarthRights uses the power of law and of grassroots organizing to support communities affected by fossil-fuel extraction in Burma, the Amazon, and beyond.

ForestEthics
www.forestethics.org
> A small but highly effective grassroots environmental organization, ForestEthics made its name helping to protect the majestic Great Bear Rainforest in British Columbia, and has since added its muscle to the fight to stop Canada's tar sands expansion.

Global Community Monitor
www.gcmonitor.org
> Led by Denny Larson, GCM provides hands-on tools for affected communities to monitor the environmental health of oil refineries and other pollution sources in their own neighborhoods.

Indigenous Environmental Network
www.ienearth.org
> A network of Indigenous peoples "demanding environmental justice and maintaining the Sacred Fire of our traditions." Its Native Energy campaign has helped lead the fight to protect the Arctic National Wildlife Refuge and stop Canada's tar sands expansion, among other projects.

Keepers of the Waters
www.keepersofthewaters.org
> An alliance of Indigenous organizations working to resist tar sands development and to protect the Arctic Ocean drainage basin.

Oil Change International

www.priceofoil.org/thepriceofoil

In addition to running sophisticated campaigns aimed at restraining Big Oil, this group has a Web site that examines the high social and environmental costs of our oil dependency.

Pachamama Alliance

www.pachamama.org

Collaborates closely with the Achuar and other native communities in Ecuador to preserve the region's tropical rainforests through public education, advocacy, and lobbying. Pachamama has been a vital, long-term ally to the Kichwa and other communities resisting the incursion of oil companies into pristine forests.

Publish What You Pay

www.publishwhatyoupay.org

A coalition of more than 300 organizations worldwide that helps citizens of resource-rich countries check the corrupting influence of the oil and other industries by holding their governments accountable for the management of revenues from oil, gas, mining, and other activities.

LEARN MORE

Books, films, and other sources of information:

Beyond Oil: The View from Hubbert's Peak
Kenneth Deffeyes's book on peak oil.

Blood and Oil: The Dangers and Consequences of America's Growing Dependency on Imported Petroleum
Michael T. Klare's book on the human costs of our dependency.

Energy Bulletin
http://energybulletin.net
A clearinghouse for information about peak energy supplies.

Justicia Now
A documentary film by Martin O'Brien and Robby Proctor about Chevron's legacy of oil spills and toxic waste in the Ecuadorian Amazon.

The Long Emergency
James Howard Kunstler's book on how the coming oil crunch will put us all in a world of hurt

The Oil Drum
www.theoildrum.com
Online community that discusses ideas related to peak oil, sustainable development and growth, and the implications of these ideas on politics, economics communities, and the environment.

Oil on Ice
Documentary film by Dale Djerassi about proposed oil drilling in the Arctic Refuge.

Oil Sands Watch
www.oilsandswatch.org
Provides current information on Canada's tar sands, sponsored by the Pembina Institute.

The Prize: The Epic Quest for Oil, Money, and Power
Daniel Yergin's book on the oil industry's rise to dominance.

Syriana
Stephen Gaghan's film examining Big Oil's corrupting influence.

Winning the Oil Endgame
A hopeful collection of clean-energy strategies by the Rocky Mountain Institute (Amory Lovins et al.).

Coal Industry

SUPPORT THESE ORGANIZATIONS AND PROGRAMS

Appalachian Voices
www.appvoices.org
A grassroots environmental organization based in Boone, North Carolina, working to stop mountaintop-removal mining and restore the Appalachian forests.

Black Mesa Water Coalition
www.blackmesawatercoalition.org
BMWC has been working to end Peabody Coal's wasteful use of scarce and sacred groundwater in the Black Mesa Diné (Navajo) and Hopi lands, calling for a transition to renewable energy practices and sources.

Coal River Mountain Watch
www.crmw.net
Based in Appalachia; works to stop the destruction of communities and the environment by mountaintop-removal mining and to help rebuild sustainable communities.

Greenpeace International's "Quit Coal" campaign
www.greenpeace.org/international/campaigns/climate-change/coal?page=2
An international effort by one of the world's largest environmental organizations to stop coal-industry expansion and kick-start a rapid transition to renewables and greater energy efficiency.

Little Village Environmental Justice Organization
www.lvejo.org
A community organization in Chicago working for clean air and environmental justice.

Ohio Valley Environmental Coalition
www.ohvec.org
Another effective grassroots group fighting in Appalachia to protect the environment and stop mountaintop removal.

Pilsen Environmental Rights and Reform Organization
www.pilsenperro.org
An ally of Little Village Environmental Justice Organization in Chicago, Pilsen fights for citizens' right to clean air and a healthy environment.

Respiratory Health Association of Metropolitan Chicago
www.lungchicago.org
Formerly part of the American Lung Association, this Chicago-based organization provides support to asthma patients and their families while also advocating for more stringent measures to reduce emissions in the region.

LEARN MORE

Books, films, and other sources of information::

Big Coal: The Dirty Secret behind America's Energy Future
Jeff Goodell's entertaining but unnerving book revealing the high cost of cheap coal.

Burning the Future
David Novack's film depicting West Virginia as ground zero in the fight to stop mountaintop removal and create a clean-energy future.

Coal: A Human History
Barbara Freese's book tracing coal's use from ancient Britain to modern China and exploring how coal will impact our future as a species.

coalSwarm
www.sourcewatch.org/index.php?title=Portal:Coal_Issues
A project of SourceWatch and the Center for Media and Democracy, coalSwarm is a wiki that allows users to share the latest information about proposed coal plants, sample testimony, campaign videos, renewable energy developments, and more.

"The Dirty Rock"
April 2007 article by Jeff Goodell in *The Nation* outlining the challenges to safe underground storage of carbon from coal plants.

Environmental Integrity Project
www.environmentalintegrity.org
   Founded by former EPA enforcement attorney Eric Schaeffer, this nonpartisan organization helps local communities gain the protection of environmental laws while holding state and federal government officials accountable for failing to enforce or comply with those laws.

"Global Boom in Coal Power—and Emissions"
   Mark Clayton's March 22, 2007, article in the *Christian Science Monitor* about the impact of proposed new coal plants on global greenhouse gas emissions.

iLoveMountains.org
   Online tool enabling users to determine whether their power is connected to mountaintop removal.

KilowattOurs
   Jeff Barrie's film on how to create an energy revolution, one kilowatt at a time.

Who's Got the Power?
   Casey Coates Danson's film contrasting the promise of clean power with the perils of fossil fuels.

Clean Government

SUPPORT THESE ORGANIZATIONS AND PROGRAMS

Center for Public Integrity
www.publicintegrity.org
   A nonpartisan organization that provides excellent investigative reports to help promote transparency and good governance.

Center for Responsive Politics
www.opensecrets.org
   Nonpartisan guide to how much oil and coal companies and utilities spend on lobbying and direct corporate contributions.

Friends of the Earth
www.foe.org
   For years, Friends of the Earth's "Green Scissors" program has united conservatives and progressives seeking to end subsidies for polluters. FOE continues as an ally of clean energy and clean government by exposing government subsidies to Big Oil.

Greenpeace USA's Project Hot Seat

www.greenpeaceusa.org

Will Congress continue to delay taking action on climate change, or will it make a break from the fossil-fuel industry? Greenpeace organizers relentlessly push Congress members to become climate heroes.

MAPLight.org

www.maplight.org

Group that shines a spotlight on the connections between money and politics.

MoveOn.org

www.moveon.org

A progressive organization of more than 3 million advocating for clean energy, including an effort to promote an "oil-free Congress."

Oil Change International

www.priceofoil.org

Runs the grassroots campaign "Separate Oil and State," which organizes Americans to persuade lawmakers to refuse Big Oil political donations. Visit this Web site to find out how much your representative is taking from the oil industry.

LEARN MORE

Crimes against Nature: How George W. Bush and His Corporate Pals Are Plundering the Country and Hijacking Our Democracy

Robert F. Kennedy, Jr.'s book about how the Bush administration "plundered the country" and how we can't let it happen again.

Earth Track

www.earthtrack.net

Doug Koplow's project to itemize state, federal, and international energy subsidies.

League of Conservation Voters' Environmental Scorecards

www.lcv.org/scorecard

Provides clear information for how your representatives voted on the most important environmental bills in Congress and state by state.

"Some Like It Hot"

Chris Mooney's May/June 2005 article in *Mother Jones* detailing how ExxonMobil has funded groups seeking to undermine scientific consensus on global warming.

Banking and Finance

As You Sow's Corporate Responsibility Program
www.asyousow.org
   Promotes corporate responsibility by engaging publicly held companies to adopt stronger
   social and environmental policies. If you're a shareholder of a publicly traded corporation and
   want to use your voice, As You Sow can help.

Bank Information Center
www.bicusa.org
   Supports communities and nonprofits in developing countries to push the World Bank and
   other international financial institutions to develop stronger social and environmental safe-
   guards.

BankTrack
www.banktrack.org
   An international network of organizations and individuals acting as a watchdog for the global
   banking industry. Its members have pressured dozens of banks to tighten their environmental
   and social regulations, and have developed a set of principles for responsible banking known
   as the Collevecchio Declaration.

Co-op America
www.coopamerica.org
   A member-based organization that assists consumers, business owners, investors, and others to take individual and collective action to promote social and environmental justice. Its
   Climate Action campaign has challenged America's largest banks to show stronger leadership
   to replace dirty energy with clean-energy sources.

End Oil Aid
www.endoilaid.org
   A coalition of organizations including Jubilee USA Network, Oil Change International,
   Friends of the Earth, and others that address the interrelated issues of oil, climate change, and
   international debt, and seek policy solutions to eliminate all international subsidies for the oil
   industry.

Interfaith Center on Corporate Responsibility
www.iccr.org
   This association of 275 faith-based institutional investors has long been a leader in the corporate social responsibility movement. ICCR's Global Warming and Environmental Justice
   programs compel corporate leaders to accelerate a transition to clean energy while alleviating
   the burden of pollution borne by low-income communities and communities of color.

International Forum on Globalization
www.ifg.org
  A research and educational institution that, among other issues, confronts the "global triple crisis" of climate change, peak oil, and resource depletion and extinction. IFG's *Alternatives to Economic Globalization* is an excellent compendium of development strategies that can create wealth without sacrificing the health of people or planet.

LEARN MORE

"Aiding Oil, Harming the Climate"
http://priceofoil.org/2007/12/06/aiding-oil-harming-the-climate/
  An Oil Change International report detailing the impacts of the World Bank's loans and investments in Big Oil.

"Don't Get Burned"
  An Interfaith Center on Corporate Responsibility report for investors about the high economic risks of financing coal-fired power plants.

Globalization and Its Discontents
  Nobel Prize–winning economist Joseph Stiglitz's book shows how the World Bank and International Monetary Fund often undermined national sovereignty and environmental and labor standards in service to a discredited economic policy.

Green banking
  For green banking options, visit New Resource Bank at www.newresourcebank.com, ShoreBank Pacific at www.shorebankcorp.com, or www.creditunionsonline.org, as noted in chapter 4.

"U.S. Sends Mixed Message on Climate"
  August 12, 2007 article by Judy Pasternak in the *Los Angeles Times* revealing hypocrisy in U.S. climate policy.

Public Transportation and Urban Planning

SUPPORT THESE ORGANIZATIONS AND PROGRAMS

Bus Riders Union
www.busridersunion.org
  Environmental justice organization that promotes sustainable transportation options for all Los Angeles residents, based on the belief that "affordable, efficient, and environmentally sound mass transit is a human right."

Center for Neighborhood Technology
www.cnt.org
A Chicago-based research and policy organization—"part think tank, part incubator"–to promote more livable and sustainable communities.

Congress for the New Urbanism
www.cnu.org
A member-based organization of planners, architects, designers, activists, and others working together to encourage the development, or redevelopment, of walkable, mixed-use neighborhoods as an alternative to sprawl.

League of American Bicyclists
www.bikeleague.org
Its membership of 300,000 affiliated cyclists uses education and advocacy to promote a bicycle-friendly America. Publishes the *American Bicyclist* magazine.

Midwest High Speed Rail Association
www.midwesthsr.org
A membership-based organization promoting fast and frequent rail service connecting the entire Midwest.

National Association of Railroad Passengers
www.narprail.org
The nation's largest advocacy organization for train and rail transit passengers. For too many years, NARP has had to fight tenaciously in Congress to maintain even minimum funding levels for passenger rail. Join them to promote a modern, national train network that "provides a travel choice Americans want."

National Center for Safe Routes to School
www.saferoutesinfo.org
A clearinghouse of information for how to start a Safe Routes to School program in your neighborhood. Runs the annual Walk to School events nationwide, which promote safe walking and cycling routes for students in their hometowns.

Reconnecting America
www.reconnectingamerica.org
A national organization based in Oakland working to "integrate transportation systems and the communities they serve." Reconnecting America operates the Center for Transit-Oriented Development, which seeks to catalyze greater public and private investment into creating walkable, transit-friendly communities.

Thunderhead Alliance
www.thunderheadalliance.org
A national coalition of state and local pedestrian and cycling advocacy organizations working to promote safe cycling and walking in North America.

Transportation Alternatives

www.transalt.org

The leading voice for promoting safe and convenient cycling and for reducing car use in New York City.

Urban Habitat

www.urbanhabitat.org

Based on the belief that an affordable, dependable, efficient transportation system is prerequisite to the economic and social health of a region, Urban Habitat advocates for smart growth and sustainable transportation investments as part of a multifaceted program promoting equitable development and environmental justice.

U.S. PIRG

www.uspirg.org/issues/transportation

The federation of state Public Interest Research Groups. In almost every state, grassroots organizers affiliated with state PIRGs work to increase the share of public transportation dollars devoted to transit and prioritize a modern, efficient transportation network.

LEARN MORE

Bike 2015 Plan, City of Chicago

www.bike2015plan.org

Quite possibly the best bicycle plan in the country.

"Building a Better Bike Lane"

May 4, 2007, *Wall Street Journal* article by Nancy Keates reports on how cities in Europe continue to innovate to make cycling more safe and convenient.

The End of Suburbia

Documentary film by Gregory Greene that predicts the energy crisis will intensify and suggests steps for action.

Online Transportation Demand Management (TDM) Encyclopedia

www.vtpi.org/tdm/tdm12.htm

Operated by the Victoria Transport Policy Institute. The most comprehensive resource for sustainable transportation systems.

Race, Poverty, and the Environment

A journal of environmental justice, produced by Urban Habitat.

Street Smart: Street Cars and Cities in the 21st Century

Beautifully illustrated book by Shelley Poticha and Gloria Ohland, showing how urban planners are creating a renaissance for the American street car.

Cars and Trucks

SUPPORT THESE ORGANIZATIONS AND PROGRAMS

CalCars
www.calcars.org
A California-based "start-up" nonprofit group of engineers and entrepreneurs that is organizing customer demand and advocating for strong public policy incentives to promote the development of plug-in hybrid vehicles that can earn more than 100 mpg.

Friends of the Earth's Transportation campaign
http://action.foe.org/content.jsp?content_KEY=2710&t=2007_Smarter-Transportation.dwt
This project of Friends of the Earth works aggressively to uphold California's precedent-setting legislation to reduce auto emissions, while pushing Congress to follow California's lead. Also a leading advocate for plug-in hybrid vehicles.

Global Exchange's Freedom from Oil campaign
www.globalexchange.org
Global Exchange earned its reputation fighting sweatshops and the World Trade Organization. This project challenges automakers at North American locations, such as auto shows, dealerships, and industry conferences, to produce zero-emission vehicles as soon as possible..

Plug In America
www.pluginamerica.org
A collection of electric-vehicle drivers and clean-energy advocates who know a good thing when they see it and drive it. Plug In America is one of the country's most effective advocates for electric vehicles, and is a big reason why plug-in hybrid cars and trucks will be seen on America's roadways in increasing numbers.

Ruckus Society
www.ruckus.org
Ruckus works closely with Global Exchange and Rainforest Action Network's Freedom from Oil campaigns, giving training and strategic advice to individuals and organizations working for human rights and social and environmental justice.

Set America Free Coalition
www.setamericafree.org
One of the country's most diverse coalitions; includes conservative hawks and green energy activists working together to fight climate change and secure energy independence by advancing automotive fuel efficiency.

SmartTransportation.org
www.smarttransportation.org
A leading voice for converting New York City's taxi fleet to hybrid vehicles and encouraging other cities to do the same. Also advocates for congestion pricing and other strategies to reduce congestion and gridlock in New York.

"Drilling in Detroit"
www.ucsusa.org/clean_vehicles/fuel_economy/drilling-in-detroit.html
   A 2001 report from the Union of Concerned Scientists showing how practical, off-the-shelf technologies can be used by automakers to dramatically increase fuel efficiency.

Freedom from Oil: How the Next President Can End the United States' Oil Addiction
   David Sandalow's book gives a step-by-step guide for how the next president can help kick our oil habit. Several of Sandalow's steps were suggested in this book.

Who Killed the Electric Car?
   Chris Paine's critically acclaimed documentary exploring the rise, fall, and potential comeback of the electric car.

Agrofuels

SUPPORT THESE ORGANIZATIONS AND PROGRAMS

Earth Policy Institute
www.earth-policy.org
   An organization that has been one of the most influential and powerful voices warning of the dangers of the growing biofuel craze; founded by Lester Brown.

Food First
www.foodfirst.org
   Institute for food and development policy. Works to eliminate the injustices that cause hunger, poverty, and environmental degradation globally. An activist think tank, Food First amplifies the voices of communities being impacted by transnational agribusinesses and advocates for sustainable food—and fuel—production.

Forest Peoples Programme
www.forestpeoples.org
   An expert team based in the United Kingdom that supports forest peoples to secure land rights and sustainably manage their forests and livelihoods.

Grassroots International
www.grassrootsonline.org
   A human rights and international development organization that provides grants to organizations and communities in the Global South to support community-led sustainable development projects.

Greenpeace International's soy and palm oil campaigns
www.greenpeace.org/international/campaigns/forests
  In Brazil, Greenpeace campaigners helped secure a temporary moratorium on the further
  expansion of the soy industry into the Brazilian Amazon. In Europe, Greenpeace organizers
  are pressuring leading food and consumer products manufacturers to cease using palm oil
  from endangered forests.

Institute for Agriculture and Trade Policy
www.iatp.org
  A long-time advocate for family farmers and responsible U.S. agriculture policy, IATP carefully bridges the divide between farmers and agrofuel critics in the United States.

Oakland Institute
www.oaklandinstitute.org
  A policy think tank that specializes in strengthening multicultural social movements. A leading voice warning of the dangers of agrofuels.

Sustainable Biodiesel Alliance
www.sustainablebiodieselalliance.org
  An organization of farmers, biodiesel enthusiasts, environmental groups, and others working
  together to try to do it right: developing strong life-cycle standards for sustainable biodiesel
  production and distribution so that consumers can "fuel responsibly."

World Rainforest Movement
www.wrm.org.uy
  One of the earliest critics of how the growth in agrofuel production was increasing deforestation and human rights violations, this international network defends the world's rainforests.

LEARN MORE

"The Clean Energy Scam"
  March 27, 2008, report by Michael Grunwald in *Time,* taking a highly critical look at the
  ethanol craze.

"Green Dreams"
  October 2007 article by Joel K. Bourne, Jr., in *National Geographic* exploring the social and
  environmental impacts of the agrofuel industry.

"How Biofuels Could Starve the World's Poor"
  May/June 2007 article in *Foreign Affairs* by C. Ford Runge and Benjamin Senauer.

"How the Palm Oil Industry Is Cooking the Climate"
www.greenpeace.org/international/news/palm-oil_cooking-the-climate
  Report by Greenpeace in October 2007.

"Palm Oil: The Biofuel of the Future Driving an Ecological Disaster Now"
April 4, 2007, article by Ian McKinnon in the *Guardian*.

Plan B 3.0: Mobilizing to Save Civilization
Wide-ranging book by Lester Brown that highlights many of the dangers of agrofuel production and advocates for sustainable alternatives.

Science, February 29, 2008, issue
Two important articles: "Use of U.S. Croplands for Biofuels Increases Greenhouse Gas Emissions from Land-Use Change," by Searchinger et al., and "Land Clearing and the Biofuel Carbon Debt" by Fargione et al.

Renewable Energy

SUPPORT THESE ORGANIZATIONS AND PROGRAMS

1Sky.org
www.1sky.org
A diverse coalition of elected officials, students, faith-based institutions, and health and environmental organizations working to promote bold federal action by 2010 on climate change and green jobs.

American Council on Renewable Energy
www.acore.org
A nonprofit organization with members from the wind, solar, biomass, and other clean-power sectors; seeks to advance trade and policy tools to promote all forms of renewable energy.

ClimateChallenge.org
www.climatechallenge.org
Students, faculty members, and administrators taking action on climate change at high schools and college campuses across the country. A project of Energy Action and more than six hundred local organizations.

Community-Based Energy Development
www.c-bed.org
A coalition of farmers, clean-power advocates, business owners, and others working to promote clean energy along with local economic development, so that local ownership of renewable resources will keep the financial benefits in the community.

Environment America
www.environmentamerica.org
State by state, this collection of grassroots organizations advocates for laws to promote solar and wind power and forces fossil-fuel companies and utilities to cut emissions.

Green for All
www.greenforall.org
Advocates for local, state, and federal resources to create economic opportunities and job training for green-collar jobs, especially in low-income communities.

New Voice of Business
www.newvoiceofbusiness.org
Seeks to amplify the voices of business people who want to be part of the solution on climate change and other issues.

Vote Solar
www.votesolar.org
Starting in San Francisco and spreading across the country, one of the country's most effective advocates for strong public policies promoting solar power.

Western Resource Advocates
www.westernresourceadvocates.org
An environmental law and policy organization working to restore and protect the natural environment of the interior American West. Works to challenge coal-plant proposals and advocate for clean-energy solutions.

LEARN MORE

Carbon-Free and Nuclear-Free: A Roadmap for U.S. Energy Policy
An excellent book by Arjun Makhijani and the Institute for Energy and Environment Research that gives a detailed analysis of America's untapped clean-energy potential.

"Cashing in on Clean Energy"
www.ucsusa.org/clean_energy/clean_energy_policies/cashing-in.html
A 2007 Union of Concerned Scientists report on the economic benefits of clean energy.

"Clean Energy Trends"
www.cleanedge.com/reports/
These annual reports by Clean Edge track the rapid growth rates and new developments in the renewable energy sector.

Green-Collar Jobs in America's Cities
Resource guide produced by the Apollo Alliance and Green for All to help policymakers in urban areas develop local strategies to create and support green job growth.

"Solar Generation IV"
www.greenpeace.org/international/press/reports/solar-generation-iv
Report by Greenpeace International in 2007 predicting the creation of 2 million solar jobs by 2020.

"A Solar Grand Plan"
    January 2008 *Scientific American* article by Ken Zweibel, James Mason, and Vasilis Fthenakis
    proposing how solar technology (the article mostly focuses on solar photovoltaics) can meet a
    substantial portion of our energy needs.

Solar Revolution: The Economic Transformation of the Global Energy Industry
    Industry analyst Travis Bradford develops a compelling business case for why distributed
    solar power will upend the way power is produced and delivered in the twenty-first century.

"Tackling Climate Change"
www.ases.org/climatechange/
    A comprehensive 2007 report by the American Solar Energy Society showing the potential for
    greenhouse gas reductions through clean energy and efficiency through 2030.

SOLAR PROVIDERS

There will soon be hundreds of solar power installers operating around the country. Most of
them will help you secure local, state and federal rebates and even help arrange financing. Here
are a few:

SolarCity
www.solarcity.com
    A rapidly growing company, awarded the 2008 Aspen Energy and Environment Award for
    Corporate Energy Generation.

SunEdison
www.sunedison.com
    SunEdison works with businesses and municipalities and takes a different approach to
    providing solar power. They own the solar panels; will install them on the rooftop of your
    business, university, or government building; and will sell you clean, secure power at competi-
    tive rates.

Sungevity
www.sungevity.com
    California-based installers led by some of the country's most experienced environmental
    advocates.

Energy Efficiency

SUPPORT THESE ORGANIZATIONS AND PROGRAMS

Alliance to Save Energy
www.ase.org
    A national coalition of high-profile politicians, business leaders, and others providing
    research and policy advice to promote the efficient use of clean energy.

American Council for an Energy-Efficient Economy
www.aceee.org
A nonprofit that provides research materials to consumers and policymakers to promote prosperity and sustainability through energy efficiency. Produces the *Consumer Guide to Home Energy Savings* and other resources highlighting businesses and municipalities that are leading innovators in energy efficiency.

Architecture 2030
www.architecture2030.org
Founded by architect Ed Mazria in 2002 to transform the U.S. building sector from a major contributor of climate change to a potential cure. Aims to change the ways in which buildings are planned, designed, and constructed, taking a vocal and determined stance against new coal plant construction.

Climate Group
www.theclimategroup.org
An international organization based in the United Kingdom, United States, and Australia that helps businesses and governments to share knowledge of new technologies and techniques to reduce energy consumption and greenhouse gas emissions. Also advocates for clean-energy policies.

Rocky Mountain Institute
www.rmi.org
Colorado-based organization founded by Amory Lovins that has long been an efficiency pioneer, providing advocacy, research, and consultancy services. RMI's mission statement says that its work is "independent, nonadversarial, and transideological, with a strong emphasis on market-based solutions."

LEARN MORE

"More Profit with Less Carbon"
September 2005 *Scientific American* article by Amory Lovins that reshapes the climate debate by showing how reducing greenhouse gas emissions can significantly improve a company's bottom line.

"Reducing Greenhouse Gas Emissions"
www.mckinsey.com/clientservice/ccsi/greenhousegas.asp
December 2007 report by McKinsey and Company showing how efficiency combined with renewable power can significantly reduce greenhouse gas emissions in the short term.

Notes

Introduction: It's Time to Refuel

Page 11. Victor Hugo epigraph: *History of a Crime,* written in 1852, published in 1877. Quotation taken from English translation by T. H. Joyce and Arthur Locker (New York: Mondial, 2005), p. 409.

Page 11. Sports Illustrated cover story: Alexander Wolff, "Going, Going Green," *Sports Illustrated,* March 2007.

Page 11. "Green" is "the new red, white and blue": Thomas Freidman, "Green: The New Red, White and Blue," *New York Times,* January 6, 2006.

Page 11. "Al, it's cold outside": The original context for this quote was Al Gore speaking at an event hosted by MoveOn.org at Beacon Theater in Manhattan, on a cold winter day in New York City. So House Majority Whip Roy Blunt, a Missouri Republican, said it was "fitting that Mr. Gore chose one of the coldest days of the year to spread false information about the Bush administration's record on global warming. Mother Nature didn't agree with his message, and neither do I." The congressman added, "Al, it's cold outside." This is an excerpt from Robert Yoho's article in the *American Partisan* entitled, "Al, It's Cold Outside," January 20, 2004, available at www.american-partisan.com/cols/2004/yoho/qtr1/0120.htm.

Page 11. In 2007, sales of hybrid vehicles increased by 38 percent: HybridCars.com, "December 2007 Dashboard," www.hybridcars.com/market-dashboard/dec07-overview.html. Cars outpacing trucks: Chris Woodward, "Drivers Choose Cars over Trucks as Auto Sales Plunge," *USA Today,* June 3, 2008.

Page 12. 18seconds.org: The Web site's creators estimate that it takes only eighteen seconds to change a light bulb. Check out how "enlightened" your town is at www.18seconds.org.

Page 12. Sixty percent of U.S. citizens believe we must take action now: John Podesta, Daniel J. Weiss, and Laura Nichols, "Americans Urgently Want Action on Energy Independence and Global Warming," Center for American Progress, Issues page (April 18, 2007), www.americanprogress.org/issues/2007/04/environment_poll.html.

Page 12. Ecomagination: Excerpted from General Electric's Web site, the Our Company page, www.ge.com/company/citizenship/ecomagination/index.html.

Page 12. Ford fuel economy below the industry norm: From U.S. Environmental Protection Agency Web site, "Light-Duty Automotive Technology and Fuel Economy Trends: 1975 through 2007," appendix L, "Data Stratified by Vehicle Type and Marketing Group," www.epa.gov/oms/cert/mpg/fetrends/420r07008l.pdf, table L-8, p. 9. The Model T Ford earned between twenty and twenty-five miles per gallon in the early twentieth century (Model T Ford Register of Great Britain Web site, www.modeltregister.co.uk/the-model-t-ford.html). By comparison, over the past twelve years, Ford Motor Company's fleet average has not exceeded twenty miles per gallon.

Page 13. California's vehicle emissions regulations: Details on the Pavley Law can be found on Union of Concerned Scientists (UCS) Web site, and in "California Regulates Global Warming Emissions from Motor Vehicles," available at the UCS site: www.ucsusa.org/clean_vehicles/vehicles_health/californias-global-warming-vehicle-law.html.

Page 13. Washington Post op-ed: Arnold Schwarzenegger and Jodi Rell, "Lead or Step Aside, EPA: States Can't Wait on Global Warming," *Washington Post,* May 21, 2007.

Page 14. Bush administration rules in favor of the automakers: Juliet Eilperin, "EPA Chief Denies Calif. Limit on Auto Emissions," *Washington Post,* December 20, 2007.

Page 14. Frederick Douglass quote: Frederick Douglass, "The Significance of Emancipation in the West Indies," speech, Canandaigua, New York, August 3, 1857, taken from the Building Equality Web site, a cooperative project of the Center for Democratic Renewal, Political Research Associates, National Center for Human Rights Education, and the Gustavus Myers Center: see the Quotes page, www.buildingequality.us/Quotes/Frederick_Douglass.htm.

Page 14. Nearly half of our electricity comes from coal: Energy Information Administration (EIA), "Electric Power Annual," EIA Web site, data for 2006 (October 22, 2007), www.eia.doe.gov/cneaf/electricity/epa/epa_sum.html.

Page 14. Oil accounts for 97 percent of transportation: International Energy Agency (IEA), "Transportation and Energy," report for the World Summit on Sustainable Development, in Johannesburg, August–September 2002, p. 5. View the full report at IEA Web site, http://iea.org/textbase/work/2002/johannesburg/transportation.pdf.

Page 15. Coal-fired power plants kill an estimated twenty-four thousand Americans each year: American Lung Association, "State of the Air: 2007." You can view a full copy of the report at the American Lung Association of Rhode Island's Web site, www.lungusa2.org/embargo/sota07/ALA_SOTA_07.pdf.

Page 15. Strip mining in Appalachia has leveled more than 450 mountains: See "End Mountaintop Removal," at the iLoveMountains.org Web site. On the Web site there is a map that shows the locations where mountains have been leveled since 1985, http://ilovemountains.org/resources.

Page 15. Over a hundred thousand Americans died mining coal in the last century: Jeff Goodell, *Big Coal: The Dirty Secret behind America's Energy Future* (Boston: Houghton Mifflin, 2006), p. xx.

Page 15. Saudi Arabia human rights record: Records of Saudi Arabia's human rights violations can be found at Human Rights Watch (HRW), "World Report 2007: Saudi Arabia, Events of 2006," HRW Web site, http://hrw.org/englishwr2k7/docs/2007/01/11/saudi14717.htm. Statistics can also be found in Amnesty International USA, "Saudi Arabia: Human Rights Concerns," www.amnestyusa.org/By_Country/Saudi_Arabia/page.do?id=1011230&n1=3&n2=30&n3=980.

Page 15. U.S. Agreement with Saudi Arabia since 1945: PBS series *Frontline,* "A Chronology: House of Saud," February 8, 2005, www.pbs.org/wgbh/pages/frontline/shows/saud/cron.

Page 21. Arundhati Roy quote: "Confronting Empire," talk delivered January 27, 2003, at the World Social Forum in Porto Alegre, Brazil.

Chapter 1: Getting Our Fix

Page 22. Al Gore quote: "Al Gore 3.0," *Rolling Stone,* July 13, 2006, online at www.rollingstone .com/politics/story/10688399/al_gore_30/1.

Page 23. More than half of the oil Ecuador produces is shipped to the United States: Energy Information Administration (EIA), "Country Analysis Brief: Ecuador, 'Oil,'" EIA Web site, Energy Information Sheets page (March 2007), www.eia.doe.gov/emeu/cabs/Ecuador/ Oil.html/, p. 2.

Page 24. America consumes its oil imports from Ecuador in less than twenty minutes: This is the author's calculation. The United States consumes about 20.5 million barrels per day, more than 850,000 barrels per hour. Ecuador exported 274,000 barrels into the United States each day in 2006.

Page 25. Oil consumption expected to increase: EIA, *International Energy Outlook, 2007,* chapter 3, "Petroleum and Other Liquid Fuels," EIA Web site, Energy Information Sheets page (May 2007), www.eia.doe.gov/oiaf/ieo/oil.html/, p. 3.

Page 25. Hubbert's prediction: M. King Hubbert, "Nuclear Energy and Fossil Fuels," *American Petroleum Institute and Production Practice Proceedings* (Spring 1956): 5–75.

Page 26. U.S. oil production topped out at 9.6 million barrels: EIA, "Crude Oil Production," EIA Web site, Energy Information Sheets page (January 2008), www.eia.doe.gov/neic/ infosheets/crudeproduction.html/, p. 3.

Page 26. Global oil discoveries peaked in the mid-1960s: Lester Brown, "Is World Oil Production Peaking?" at Earth Policy Institute Web site (November 15, 2007), www.earth-policy.org/ Updates/2007/Update67.htm.

Page 26. Deffeyes quote: Kenneth S. Deffeyes, *Beyond Oil: The View from Hubbert's Peak* (New York: Hill and Wang, 2005), p. 3.

Page 26. Consuming oil at a far faster rate than it can be replaced: Brown, "Is World Oil Production Peaking?"

Page 26. Oil production has leveled off: Kjell Aleklett, "The Oil Supply Tsunami Alert," Association for the Study of Peak Oil and Gas (April 25, 2005), www.peakoil.net/Oil_tsunami.html.

Page 27. Daniel Yergin quote: Daniel Yergin, "It's Not the End of the Oil Age: Technology and Higher Prices Drive a Supply Buildup," *Washington Post,* op-ed, July 31, 2005.

Page 27. Michael Rodgers quote: Jeffery Ball, "Dire Prophecy: As Prices Soar, Doomsayers Provoke Debate on Oil's Future," *Wall Street Journal,* September 20, 2004.

Page 27. No new refineries have been built since 1976: Deffeyes, *Beyond Oil,* p. xiv.

Page 27. Al-Huseini says global oil production reached peak in 2006: David Strahan, interview with Sadad al-Huseini (October 29, 2007). You can listen to the full podcast on the articles page of David Strahan's Web site, www.davidstrahan.com/blog/?p=67.

Page 28. For every barrel of oil we discover, we now consume three: David Strahan Web site, Home page, information from Strahan's book *The Last Oil Shock: A Survival Guide to the Imminent Extinction of Petroleum Man* (2007), www.davidstrahan.com.

Page 28. Global demand for oil is expected to increase: *International Energy Outlook, 2007,* chapter 3, "Petroleum and Other Liquid Fuels," p. 3.

Page 29. Drilling advocates argue that any incursion will impact as little as two thousand acres: Artic National Wildlife Refuge (ANWR), "Top 10 Reasons to Support Development in ANWR," ANWR Web site, Basics page, www.anwr.org/topten.htm.

Page 29. Oil may be scattered in thirty deposits: *U.S. Geological Survey, 1999,* "Oil and Gas Potential of the Arctic National Wildlife Refuge 1002 Area, Alaska," U.S. Department of the Interior, U.S. Fish and Wildlife Service Web site, Arctic National Wildlife Refuge page, open file report 98-34 (January 17, 2001), http://arctic.fws.gov/issues1.htm. A map of the potential impacts of drilling in the refuge can be found at the National Resources Defense Council Web page, www.nrdc.org/land/wilderness/arcticmap_2000acres.pdf.

Page 29. Exporting oil from ANWR would require infrastructure: U.S. Fish and Wildlife Service (USFWS): Alaska, "Potential Impacts of Proposed Oil and Gas Development on the Arctic Refuge's Coastal Plain: Historical Overview and Issues of Concern," USFWS Web site, Arctic National Wildlife Refuge page (2001), http://arctic.fws.gov/issues1.htm#section4.

Page 29. It would take at least ten years for the oil of ANWR to reach American gas tanks: Natural Resource Defense Council (NRDC), "Arctic National Wildlife Refuge: Why Trash an American Treasure for a Tiny Percentage of Our Oil Needs?" NRDC Web site, Water page (November 10, 2005), www.nrdc.org/land/wilderness/arctic.asp.

Page 29. Drilling for much less oil than the United States consumes in a year: U.S. Geological Survey (USGS), "Arctic National Wildlife Refuge, 1002 Area, Petroleum Assessment, 1998, Including Economic Analysis," USGS Web site, http://pubs.usgs.gov/fs/fs-0028-01/fs-0028-01.pdf/, p. 4. The USGS estimates that there is a 95 percent probability of finding 4.3 billion barrels of oil within the Arctic National Wildlife Refuge. U.S. oil consumption in 2006 totaled 7.55 billion barrels. Energy Information Administration, "Product Supplied," EIA Web site, Consumption/Sales page, http://tonto.eia.doe.gov/dnav/pet/pet_cons_psup_dc_nus_mbbl_a.htm.

Page 30. Adam quote: Telephone interview, September 16, 2007.

Page 30. O'Conner calls for epidemiological studies: CBC News Canada, "High Illness Rate near Oil Sands Worrisome, Says Alberta Health Official," cbsnews.ca (March 10, 2006), www.cbc.ca/story/canada/national/2006/03/10/oilsands-chipewyan060310.html.

Page 30. Donna Cyprien quote: Ian Austen, "Study Finds Carcinogens in Water Near Alberta Oil Sands Projects," *New York Times,* November 9, 2007.

Page 30. Elsie Fabian quote: Doug Struck, "Canada Pays Environmentally for U.S. Oil Thirst: Huge Mines Rapidly Draining Rivers, Cutting into Forests, Boosting Emissions," *Washington Post,* May 31, 2006.

Page 31. Tar sands landscape excavation: Knudson, "Grubbing for Oil."

Page 31. Four tons of dirt is dug up for every barrel of oil refined: Dan Woynillowicz, "Oil Sands Fever: The Environmental Implications of Canada's Oil Sands Rush," Pembina Institute Web site, Publications page (November 2005), http://pubs.pembina.org/reports/OilSands72.pdf/, p. 12.

Page 31. Waste from tar sands in two days can fill Yankee Stadium: Justin Bloom, "Where Oil Is Mined, Not Pumped," *Washington Post,* June 15, 2005.

Page 31. Mining of tar sands is energy intensive: Woynillowicz, "Oil Sands Fever," p. 22. Report authors calculate that the average greenhouse gas (GHG) intensity for conventional oil is 28.6 GHG/barrel of oil, versus 85.8 GHG/barrel of oil from the tar sands.

Page 31. Tar sands contribute to growth of climate-change pollution in Canada: Ibid., p. 19.

Page 31. Largest strip mine: Byron W. King, "2006 Boston ASPO: The Canadian Tar Sands" (November 13, 2006), originally published by Whiskey and Gunpowder and by Energy Bulletin, available at Energy Bulletin, www.energybulletin.net/22358.html.

Page 31. Strip mine that will be six miles in diameter: Elizabeth Kolbert, "Unconventional Crude: Canada's Synthetic Fuels Boom," *New Yorker,* November 12, 2007, p. 46.

Page 31. Dozens more strip mines are planned: Woynillowicz, "Oil Sands Fever," p. 5.

Page 31. For every three barrels of oil produced the energy equivalent of one is consumed: Kolbert, "Unconventional Crude," p. 46.

Page 31. Enough gas will be consumed each year to heat every home in Canada: Woynillowicz, "Oil Sands Fever," p. 15.

Page 31. Reguly quote: Eric Reguly, "Oil Sands Mother Lode Could Doom Gas Reserves," *Globe and Mail* (Toronto), May 28, 2005.

Page 32. In 2007 tar sands produced 1.3 million barrels per day: Tom Knudson, "Grubbing for Oil," *Sacramento Bee,* December 10, 2007.

Page 32. Expansion plans for tar sands: Woynillowicz, "Oil Sands Fever," p. 5.

Page 32. Norwegian quote: Tim Reiterman, "A Stand in the Forest," *Los Angeles Times,* July 2, 2006.

Page 32. Tar sands oil production is water intensive: Woynillowicz, "Oil Sands Fever," p. 29.

Page 32. Millions of feet of cubic water is diverted: Ibid., p. 34.

Page 32. Natural systems are not restored: Ibid., p. 38.

Page 32. First Nations Keepers Declaration, "Keepers of the Water Declaration," Kairos: Canadian Ecumenical Justice Initiatives Web site, Ecology page (September 7, 2006), www.kairoscanada.org/e/ecology/water/Declaration_KeepersWater_Sept06.pdf.

Page 33. Output could reach 11 million barrels per day by 2047: Woynillowicz, "Oil Sands Fever," p. 5.

Page 33. Adam quote: Telephone interview, September 16, 2007.

Page 34. Investigative report by the Ecological Integrity Project and the Houston Galveston Association for Smog Prevention: "Who's Counting? The Systematic Underreporting of Toxic Air Emissions" (June 2004), a joint project by the Environmental Integrity Project and Galveston-Houston Association for Smog Prevention, available at Environmental Integrity Project Web site, Publications page, www.environmentalintegrity.org/pubs/TRIFINALJune_22.pdf.

Page 34. Ortiz quote: Monica Rohr, "Texas Town Has Been Defined by Oil Refineries," Associated Press, October 23, 2007, www.msnbc.msn.com/id/21420793.

Page 35. Larson quote: Telephone interview, January 9, 2008.

Page 35. Rolfes quote: Michelle Nijhuis, "Passing the Bucket: How the Five-Gallon Plastic Bucket Came to the Aid of Grassroots Environmentalists," *Grist: Environmental News and Commentary,* News page (July 23, 2003), www.grist.org/news/maindish/2003/07/23/the.

Page 35. Larson quote: Ibid.

Page 36. Christian Aid report: Christian Aid, "Fuelling Poverty: Oil, War, and Corruption," Christian Aid Web site (May 2003), http://212.2.6.41/indepth/0305cawreport/fuellingpoverty.htm/, p. 2.

Page 36. Each fifteen gallons would add an additional three hundred pounds of carbon dioxide to the atmosphere: Environmental Protection Agency (EPA), "Emission Facts: Greenhouse Gas Emissions from a Typical Passenger Vehicle," EPA Web site, Transportation and Air Quality page (February 2005), www.epa.gov/oms/climate/420f05004.htm.

Chapter 2: Smokescreen

Page 40. Abraham Lincoln epigraph: From a speech delivered in Clinton, Illinois, September, 1858, taken from the Gaia Community Web site, Wisdom page, http://quotes.gaia.com/184/you_can_fool_all_the_people_so/by_abraham_lincoln.

Page 40. Gibson quote: In-person interview, July 14, 2007.

Page 41. Hitt quote: Telephone interview, July 20, 2007.

Page 41. Coal mining accounted for 65 percent of all explosives use in the United States in 2006: Deborah A. Kramer, "Explosives," U.S. Geological Survey, 2006 minerals yearbook (September 2007), http://minerals.usgs.gov/minerals/pubs/commodity/explosives/600495.pdf/, p. 1.

Page 41. Explosives can be set off within three hundred feet of a home: West Virginia Secretary of State, Code of State Rules, Environmental Protection, Series 1 Surface Mining Blasting Rule, sec. 3.6h, p. 7: available at www.wvsos.com/csr/verify.asp?TitleSeries=199-01.

Pages 41–42. Dennis Davidson story: Carol Morello, "Mining Town Rises in Anger," *Washington Post,* January 6, 2005. Also listen to the story on NPR, by Noah Adams, "Virginia Strip-Mining Death Brings Reforms," www.npr.org/templates/story/story.php?storyId=4489461.

Page 42. Mountaintop-removal coal mining described as "strip mining on steroids": This term is commonly used in describing mountaintop removal and you will find it referred to this way on numerous Web sites. One of the originating articles in which mountaintop removal was referred to this way was Peter Galuszka's "Strip-Mining on Steroids," *Business Week,* November 17, 1997, p. 70.

Page 42. More than 450 mountains have been leveled throughout Appalachia: From the End Mountaintop Removal page of the iLoveMountains.org Web site, where there is a map that shows the locations where these mountains have been leveled since 1985: http://ilovemountains.org/resources.

Page 42. In that same period, more than seven hundred miles of rivers and streams have been buried: Joby Warrick, "Appalachia Is Paying Price for White House Rule Change," *Washington Post,* August 14, 2004.

Page 42. U.S. Fish and Wildlife Service report: Ibid.

Page 42. Gibson quote: In-person interview, July 14, 2007.

Page 43. Gunnoe quote: In-person interview, July 16, 2007.

Page 43. Maria Gunnoe is fighting back: Maria Gunnoe, "My Life Is on the Line: A Personal Story." Read the full story on the Stop Mountaintop Removal Web site, at the Read Their Stories page, www.stopmountaintopremoval.org/marias-story.html.

Page 44. Gunnoe quote: Personal communication, July 16, 2007.

Page 44. Not a single power plant has ever captured all of its carbon dioxide emissions: While a few power plants have started to experiment with capturing some of their emissions, none has been able to successfully capture all of them or to store those emissions underground.

Page 45. From 1985 to 2005, coal-mine production increased by 28 percent, while the number of coal-mining jobs decreased by 44 percent in that same period: The National Mining Association's (NMA) "Mining Industry Employment by Sector, 1985–2005" shows how total coal mining employment has declined from 184,373 in 1985 to 81,891 in 2005, a drop of 44 percent. See the NMA Web site, Statistics page, www.nma.org/pdf/e_sector.pdf. Meanwhile, according to the National Mining Association's "Trends in U.S. Coal Mining, 1923–2006," total U.S. coal production increased from 883.6 million tons in 1985 to 1,132 million tons in 2005, an increase of 28 percent. See the NMA site, www.nma.org/pdf/c_trends_mining.pdf.

Page 45. More than a hundred thousand miners died in coal mines in the twentieth century: Jeff Goodell, *Big Coal: The Dirty Secret behind America's Energy Future* (New York: Houghton Mifflin, 2006), introduction, p. xiii. The statistic about twelve thousand miners dying from black lung comes from the Sierra Club, "The Dirty Truth about Coal: Why Yesterday's Technology Should Not Be Part of Tomorrow's Energy Future," sierraclub.org, Moving beyond Coal page, www.sierraclub.org/coal/dirtytruth/coalreport.pdf/, p. 4.

Page 45. Coal is also the dirtiest and most carbon-intensive fossil fuel: Goodell, *Big Coal,* p. xvi.

Page 45. Three tons of carbon dioxide are produced for every ton of coal that is burned: U.S. Environmental Protection Agency (EPA), "Green Power Equivalency Calculator Methodologies," EPA Web site, Tools and Calculators page (2003), www.epa.gov/grnpower/pubs/calcmeth.htm.

Page 45. Coal is the largest and one of the fastest-growing sources of greenhouse gas emissions in the country: Union of Concerned Scientists (UCS), "The Costs of Coal," UCS Web site, Clean Energy page, www.ucsusa.org/clean_energy/fossil_fuels/costs_of_coal.html; and Mark Clayton, "Global Boom in Coal Power—and Emissions," *Christian Science Monitor,* March 22, 2007.

Page 45. Coal plants use far more water than all other forms of electricity besides nuclear power: Union of Concerned Scientists, "Impacts of Coal Power: Water Use," UCS Web site, Clean Energy page (2005), www.ucsusa.org/clean_energy/coalvswind/c02b.html.

Page 45. Coal-fired power plants kill an estimated twenty-four thousand people prematurely each year: American Lung Association (ALA), "State of the Air, 2007," ALA Web site, www.lungusa2.org/embargo/sota07/ALA_SOTA_07.pdf.

Page 45. Department of Energy study listed 151 proposed coal plants: National Energy Technology Laboratory (NETL), "Tracking New Coal-Fired Power Plants," NETL Web site, Coal and Power Systems page (May 1, 2007), www.netl.doe.gov/coal/refshelf/ncp.pdf.

Page 45. Goodell quote: Goodell, *Big Coal,* p. xiii.

Page 45. More than a billion tons of coal is mined in the United States each year: Energy Information Administration (EIA), "Annual Coal Report: Executive Summary," EIA Web site (2006), www.eia.doe.gov/cneaf/coal/page/acr/acr_sum.html. Electricity statistic comes from the EIA, "Electricity Power Annual" (2006), www.eia.doe.gov/cneaf/electricity/epa/epa_sum.html.

Page 46. On average, every man, woman, and child in the United States uses about twenty pounds of coal each day: Goodell, *Big Coal,* p. xx.

Page 47. Americans for Balanced Energy Choices advertisement: These ads were on learnaboutcoal.com, but were pulled in early 2008. Read about the ads at the Center for American Progress Action Fund blog, Think Progress, http://thinkprogress.org/2008/02/14/coal-kids.

Page 48. "Clean Coal" PR firms and their activities: See SourceWatch Web site, a project of the Center for Media and Democracy, www.sourcewatch.org/index.php?title=Pac/West_Communications.

Page 48. GE Energy ad: Available on YouTube at http://youtube.com/watch?v=J1A146sANdg.

Page 49. An IGCC plant that captured its carbon would increase the cost of power production by 20 to 55 percent: Intergovernmental Panel on Climate Change (IPCC), *IPCC Special Report on Carbon Dioxide Capture and Storage* (Cambridge: Cambridge University Press, 2005), p. 342, sec. 8.2.1, "Capture and Compression," available at IPCC Web site, http://arch.rivm.nl/env/int/ipcc/pages_media/SRCCS-final/IPCCSpecialReportonCarbondioxideCaptureandStorage.htm.

Page 49. IGCC plants are more costly to construct: As of this writing, there were only two IGCC plants in operation in the United States, although several more were planned. The Electric Power Research Institute estimated that the capital costs of an IGCC plant were at a 20 percent premium compared to pulverized plants: Electric Power Research Institute (EPRI), *Feasibility Study for an Integrated Gasification Combined Cycle Plant at a Texas Site,* EPRI Web site, Technical Update page (October 2006), www.epriweb.com/public/000000000001014510.pdf/, p. v. See also William G. Rosenberg, Dwight C. Alpern, and Michael R. Walker, "Deploying IGCC in This Decade with 3Party Covenant Financing: Volume I," revised version (May 2005), Belfer Center for Science and International Affairs, Kennedy School of Government, Harvard University, http://belfercenter.ksg .harvard.edu/publication/2100/deploying_igcc_in_this_decade_with_3party_covenant _financing.html/, p. 2.

Page 49. IGCC plants that capture carbon will require 14 to 25 percent more power: See the *IPCC Special Report on Carbon Dioxide Capture and Storage,* p. 343. table 8.1, "Summary of New Plant Performance and CO2 Capture Cost Based on Current Technology."

Page 49. A coal plant emits about 3 million tons of carbon dioxide per year: Interdisciplinary study, Massachusetts Institute of Technology, *The Future of Coal: Options for a Carbon Constrained World,* box 1, "Illustrating the Challenge of Scale for Carbon Capture," MIT Web site, Future of Coal page (2007), http://web.mit.edu/coal/, p. ix.

Page 49. Burning coal in the United States caused the release of more than 2 billion tons of CO_2 in 2006: Energy Information Administration, "U.S. Carbon Dioxide Emissions from Energy Sources, 2006: Flash Estimate," slide 11 (entitled "Carbon Dioxide Emissions by Fossil Fuel Type") of a Powerpoint presentation, EIA Web site (May 2007), www.eia.doe.gov/oiaf/1605/flash/flash.html.

Pages 49–50. A 2007 study from MIT: *The Future of Coal,* p. ix.

Page 50. In Cameroon in 1986, a natural release of poisonous CO_2 at Lake Nyos caused the deaths of more than seventeen hundred people: Keith Schneider "Cameroon Disaster: A U.S. Team Sifts Causes," *New York Times,* September 14, 1986.

Page 50. Massey Energy violated Clean Water Act more than forty-five hundred times: As reported by EPA in its 2007 decision to fine Massey for the violations; see http://yosemite .epa.gov/opa/admpress.nsf/dc57b08b5acd42bc852573c90044a9c4/6944ea38b888dd038 52573d3005074ba!OpenDocument.

Page 51. Quote from Kidshealth.org: See the Kidshealth.org Web site, Asthma Basics page, www.kidshealth.org/parent/asthma_basics/what/asthma_basics.html.

Page 51. Approximately 20 million Americans suffer from asthma each year: American Academy of Allergy, Asthma, and Immunology (AAAAI), "Tips to Remember: Exercise-Induced Asthma," AAAAI Web site, Patients and Consumers page, www.aaaai.org/patients/publicedmat/tips/exerciseinducedasthma.stm.

Page 51. Asthma leads to 2 million emergency room visits and five thousand deaths each year in the United States: U.S. Environmental Protection Agency, "Basic Information about Asthma," EPA Web site, Asthma page, www.epa.gov/asthma/about.html.

Page 51. American Lung Association estimates: American Lung Association, "State of the Air, 2007," p. 53.

Page 52. Damitz quote: Telephone interview, October 25, 2007.

Page 52. Solid waste and hazardous air pollutants from burning coal: Goodell, *Big Coal,* pp. 122–23.

Page 52. Mercury emissions from coal and power plants: See the U.S. Environmental Protection Agency (EPA) Web site, Mercury page, www.epa.gov/mercury/about.htm.

Page 52. Air pollution can significantly increase the risk of ischemic strokes: Gregory A. Wellenius et al., "Air Pollution and Hospital Admissions for Ischemic and Hemorrhagic Stroke among Medicare Beneficiaries." *Journal of the American Heart Association* 36, no. 12 (December 2005): 1.

Pages 52–53. Report by Clear the Air: Black Leadership Forum, Clear the Air, Georgia Coalition for the People's Agenda, and Southern Organizing Committee for Economic and Social Justice, "Air of Injustice: African Americans and Power Plant Pollution," Clear the Air Web site, Publications page (October 2002), www.catf.us/publications/reports/Air_of_Injustice.pdf/, p. 3.

Page 53. Harvard University study released in 2001: John Spengler and Jonathan Levy, "Estimated Public Health Impacts of Criteria Pollutant Air Emissions from Nine Fossil-Fueled Power Plants in Illinois," Harvard School of Public Health press release, 2001 Releases page, www.hsph.harvard.edu/news/press-releases/archives/2001-releases/press01032001.html.

Page 53. In 2006, the Crawford and Fisk plants released more than fourteen thousand tons of sulfur dioxide and nearly four thousand tons of nitrogen oxide: U.S. Environmental Protection Agency, "Clean Air Markets—Data and Maps, 1980–2006 Emissions," facility level emissions quick report, for Fisk and Crawford plants in Illinois, EPA Web site, Clean Air Markets page, www.epa.gov/airmarkets (go to Data and Maps, click on Emissions, then Quick Reports, and do search).

Page 53. Villasenor quote: Telephone interview, October 24, 2007.

Page 53. Coal consumption tripled in the United States between 1970 and 2000: National Mining Association (NMA), "Fast Facts about Coal," NMA Web site, Statistics page (January 28, 2008), http://nma.org/statistics/pub_fast_facts.asp.

Page 53. Statistics on the 150 new coal-fired power plants: Mark Clayton, "Global Boom in Coal Power—and Emissions," *Christian Science Monitor,* March 22, 2007.

Page 54. Hansen call for a moratorium: James E. Hansen, "How Can We Avert Dangerous Climate Change?" based on testimony to Select Committee on Energy Independence and Global Warming, U.S. House of Representatives (April 26, 2007), available at Columbia University Web site, Dr. James E. Hansen page, www.columbia.edu/~jeh1/2007/CanWeAvert_20070625.pdf/ (his call for a moratorium is on p. 2).

Page 55. Proposed new coal plants have already been rejected: The closing of these plants is referenced in the following articles: Oklahoma: American Electric Power (AEP) news release,

"OCC Denies Application for Red Rock Power Plant," AEP Web site, Newsroom page (September 10, 2007), www.aep.com/investors/newsreleases/print.asp?ID=1396; Kentucky: *Sierra Club v. Environmental and Public Protection Cabinet*, civ. action no. 06-CI-00640 (Franklin County Circuit Court, August 6, 2007); Florida: Marcia Lane, "Seminole Electric Plans to Appeal Rejection of Coal-Burning Unit," *St. Augustine Record,* August 22, 2007; North Dakota: Dakota Council, "South Heart on Life Support" (August 2007), available at the Dakota Resource Council Web site, Documents page, www.drcinfo.com/documents/DRC%20newsletterAug07.pdf. Illinois: Alison Carney Brown, "EPA Denies Permit for Coal Plant Near Midewin," *Chicago Wilderness Magazine* (Winter 2007), available at the dirtykilowatts.org Web site, www.dirtykilowatts.org/Dirty_Kilowatts.pdf.

Page 55. Coal-plant statistics: Ilan Levin and Eric Schaeffer, "Dirty Kilowatts: Americas Most Polluting Power Plants," Environmental Integrity Project (July 2007), www.environmentalintegrity.org/pubs/2007 percent20Dirty percent20Kilowatts.pdf. The greenhouse gas figures are on p. 10, table 2; the sulfur dioxide figures are on p. 16, table 4; the mercury figures on p. 25, table 8; the nitrous oxide figures on p. 20, table 6; and the emission rates by pounds of CO_2 on p. 9, table 1.

Chapter 3: Separate Oil and State

Page 59. Supreme Court Justice Louis D. Brandeis epigraph: *Other People's Money, and How the Bankers Use It* (1914).

Page 59. U.K. government report: "The Stern Review on the Economics of Climate Change" (2006), 1, "Summary of Conclusions." This particular quote is by Sir Nicolas Stern; one of the lead authors of the in the seven-hundred-page report, he is also former chief economist of the World Bank. You can download a version of the report at the HM Treasury Web site, www.hm-treasury.gov.uk/independent_reviews/stern_review_economics _climate_change/sternreview_index.cfm.

Page 59. Need to reduce greenhouse gas emissions by 80 percent: Alister Doyle, "World Needs to Axe Greenhouse Gases by 80 Percent," Reuters, April 19, 2007, http://uk.reuters.com/article/topNews/idUKL194440620070419.

Page 59. U.S. greenhouse gas emissions have increased by more than 17 percent since 1990: Energy Information Administration (EIA), "Emissions of Greenhouse Gases in the United States, 2006," EIA Web site, Office of Integrated Analysis and Forecasting page (November 2007), www.eia.doe.gov/oiaf/1605/ggrpt/pdf/agge.pdf.

Page 60. F-series Ford truck gets less gas mileage than the Model T: The Model T Ford got between twenty and twenty-five miles per gallon in the early parts of the twentieth century: Model T Ford Register of Great Britain, www.modelregister.co.uk/the-model-t-ford.html. In comparison, the 2007 Ford F-150 gets just 17 mpg, and that's not even for four-wheeled drive vehicles: Ford Motors Web site, F-150 Detailed Comparison page, www.fordvehicles.com/trucks/f150/compare/details/?vehicles=20089|22066|23551|23402.

Page 60. Improve gas mileage in America's cars, trucks, and SUVs by 2020 to reach China's fuel efficiency today: John M. Broder and Micheline Maynard, "Lawmakers Set Deal on Raising Fuel Efficiency," *New York Times*, December 1, 2007.

Page 60. Oil could be saved by using hybrid technology: Sierra Club, "Global Warming and Energy: The Biggest Single Step," Sierra Club, Global Warming and Energy page, www.sierraclub.org/globalwarming/biggest_single_step/intro.asp.

Page 61. Massey Energy violating state and federal regulations: In May 2007, Massey Energy Corporation was accused by federal environmental regulators of thousands of violations of water pollution standards, leading to a proposed $20 million penalty in January 2008. From Ken Ward, Jr., "$20 Million Fine, Improvements Part of Massey Deal: Feds Believe Company Will Now Have to Change," *Charleston Gazette*, January 18, 2008. Also in 2003, Massey CEO Don Blankenship told a Forbes reporter, "We don't pay much attention to the violation count." Quote from Bernard Condon, "Not King Coal," Forbes.com, May 26, 2003, www.forbes.com/forbes/2003/0526/080_print.html.

Page 61. Utilities and coal companies spend millions on teams of lawyers: Countless lawsuits and regulatory battles have been wages for decades. Most recently, Massey Energy settled with regulators for $30 million in January of 2008. See Clem Guttata, "Massey Energy Settles Clean Water Act Lawsuit for $30 Million," at the West Virginia Blue Web site (January 17, 2008), www.wvablue.com/showDiary.do?diaryId=1569.

Page 61. Oil companies spent a total of $75 million in lobbying expenses in 2006: Center for Responsive Politics, "Oil and Gas: Industry Profile, 2006," opensecrets.org, Lobbying Database, www.opensecrets.org/lobbyists/indusclient.asp?code=E01&year=2006. Totals for Exxon are a summation of their reported lobbying expenses from 1999 to 2007.

Page 61. Oil companies spent a total of $574 million from 1998 to 2007 on politicians, political parties, and lobbyists: Center for Responsive Politics, "Influence and Lobbying, Industry List by Sector, Oil and Gas," opensecrets.org, www.opensecrets.org/industries/indus .php?ind=E01.

Page 62. Enron and Kenneth Lay donations: CBS News Online, "Bush Edges Away from 'Kenny Boy': Indicted Ex-Enron Boss Ken Lay, and Bush Pal, Made Big GOP Donations," cbsnews.com, Politics page (July 8, 2004), www.cbsnews.com/stories/2004/07/08/ politics/main628320.shtml.

Page 62. Lay appoints two out of five members of the Federal Energy Regulatory Commission: Winning Argument Blogspot, "Ken Lay's Influence in the Bush Administration Continues to Undermine America's Energy Policy," Winning Argument Blogspot (July 28, 2004), http://winningargument.blogspot.com/2004/07/ken-lays-influence-in-bush.html.

Page 62. Investigation by Representative Henry Waxman: Scott Lindlaw, "Cheney's Energy Plan Benefited Enron in 17 Ways, Top Democrat Says," Associated Press, January 18, 2002, available at seattlepi.com, http://seattlepi.nwsource.com/national/54921 _energy18.shtml.

Page 62. Kenneth Lay memo: John Nichols, "Enron: What Dick Cheney Knew," *The Nation*, April 15, 2002.

Page 62. Cheney announces that the Bush administration would not support price caps on California's energy prices: Here in Reality, "Enron Photo Album," Enron page, www.hereinreality.com/enron.html.

Page 62. Oil industry give more than $70 million to politicians: Center for Responsive Politics, "Oil and Gas: Long-Term Contribution Trends," opensecrets.org, Industries page, www.opensecrets.org/industries/indus.asp?Ind=E01.

Page 63. Top twenty recipients of oil industry cash in the 2006 election cycle: Center for Responsive Politics, "Oil and Gas: Top 20 Recipients," Opensecrets.org, Industries page, www.opensecrets.org/industries/recips.asp?Ind=E01&Cycle=2006recipdetail=A& Mem=N&sortorder=U.

Page 63. All recipients sided with oil industry: League of Conservation Voters, "Second Session 109th Congress, National Environmental Scorecard, 2006," www.lcv.org/images/client/ pdfs/LCV_2006_Scorecard_final.pdf/, Senate votes listed by state and individual senator at pp. 10–15, House votes at pp. 20–35.

Page 63. Since 2001 mining companies have given more than $180,000 to Kentucky's Republican senator Mitch McConnell: OpenSecrets.org, Center for Responsive Politics, "Mitch McConnell: Campaign Finance/Money—Contributions—Senate 2006," opensecrets.org, Mitch McConnell—Top Industries page, www.opensecrets.org/politicians/indus.asp? CID=N00003389&cycle=2006.

Page 63. Crandall Canyon Mine in Utah gained notoriety: Kirk Johnson, "Safety Issues Slow Mine Rescue Efforts," *New York Times,* August 8, 2007.

Page 63. Galatia mine in southern Illinois cited more than twenty-seven hundred times in two years: Rachel Sklar, "CNN Delves into Robert Murray's Safety Record—17 Days Later," *Huffington Post,* August 23, 2007. Watch the full news report at www.huffingtonpost.com/ 2007/08/23/cnn-delves-into-robert-mu_n_61609.html.

Page 63. Ken American Resources: Susan Saulty and Carolyn Marshall, "Mine Owner Has History of Run-ins on Work Issues," *New York Times,* August 24, 2007.

Page 63. Murray quote and information about the transfer of Tim Thompson: "Two for the Money," *Kentucky Herald-Leader* (Lexington), October 20, 2006.

Page 63. Thompson quote: Ibid.

Page 64. Seattle Times report on Oreskes study: Sandi Doughton, "The Truth about Global Warming," *Seattle Times,* October 11, 2005.

Page 64. Analysis of newspaper articles: Jennifer McNulty, "Top U.S. Newspapers' Focus on Balance Skewed Coverage of Global Warming, Analysis Reveals," University of California, UC Newsroom (August 25, 2004), www.universityofcalifornia.edu/news/article/6572.

Page 64. EPA chief Christine Todd Whitman: Cnn.com, "Climate Talks Secure U.S. Support." Whitman assured international leaders that Bush would take climate change seriously: "The president has said global climate change is the greatest environmental challenge that we face and that we must recognise that and take steps to move forward." See Cnn.com, World page (March 5, 2001), http://archives.cnn.com/2001/WORLD/europe/italy/03/04/ environment.climate/index.html.

Page 65. Competitive Enterprise Institute and Exxon: Chris Mooney, "Some Like It Hot," *Mother Jones,* May–June 2005.

Page 65. Memo from Myron Ebell to Phil Cooney: A copy of the memo can be read in full on Greenpeace International's Web site at www.greenpeace.org/international/assets/ binaries/ceimemo.swf.

Page 65. Internal White House documents leaked: Andrew C. Revkin, "Bush Aide Softened Greenhouse Gas Links to Global Warming," *New York Times,* June 8, 2005.

Page 65. Cooney quote: Robert Lusetich, "Climate Science Was Doctored," *The Australian* (Sydney), *March 21, 2007.*

Page 66. Kennedy, Jr., quote: From speech given at Rebekka Chapel in Rock Creek, WV, July 16, 2007.

Page 66. Exxon in 2006 was the most profitable corporation in history: Cnnmoney.com, "20 Most Profitable Companies," 2007 Fortune 500, cnnmoney.com (April 30, 2007), http://money .cnn.com/galleries/2007/fortune/0704/gallery.F500_profitable.fortune/index.html.

Page 66. John Drosdick, Don Blankenship, and Ray Irani salaries: Forbes.com, "CEO Compensation: Oil and Gas Operations," Forbes.com, Lists page (December 2006), www.forbes.com/ lists/2006/12/Oil_Gas_Operations_Rank_1.html.

Page 66. Lee Raymond's parting gift from Exxon: ABC News, "Oil: Exxon Chairman's $400 Million Parachute," abcnew.go.com, *Good Morning America* page (April 14, 2006), www.abcnews.go.com/GMA/story?id=1841989.

Page 66. Friends of the Earth federal policies study: Friends of the Earth (FOE), "Big Oil, Bigger Giveaways," FOE (February 22, 2007), www.saveourenvironment.org/FriendsOfEarth _Report.pdf/, p. 1.

Page 67. Earth Track report for the Organization for Economic Cooperation and Development: Doug Koplow, "Subsidies in the US Energy Sector: Magnitude, Causes, and Options for Reform," Earth Track library (November 2006), www.earthtrack.net/earthtrack/library/ SubsidyReformOptions.pdf.

Page 67. U.S. federal energy subsidies in 2006 were $74 billion, in Kaplow's estimate: Mark Clayton, "US House Takes on Big Oil," *Christian Science Monitor,* January 18, 2007.

Page 67. Spadaro quote: Interview with Clara Bingham, "Under Mined: When a Flood of Toxic Mining Sludge Wreaked Havoc in Appalachia, How Did the White House Respond? By Letting the Coal Company off the Hook and Firing the Whistleblower," *Washington Monthly,* January–February 2005, p. 5. Also see http://www.wvgazette.com/static/series/ buffalocreek/.

Page 68. Spadaro was asked to help lead an investigation: Ibid., p. 2.

Page 68. Coal executives gave $3.65 million in the 2000 election: Center for Responsive Politics: "Coal Mining: Long-Term Contribution Trends," opensecrets.org, Industries page (2002), www.opensecrets.org/industries/indus.asp?Ind=E1210.

Page 68. James H. "Buck" Harless: Spadaro interview with Bingham, p. 6.

Page 68. Harless quote: Tom Hamburger, "A Coal-Fired Crusade Helped Bring Crucial Victory to Candidate Bush," *Wall Street Journal,* June 13, 2001.

Page 69. Massey Energy fined $55,000 for one of the worst environmental disasters in the history of the southeastern U.S.: Phillip Babich, "Dirty Business: How Bush and His Coal Industry Cronies Are Covering Up One of the Worst Environmental Disasters in U.S. History," Salon.com (November 13, 2003), http://dir.salon.com/story/tech/feature/2003/11/13/slurry_coverup/index.html?source=search&aim=/tech/feature.

Page 69. Providing for Head Start and for medical care for uninsured U.S. kids: Head Start is a national program to help the advancement of low-income students. Read more at www.acf.hhs.gov/programs/hsb. The $2 billion figure for the cost of this program can be found on the National Institute for Early Education Research (NIEER) Web site at the Facts and Figures page, http://nieer.org/resources/facts/index.php?FastFactID=12. The $6 billion figure for health-care costs for uninsured children can be found in an article by Pam Pohly, "Bush May Require 4 Million Uninsured Children to Suffer," Everyday Citizen's Web site (September 22, 2007), www.everydaycitizen.com/2007/09/bush_may_require_4_million_uni.html.

Page 70. Steve Kretzmann and *Rolling Stone:* Dan Baum, "Revolution 101: The Ruckus Society," *Rolling Stone,* July 5, 2001, p. 83.

Page 71. Midterm election results in 2006: Lindsay Renick Mayer, "Big Oil, Big Influence," PBS, *Now* page (November 23, 2007), www.pbs.org/now/shows/347/oil-politics.html.

Page 71. Kretzmann quote: Telephone interview, October 10, 2007.

Page 71. Newman quote: Telephone interview, October 12, 2007.

Page 72. After some experimentation and exploration on MAPLight.org, the reader will be able to track what contributions were made—and when—for many bills in Congress. Here are the specific steps to take to get more information on the Pombo bill: Visit MAPLight.org, click "U.S. Congress," then "Bills," then enter "American-Made Energy and Good Jobs Act" into the search engine. Select the bill number: H.R. 5429. You'll come to a screen that lists the groups that did—and did not—want this bill to pass. To determine the role that the oil and gas industry played, take the following steps. Click "Customize" on the bottom, right-hand portion of your screen. Select "Energy/Nat resources," then "Oil and Gas," then click "support" next to "major (multinational) oil and gas producers" and "Oilfield service, equipment, and exploration" to see which oil and gas companies supported the bill. Then scroll down to the bottom of the screen and click "remove" next to all the other industries that may have supported the bill, including "trucking," the "Teamsters union," and so on. Once you've isolated just "major (multinational) oil and gas producers" and "oilfield service, equipment and exploration," click the "Votes" tab at the top of the page to find out how much each legislator that voted yes received from those sectors. Click on another tab at the top, "Timeline of Contributions" to learn more about when these donations were made.

Page 72. Newman quote: Telephone interview, October 12, 2007.

Page 73. Newman quote: Ibid.

Page 73. The House passed a bill: "House Rolls Back Oil Company Subsidies," *USA Today,* January 18, 2007, www.usatoday.com/news/washington/2007-01-18-house-oil_x.htm.

Page 73. Senate nearly defeated a similar provision: Steven Mufson and Jonathan Weisman, "Senate to Rework Ambitious Energy Bill," *Washington Post,* December 8, 2007.

Page 73. Bush quote: President George W. Bush, State of the Union Address, January 31, 2006. View the full address at www.whitehouse.gov/stateoftheunion/2006.

Chapter 4: Follow the Money

Page 75. Mayer Anselm Rothschild epigraph: U.S. Senate document no. 23, 76th Congress, 1939.

Page 76. Bank of America press materials: Anne Finucane, "Bank of America Climate Change Position," Bank of America Web site, Environment page, www.bankofamerica.com/environment/index.cfm?template=env_clichangepos.

Page 76. Bank of America announces $20 billion commitment to climate change: Bank of America press release, "Bank of America Announces $20 Billion Environmental Initiative," Bank of America Web site, Newsroom page (Charlotte, NC, March 6, 2007), http://newsroom.bankofamerica.com/index.php?s=press_releases&item=7697.

Page 76. Citi pledges $50 billion toward climate change: Dominic Rushe, "Green Ideals Inflate Bottom Line," *Australian Business,* May 15, 2007.

Page 77. AES Corporation seeks to build new coal-fired power plants in four states: Coal Moratorium Now! "State-by-State Descriptions of Proposed Coal-Fired Power Plants," Coal Moratorium Now! Web site, Proposed Coal Plants page (January 15, 2008), http://cmnow.org/Proposed%20Coal%20Plants.pdf.

Page 77. Dynergy plans to build up to eight or more new coal-fired power plants: Ibid.

Page 77. Peabody Energy has poisoned the groundwater for Hopi and Navajo and plans to build new power plants: Information on the poisoning of groundwater can be found in a paper written by Kimberly Smith of Black Water Mesa Coalition, "Pollution of the Navajo Nation Lands," presented to the United Nations Department of Economic and Social Affairs at an International Expert Group Meeting on Indigenous Peoples and Protection of the Environment, Khabarovsk, Russian Federation, August 27–29, 2007. The full document can be accessed at the UN Department of Economic and Social Affairs Web site, www.un.org/esa/socdev/unpfii/documents/workshop_IPPE_smith.doc. Information about Peabody Energy's plans to build new coal-fired power plants can be found at Coal Moratorium Now! "State-by-State Descriptions of Proposed Coal-Fired Power Plants."

Page 77. American Electric Power: Coal Moratorium Now! "State-by-State Descriptions of Proposed Coal-Fired Power Plants."

Page 77. Florida Power and Light: Ibid.

Page 77. Southern Company: Environmental Integrity Project (EIP), "Dirty Kilowatts: America's Most Polluting Power Plants," available at dirtykilowatts.org, "Dirty Kilowatts" 2007

Database (July 2007), www.dirtykilowatts.org/Dirty_Kilowatts2007.pdf/, p. 10, table 2, "Top 50 Most Polluting Power Plants for CO2 by Tons CO2" (2006).

Page 77. TXU: Ibid.

Page 78. Citi's largest shareholder is Abu Dhabi: Dan Wilchins and James Cordahi, "Citigroup to Sell $7.5 Billion Stake to Abu Dhabi," Reuters, November 27, 2007, www.reuters.com/article/wtMostRead/idUSSP7190720071127. Another large shareholder: Eric Dash, "Citigroup to Sell $7.5 Billion Stake to Abu Dhabi," *New York Times,* November 27, 2007.

Page 78. Leslie Lowe quote: E-mail, November 14, 2007.

Page 78. One plant produces more carbon dioxide in three weeks than Citi will reduce in one year: From calculations by RAN campaigner Matt Leonard: Citi's operational emissions were 1,243,800 metric tons in 2005, according to Citi, "Citizenship Report, 2006," citigroup.com, Corporate Citizenship page, www.citigroup.com/citigroup/citizen/community/data/citizen06_en.pdf. On May 16, 2007, Citi announced it is "committing to reduce our carbon emissions by 10 percent from our 2005 level by 2011" ("The Environment," citigroup.com, Corporate Citizenship page, www.citigroup.com/citigroup/environment/climatechange.htm). If this goal is met, Citi would reduce its CO_2 footprint by approximately 124,380 metric tons by 2011. In comparison, a single medium-sized coal-fired power plant will emit more than 3 million tons of CO_2 annually.

Page 78. One large plant releases as much carbon as six hundred thousand cars and trucks: Union of Concerned Scientists (UCS), "The Costs of Coal," UCS Web site, Clean Energy page, www.ucsusa.org/clean_energy/fossil_fuels/costs_of_coal.html.

Page 78. Citi will spend an average of $3.1 billion on climate change per year: Citi, "The Environment," citigroup.com, Corporate Citizenship page (May 8, 2007), www.citigroup.com/citigroup/environment/climatechange.htm.

Page 78. Citi's corporate credit portfolio, $63 million dedicated to petroleum sectors: Citi Web site, Investor Relations, Financial Information, Annual Reports, and Proxy Information page, Annual Report (2006), www.citigroup.com/citigroup/fin/data/ar06c_en.pdf.

Page 78. Bank of America will spend $1.8 billion a year to help clients reduce gas emissions: Bank of America press release, "Bank of America Announces $20 Billion Environmental Initiative."

Page 78. Bank of America extended $35.6 billion in credit to oil and utilities: Bank of America Web site, Shareholders and Investors page, Annual Report (2006), http://phx.corporate-ir.net/phoenix.zhtml?c=71595&p=irol-reportsannual.

Page 79. Citigroup statistics: Cnnmoney.com, "Fortune 500, 2006: Our Annual Ranking of America's Largest Corporations; Citigroup," cnnmoney.com, Fortune 500 Data page, http://money.cnn.com/magazines/fortune/fortune500/snapshots/309.html.

Page 79. Bank of America statistics: Cnnmoney.com, "Fortune 500, 2006: Our Annual Ranking of America's Largest Corporations; Bank of America," Cnnmoney.com, Fortune 500 Data page, http://money.cnn.com/magazines/fortune/fortune500/snapshots/164.html.

Page 80. Time names Home Depot story as top environmental story of 1999: Published in the Canadian version of *Time,* December 20, 1999, p. 60.

Page 80. Citi's "Live Richly" campaign: In 2003 Citi launched the Live Richly campaign. From May to August 2003, Citi ran a series of ads. Copies of the ads can be viewed on Citi's Web site, Citigroup Advertising Showcase page, www.citi.com/citigroup/showcase/liverichly.htm.

Page 81. Joe Chemo campaign: Adbusters, "Joe Chemo," Adbusters Web site, Spoof Ads page, www.adbusters.org/spoofads/tobacco/jc2.

Page 81. Absolute on Ice ad: Adbusters, "Absolute on Ice," Adbusters Web site, Spoof Ads page, www.adbusters.org/spoofads/alcohol/absolutonice.

Page 81. Lowe's agrees to phase out wood products from endangered forests: Commitment made on October 13, 1999, in a letter to Rainforest Action Network.

Page 81. Kinko's adopts strongest environmental policy in the country: Kinko's adopted its Environmental Vision Statement, committing to not purchase paper or wood products from old-growth or endangered forests, and to increase the use of recycled and tree-free paper. Several years later, the policy was further strengthened: FedEx Kinko's press release, "Kinko's Forest-Based Products Policy Sets New Standard for Protecting the World's Forests," Corporate Social Responsibility Newswire, News Archive (March 11, 2003), www.csrwire.com/PressRelease.php?id=1650.

Page 81. Hogue quote: Telephone interview, October 11, 2007.

Page 81. Citi executive quote: In-person interview, 2004.

Pages 81–82. Chan quote: Telephone interview, November 8, 2007.

Pages 82–83. Firger quote: E-mail, November 14, 2007.

Page 83. New York Times ad: RAN placed the advertisement on November 13, 2002.

Page 84. International Herald Tribune ad: RAN placed the advertisement on August 30, 2002.

Page 84. Sandy Weill's speech at Cornell University in 2003: Linda Myers, "Weill Calls Economic Growth an Answer to Global Poverty and Conflict," *Cornell Chronicle,* April 10, 2003; available at the *Chronicle* page on the Cornell Web site, www.news.cornell.edu/chronicle/03/4.10.03/Weill_cover.html.

Page 85. RAN Citibank ads: "Not with My Money" advertisements were placed on New York cable television, April 2003.

Page 85. Equator Principles: Equator Principles Web site, Principles page, www.equator-principles.com/principles.shtml.

Page 85. Citi goes beyond the Equator Principles: Rainforest Action Network (RAN), "Citigroup New Environmental Initiatives," RAN Web site, Campaigns, Global Finance, Resources, Bank Policies page (January 2004), http://ran.org/fileadmin/materials/global_finance/Bank_Policies/CitiEnvPolicy.pdf.

Page 85. Hogue quote: Telephone interview, October 11, 2007.

Page 86. World Bank Group has provided more than $8 billion to the oil industry since 1992: Oil Change International, "Aiding Oil, Harming the Climate: A Database of Public Funds for

Fossil Fuels" (December 2007), available at dev-zone.com, Knowledge Center page, www.endoilaid.org/wp-content/uploads/2008/01/aidingoilreport.pdf.

Page 86. U.S. Export-Import Bank and the Overseas Private Investment Corporation have given more than $21 billion: Judy Pasternak, "A Mixed Message on CO_2: Bush Seeks Overseas Curbs as U.S.-Backed Banks Help Emit More," *Los Angeles Times,* August 12, 2007.

Page 86. In the United Kingdom, it is the right-wing Conservative Party that is calling for an elimination of such "perverse subsidies": Quality of Life Policy Group, Conservative Party (U.K.), "Blueprint for a Green Economy," Conservatives.com, News page (September 13, 2007), www.conservatives.com/tile.do?def=news.story.page&obj_id=138484 (scroll down the page to download pdf file). The mention and description of "perverse subsidies" is found on page 391.

Page 86. Cameron quote: ePolitix.com, "Conservative 'Quality of Life' Report," ePolitix.com Stakeholders comment on the Conservative Party's quality of life policy review, www .epolitix.com/EN/ForumBriefs/200709/e1a74739-521b-4ae9-86d2-ea4ceca94c2a.htm.

Page 87. Joseph Stiglitz describes World Bank and IMF: "What I Learned at the World Economic Crisis," *The Insider,* April 17, 2000.

Page 87. World Bank Group: About Us section on the World Bank Group Web site, www.worldbank.org.

Page 87. World Bank Group committed $28 billion to fossil-fuel projects: Sustainable Energy and Economy Network (SEEN), "Key Facts on the G-8, World Bank, and Climate Change," SEEN Web site, Climate Change page (July 2005), www.seen.org/pages/keyfacts.shtml.

Page 88. Salim quote: E-mail, March 17, 2008.

Page 88. Kretzmann quote: Telephone interview, October 10, 2007.

Pages 88–89. Indigenous Peoples' Declaration on Extractive Industries: "Preamble to Indigenous Peoples' Declaration on Extractive Industries" (Oxford, England, April 15, 2003), available at Tebtebba Web page, www.tebtebba.org/tebtebba_files/susdev/mining/eir/eirdec.html.

Page 89. EIR official report: Extractive Industries Review, *Striking a Better Balance: Consultation on the Future Role of the World Bank Group in the Extractive Industries,* 6 vols. (December 2003), World Bank Web site, Extractive Industries Review page, http://web.worldbank.org/WBSITE/EXTERNAL/TOPICS/EXTOGMC/0,,contentMDK:2030 6686-menuPK:592071-pagePK:148956-piPK:216618-theSitePK:336930,00.html/, 1: xiii.

Page 89. Nobel Peace Prize letters: February 9, 2004, letter to World Bank president James Wolfensohn from Nobel peace laureates Jody Williams, Archbishop Desmond Tutu, Rigoberta Menchu Tum, Sir Joseph Rotblat, Betty Williams, and Mairead McGuire; reported by Bob Burton, "Nobel Laureates Ask World Bank to Curb Extractive Industries," Environmental New Service (February 13, 2004), www.ens-newswire.com/ens/feb2004/2004-02-13-01.asp.

Page 89. World Bank's response to EIR report: "Striking a Better Balance: The World Bank Group and Extractive Industries," the final report of the Extractive Industries Review,

World Bank Group Management Response, World Bank Web site, Resources page (September 17, 2004), http://siteresources.worldbank.org/INTOGMC/Resources/finaleirmanagementresponse.pdf/, p. iii.

Page 90. International Finance Corporation increased its loans: From statistics generated by Heike Mainhart-Gibbs, Bank Information Center. Quote from e-mail, December 13, 2007.

Page 90. Mainhart-Gibbs quote: Andrew Revkin, "Money for India's 'Ultra Mega' Coal Plants Approved," *New York Times,* Science, April 9, 2008. See also www.nytimes.com/2008/04/06/weekinreview/06revkin.html?scp=7&sq=april+6%2C+2008&st=nyt.

Page 90. Financing for Indian coal plant: Leslie Wroughton, "World Bank Approves Funds for Indian Coal-Fired Plant," Reuters, April 8, 2008, www.reuters.com/article/latestCrisis/idUSN08412737.

Page 90. Goodland quote: E-mail, November 17, 2007.

Page 91. Since 2000 more than $60 billion has been transferred from public coffers: Oil Change International, "Aiding Oil," p. 1.

Page 91. End Oil Aid Act, and U.K. Parliament petition: For a summary and a copy of the End Oil Aid Act (H.R. 1886), see the End Oil Aid Web site, Public Policy page, www.endoilaid.org/publicpolicy, where there are links to both. In the U.K. Parliament, petitions such as the one mentioned here are called Early Day Motions. This was Early Day Motion 1200, issued on March 22, 2007, available at the Parliament Web site, Early Day Motions page, http://edmi.parliament.uk/EDMi/EDMDetails.aspx?EDMID=32957&SESSION=885.

Page 91. Polar bears withdraw $27,000: This was part of a protest hosted by RAN on November 27, 2007. The protestors were two folks dressed up in polar bear costumes to protest Bank of America's investments in coal-fired power plants and the effect that climate change is having on polar bear habitat. Frustrated with Bank of America's policies, these two people strolled into Bank of America, cameras in tow, to withdraw all their money as a statement to the bank. You can check out a video of this action on RAN's Web site, on the Understory (RAN's blog) page (posted November 27, 2007): http://understory.ran.org/2007/11/27/polar-bears-make-a-run-on-bank-of-america.

Page 91. Local residents at Kayford Mountain, West Virginia: You can see pictures of the banner and read about the National Day of Action against Coal: RAN, "Coal Finance Day of Action in West Virginia," RAN Web site, the Understory (RAN's blog) page (posted November 18, 2007), http://understory.ran.org/2007/11/18/coal-finance-day-of-action-in-west-virginia.

Page 91. Over a hundred demonstrations were held in November 2007: RAN press release, "Thousands Take to the Streets to Protest Citi and Bank of America Coal Investments," RAN Web site, Media Center page (November 16, 2007), http://ran.org/media_center/news_article/?uid=2443.

Page 91. Carbon Principles: Jeffrey Ball, "Wall Street Shows Skepticism over Coal," *Wall Street Journal,* February 4, 2008.

Page 91. ShoreBank Pacific: Details of the EcoDeposits program can be found at the ShoreBank Pacific Web site, home page, www.eco-bank.com.

Page 92. Liu quote: Telephone interview, October 27, 2007.

Page 92. Barclay quote: In-person interview, January 7, 2007.

Page 94. Bank Track's report: See "A Challenging Climate: What International Banks Should Do to Combat Climate Change," at the Bank Track Web site, Documents page, www.banktrack.org/doc/File/banks,%20climate%20and%20energy/banktrack%20on %20climate%20and%20energy/0_071212%20A%20challenging%20climate%20final.pdf.

Chapter 5: Redesigning Mobility

Page 95. New *shinkansen* trains decrease electricity use by 19 percent over earlier models: Alex Hutchinson, "World's Fastest Train You Can Ride Dumps Energy Like a Prius," *Popular Mechanics,* September 2007, www.popularmechanics.com/technology/transportation/ 4219935.html.

Page 95. Speed of trains exceeds 350 mph during test runs: Railway Technical Research Institute (RTRI), "Overview of Maglev R and D," RTRI Web site, Maglev page (February 20, 2004), www.rtri.or.jp/rd/maglev/html/english/maglev_frame_E.html.

Page 95. Nineteen-mile demonstration line at Pudong International Airport: Shanghai Municipal Tourism Administrative Commission, New Scenes of Shanghai page, http://lyw.sh.gov.cn/en/scenic_spot/maglev.html.

Page 96. Japan has over twelve thousand miles of train tracks: Japan Railways Group, www.japanrail.com/JR_japanrailpass.html (scroll down a bit to the heading, "What Is the Japan Rail Pass?"). See the following note for the source of another statistic under this heading: that Japan's railways have twenty-six thousand runs daily.

Page 96. Eight hundred thousand daily riders: Japanese Guest Houses (JGH), "The Joy of Trains in Japan," JGH Web site, Travel Tips page, http://japaneseguesthouses.com/about/travel/ trains.htm.

Page 96. Shinkansen as safest form of transport in the world: Japan Railways Group, "Shinkansen (Bullet Train)": "In the almost 40 years since it opened, the Shinkansen network has carried over 6 billion passengers without a single major accident." See Japan Railways Web site, www.japanrail.com/JR_shinkansen.html. For Amtrak information, see the Amtrak Web site, National Fact Sheet page, www.amtrak.com/servlet/ ContentServer?pagename=Amtrak/am2Copy/Title_Image_Copy_Page&c=am2Copy& cid=1081442674300&ssid=542.

Page 96. Speed of boarding process: Boarding timed by author, August 4, 2006.

Page 97. Two-thirds of America's oil devoted to transportation: Energy Information Administration (EIA), "U.S. Consumption by Sector": "In the United States, in contrast to other regions of the world, about 2/3 of all oil use is for transportation." Official Energy Statistics from the U.S. Government. EIA Web site, Oil Demand page (scroll down), www.eia.doe.gov/pub/oil_gas/petroleum/analysis_publications/oil_market_basics/ demand_text.htm#U.S. percent20Consumption percent20by percent20sector.

Page 98. High-speed train as catalyst for economic growth: Katsumasa Harada, "Technological Innovation and the Development of Transportation in Japan," chap. 8 in *New Developments in Transportation (1955-1980)* (Tokyo: United Nations University Press, 1993), pp. 222–23.

Page 99. In 2003, Amtrak received two-thirds of what it received twenty years earlier: National Association of Railway Passengers (NARP), "Information on Amtrak Federal Funding," NARP Web site, www.narprail.org/cms/images/uploads/fund.pdf.

Page 99. Federal spending on highways and aviation has doubled in twenty years: Tim Gillespie, "Growth Capital: A Possible New Source," *Railway Age,* January 2004; available at www.bnet.com, Find Articles page, http://findarticles.com/p/articles/mi_m1215/is_l_205/ai_n6010943.

Page 99. More than $49 billion for the Federal Highway and Federal Aviation Administrations in 2007; and total budget outlays: NARP, "Information on Amtrak Federal Funding."

Page 99. Opponents say government shouldn't run railroads: John Sullivan, "New Jersey's Amtrak Blues," *New York Times,* June 30, 2002.

Page 99. China's investment in high-speed rail: William W. Millar, president of American Public Transportation Association (APTA), "The U.S. Rail Capacity Shortage," testimony before the Subcommittee on Railroads of the House Committee on Transportation and Infrastructure, APTA Web site, Government Affairs page (April 26, 2006), www.apta.com/government_affairs/aptatest/documents/testimony060426.pdf.

Page 100. Amtrak more energy efficient than domestic airlines and cars: NARP, "Oak Ridge Data on Fuel Efficiency," NARP Web site, www.narprail.org/cms/index.php/resources/more/oak_ridge_fuel. Data is contained in edition 26 of the *Transportation Energy Data Book.*

Page 100. Proposals for high-speed rail in Florida, upper Midwest, California, and eastern seaboard have been stalled by bureaucracy: For more information about these and other proposed high-speed railways, visit the U.S. PIRG (Public Interest Research Groups) Web site, at www.uspirg.org/issues/transportation, or the National Association of Railroad Passengers Web site at www.narprail.org.

Page 101. Cost in dollars, fuel, and productivity of traffic congestion: Texas Transportation Institute (TTI), "Annual Study Shows Traffic Congestion Worsening in Cities Large and Small," 2007 urban mobility report press release, TTI Web site, Urban Mobility Information page (September 18, 2007), http://mobility.tamu.edu/ums/media_information/press_release.stm.

Page 101. Mexico plans route from Guadalajara to Mexico City: Chris Hawley, "Mexico Reviving Travel by Train," *Arizona Republic,* January 6, 2006.

Page 101. Lomax quote: TTI press release, "Annual Study Shows Traffic Congestion Worsening."

Page 101. Percentage of Americans who use public transit to get to work each day: Will Sullivan, "Road Warriors," *U.S. News and World Report,* April 29, 2007.

Page 101. Streetcar lines were removed: Paul Matus, "GM and the Streetcar—American Ground Transport—Street Railways: 'U.S. vs. National City Lines' Recalled," Third Rail Online (May 1999), http://thethirdrail.net/9905/agt1.htm.

Page 101. Commute distances for Americans increase every year: Richard J. Jackson, "Driving Ourselves Sick," *Western City Magazine,* August 2005.

Page 102. Suburban development as "greatest misallocation of resources in history": James Howard Kunstler, quoted in documentary film, *The End of Suburbia: Oil Depletion and the Collapse of the American Dream* (2004). Check out the movie's Web site at www.endofsuburbia.com.

Page 102. Goal of the New Urbanist movement: Congress for the New Urbanism (CNU), "Charter of the New Urbanism," CNU Web site, www.cnu.org/charter.

Page 102. The need for transit-friendly places to be walkable: Telephone interview with Sheila Poticha, president and CEO of Reconnecting America, June 27, 2007.

Page 102. State of Maryland adopts New Urbanism as core planning element: Delaware Valley Regional Planning Commission (DVRPC), "Smart Growth," DVRPC Web site, Regional Plans and Policy page, www.dvrpc.org/planning/regional/SmartGrowth.htm.

Page 102. Examples of New Urbanist design: CNU, "Chapters," CNU Web site, www.cnu.org/chapters.

Page 102. New Urbanist critics: See Alex Marshall, author of *How Cities Work: Suburbs, Sprawl, and the Roads Not Taken* (Austin: University of Texas Press, 2001). His critiques of New Urbanism can be found at his Web page: www.alexmarshall.org/am_categoryPagesFolder/newUrbanism.htm.

Page 102. Transit-oriented development (TOD) increases property values: Federal Transit Administration (FTA), "Transit-Oriented Development and Joint Development," FTA Web site, Planning and Environment page, www.fta.dot.gov/planning/planning _environment_6932.html.

Page 102. More than a hundred cities around the country have or are planning to install streetcar lines: Overhead Wire (blog), "The Rapid Streetcar" (July 2, 2007), http://theoverheadwire.blogspot.com/2007/07/rapid-streetcar.html.

Page 102. Poticha quote: Telephone interview with Sheila Poticha, June 27, 2007.

Page 103. Denver FasTraks ballot measure: See "FasTracks 2006 Team Factbook," at the Metro Denver Economic Development Corporation Web site, www.metrodenver.org/files/Documents/Transportation-Infrastructure/Mass-Transit/Trans_Mass_FasTracks FactBook.pdf/, p. 2.

Page 103. Hickenlooper quote: Global Public Media, transcript of interview at Association for the Study of Peak Oil and Gas (ASPO), Denver World Oil Conference, Denver, November 11, 2005.

Page 103. Poticha quote: Telephone interview, June 27, 2007.

Page 104. New York City plans to have two hundred miles of bike trails by 2010: *The Villager,* "City Rolls Out Plan for 200 Miles of New Bike Lanes," www.thevillager.com (September 20–26, 2006), www.thevillager.com/villager_177/cityrollsout.html.

Page 104. Chicago is planning five hundred miles of bike trails by 2015: City of Chicago, "Bike 2015 Plan," www.bike2015plan.org./chapter1/chap1.html.

Page 104. Austin will spend $250 million: Daniel B. Wood, "Cities Build New Bike Paths: Will Cyclists Come?" *Christian Science Monitor,* June 19, 2007, www.csmonitor.com/2007/0619/p03s03-ussc.html.

Page 104. Robin Stallins, Texas Bicycle Coalition: Ibid.

Page 104. Steele quote: Telephone interview, June 18, 2007.

Page 104. Most people will walk to a bus or train if it is within a half-mile radius: Victoria Transport Policy Institute (VTPI), "Bike/Transit Integration," VTPI Web site (March 12, 2007), www.vtpi.org/tdm/tdm2.htm.

Page 105. Cost to construct a car parking space versus a bike rack: Ibid.

Page 105. Only a third of all buses in North America have bike racks: Victoria Transport Policy Institute (VTPI), "Bike/Transit Integration," VTPI Web site, *TDM Encyclopedia* (updated March 12, 2007), www.vtpi.org/tdm/tdm2.htm.

Page 105. Percentages for countries whose residents bike to work: Nancy Keates, "Building a Better Bike Lane," *Wall Street Journal,* May 4, 2007.

Page 105. Cities in Europe make bicycles available for free or at a very low cost: John Ward Anderson, "Paris Embraces Plan to Become City of Bikes," *Washington Post,* March 24, 2007.

Page 105. Paris and bikes: Ibid.

Pages 105–6. Shahum quote: Telephone interview, June 18, 2007.

Page 106. Four U.S. cities recently ordered more than seventeen hundred hybrid buses (sidebar): Jordan Schrader, "More Cities Get on Board with Hybrid Buses," *USA Today,* January 21, 2008, www.usatoday.com/news/nation/2008-01-21-masstransithybrids_N.htm.

Page 107. Hybrid buses: Jordan Schrader, "More Cities Get on Board with Hybrid Buses," *USA Today,* January 21, 2008.

Page 107. Public transportation saves 1.4 billion gallons of gasoline per year: American Public Transportation Association, Virginia Miller and Mantill Williams, "Public Transportation Saves $6,200 Per Household, 1.4 Billion Gallons of Gasoline," APTA Web site, Transit News page, (January 9, 2007), www.apta.com/media/releases/documents/070109_energy_report.pdf.

Page 107. Griffith quote: Thomas Heath, "Zipcar and Flexcar Driven Together, *Washington Post,* October 31, 2007.

Page 108. Nonprofit car shares: Carsharing.net "Where Can I Find Car Sharing?" www.carsharing.net/where.html.

Page 108. Zipcar helps people sell their cars: Zipcar.com, "Green Benefits," www.zipcar.com/carsharing-greenbenefits.

Page 108. Zipcar helps save a total of 32 million gallons of crude oil: Zipcar.com "Environmental and Community Impact," press release from Zipcar (January 2008), www.zipcar.com/press/onlinemediakit/environmental_and_community_impact.pdf.

Page 108. Car-sharing statistics: Ibid.

Page 108. Zipcars are available in many cities: Zipcar.com, Find Cars page, www.zipcar.com/find-cars.

Chapter 6: Jump-Start Detroit

Page 111. Lynn Hinkle epigraph: Telephone interview, June 29, 2007. Used by permission of Lynn Hinkle.

Page 111. Woman's voice on voicemail: Call from Heather Bernikoff-Raboy to Jennifer Krill, January 2005.

Page 111. Dave Bernikoff-Raboy quote: Telephone interview, November 17, 2007.

Page 112. Heather Bernikoff-Raboy quote: Telephone interview, November 17, 2007.

Page 112. Auto industry opposes California mandate: For a detailed explanation of industry and government objections, check out the movie *Who Killed the Electric Car?* written and directed by Chris Paine (Sony Pictures, DVD released in 2006), www.whokilledthe electriccar.com.

Page 113. Heather Bernikoff-Raboy quote: Telephone interview, November 17, 2007.

Page 113. Bernikoff-Raboys staged a round-the-clock vigil in their truck: Eric Bailey, "He Refuses to Put Down Electric-Powered Pickup: A Mariposa County Rancher Who Leases an Experimental Ford Ranger Wants to Keep It, but the Company Has Pulled the Plug on Such Vehicles, *Los Angeles Times,* January 18, 2005.

Page 114. Dave Raboy interview: Eric Bailey, "Ford Will Sell Its Electric Pickup Trucks to Lessees," *Los Angeles Times,* January 22, 2005.

Page 114. Golightly quote: Eric Bailey, "Ford Shifts Gears on Its Plan to Scrap Electric Pickup Trucks," *Los Angeles Times,* January 19, 2005.

Page 114. One out of every seven barrels of the world's oil is consumed on American highways: Thomas Friedman, "Let's Roll," *New York Times,* January 2, 2002.

Page 114. Two-thirds of American oil consumption is used for transportation: Energy Information Administration (EIA), "Energy INFOcard: United States 2006," EIA Web site, Publications and Reports page (data for 2006), www.eia.doe.gov/neic/brochure/infocard01.htm.

Page 114. Big Three automakers emit more greenhouse gasses than almost every country: Sierra Club Factsheet, "Driving Up the Heat: SUVs and Global Warming," Sierra Club Web site, Smart Energy Solutions page, www.sierraclub.org/globalwarming/suvreport/pollution.asp.

Pages 114–15. The average fuel economy for U.S. passenger vehicles: Environmental Protection Agency (EPA), "Light-Duty Automotive Technology and Fuel Economy Trends, 1975 through 2007," EPA Web site, Cars and Light Trucks page (September 2007), www.epa.gov/oms/fetrends.htm.

Page 115. Increase in number of vehicles, from 1950 to present: United Nations Environment Program (UNEP), "20 Issues to Keep You Awake at Night," UNEP Web site, GEO 2000 page, www.unep.org/GEO2000/pressrel/issues.htm.

Page 115. Analysis by Union of Concerned Scientists and the Center for Auto Safety: Union of Concerned Scientists (UCS), "Drilling in Detroit: Tapping Automaker Ingenuity to Build Safe and Efficient Automobiles," UCS-USA Web site, Clean Vehicles page (June 2001), www.ucsusa.org/assets/documents/clean_vehicles/drill_detroit.pdf/, p. xiv.

Page 115. Hitting this average would save more oil each year: Sierra Club, "The Biggest Single Step," introduction, Sierra Club Web site, Global Warming and Energy page, www.sierraclub.org/globalwarming/biggest_single_step/intro.asp.

Page 115. Rebirth of electric vehicles might change the automotive industry: Rocky Mountain Institute (RMI), "What Is a Hypercar Vehicle?" RMI Web site, Transportation page, www.rmi.org/sitepages/pid191.php.

Page 115. Golightly quote: Elizabeth Weise, "Think Drivers Strive to Save Their Cars from the Crusher," *USA Today,* September 2, 2004, www.usatoday.com/tech/news/2004-09-02 -thinkcar_x.htm.

Page 116. Dorgan quote: Zachary Coile, "House to Vote on 'Historic' Deal to Raise Fuel Economy to 35 mpg," *San Francisco Chronicle,* December 5, 2007.

Page 116. The 2007 energy bill passed by Congress: John M. Broder and Micheline Maynard, "Lawmakers Set Deal on Raising Fuel Efficiency," *New York Times,* December 1, 2007.

Page 116. Auto companies lose money: Cnnmoney.com, "Fortune 500, 2007: Our Annual Ranking of America's Largest Corporations; General Motors," Cnnmoney.com, Fortune 500 Data page, http://money.cnn.com/magazines/fortune/fortune500/2007/snapshots/ 563.html. For Ford Motor Company: http://money.cnn.com/magazines/fortune/ fortune500/2007/snapshots/529.html.

Page 116. GM loses about 150,000 workers: Thomas Friedman, "Et Tu, Toyota?" *New York Times,* October 3, 2007.

Page 117. Hinkle quote: Telephone interview, June 29, 2007.

Page 117. Ford plant shuts down: Jeff Horwich et al., Minnesota Public Radio, "Ford Confirms Shutdown of St. Paul Plant," Minnesota Public Radio Web site, New and Features page (April 13, 2006), http://minnesota.publicradio.org/display/web/2006/04/13/fordclosure. At the time of this writing there was also a news report saying that the plant closure has subsequently been delayed until 2009. Also from MPR on November 5, 2007: Martin Moylan, "Ford Plant Closing Could Be Delayed," http://minnesota.publicradio.org/ display/web/2007/11/05/ford_plant_closing_delay.

Page 117. Increased fuel efficiency creates more jobs: Union of Concerned Scientists, "Jobs, Energy, and Fuel Economy, 2004," UCS-USA Web site, Clean Vehicles page (July 2004), www.ucsusa.org/clean_vehicles/fuel_economy/jobs-energy-fuel-economy.html.

Page 117. Lawmakers resist modernizing the vehicle industry: Thomas Friedman, "The Capital Energy Crises," *New York Times,* June 24, 2007.

Page 118. Frank quote: Telephone interview, June 22, 2007.

Page 118. Toyota is largest automaker: National Public Radio (NPR), Jim Zarroli, "Toyota Moves Past GM in First-Quarter Sales," NPR Web site, Business page (April 24, 2007), www.npr.org/templates/story/story.php?storyId=9803216.

Page 118–19. U.S. Department of Energy study: "Tackling Climate Change in the U.S.," American Solar Energy Society (ASES) Web site (January 2007), www.ases.org/climatechange/climate_change.pdf/, p. 74.

Page 119. Sexton quote: Chelsea Sexton interviewed in Google.org, "RechargeIT: Plug-In Hybrids," video, produced by Google.org, RechargeIt program (2007), which can be viewed on YouTube at www.youtube.com/watch?v=oDjSbWTJbdo.

Page 119. Seventy-eight percent of commuters live within twenty miles of their employers: U.S. Department of Transportation, Bureau of Transportation Statistics, "Omnibus Household Survey," Department of Transportation Research and Innovative Technology Administration (October 2003), www.bts.gov/programs/omnibus_surveys/household_survey/2003/october/pdf/entire.pdf/, p. 1.

Page 119. Cost of plug-ins: John Fialka, "Coalition Turns On to Plug-In Hybrids," *Wall Street Journal,* January 25, 2006. Frank quote is from this article.

Page 120. Frank and his team modernize a Ford Explorer: Mark Clayton, "Hybrids? Some opt to Go All-Electric," *Christian Science Monitor,* January 27, 2005.

Page 120. Woolsey quote: Telephone interview, June 28, 2007.

Page 121. Sexton quote: Google.org, "RechargeIT: Plug-In Hybrids."

Page 121. Wynn quote: "Plug-In Partners National Campaign," Plug-In Partners Web site, Information Packet page, http://pluginpartners.org/includes/pdfs/PluginPartnersPacket.pdf/, p. 19.

Page 121. CalCars manual: Electric Auto Association (EAA), "PriusPlus," EAA Web site, Plug-In Hybrid page, www.eaa-phev.org/wiki/PriusPlus. See chapter 8 on "greening the grid."

Page 121. Kramer quote: Telephone interview, June 22, 2007.

Page 122. A hybrid conversion takes two hours: Green Car Congress, "A123Systems to Market PHEV Conversion Packs in 2008," Green Car Congress Web site (May 1, 2007), www.greencarcongress.com/2007/05/a123systems_to_.html.

Page 122. Silicon Valley Leadership Group pledges to buy plug-ins: Matt Nauman, "Valley Executives Join Plug-In Hybrid Push" *San Jose Mercury News,* September 23, 2007.

Page 122. Straubel quote: Telephone interview, November 2, 2007.

Page 122. Tesla Roadster: Read about the Tesla Roadster at www.teslamotors.com.

Page 123. Musk quote: Telephone interview, November 5, 2007.

Page 123. Google.org's RechargeIT program: You can learn more about Google's RechargeIT program on their Web site, www.google.org/recharge.

Page 123. Frank quote: Telephone interview, June 22, 2007.

Page 123. Sodium-sulfur batteries: American Electric Power and Xcel Energy have both recently announced purchases of sodium-sulfur batteries from NGK Insulators, of Japan, to store wind energy. American Electric Power purchase can be referenced in "Today in Business," from the *New York Times,* September 11, 2007; and Xcel Energy's "Xcel Energy Launches Groundbreaking Wind-to-Battery Project," available at the Xcel Energy Web site, News Releases page (February 28, 2008), www.xcelenergy.com/XLWEB/CDA/0,3080,1-1-1_1553 1_46991-45134-0_0_0-0,00.html.

Page 123. Mechanical process to store electricity: Gene Berry, "Present and Future Electricity Storage for Intermittent Renewables," from workshop proceedings, "The 10-50 Solution: Technologies and Policies for a Low-Carbon Future," prepared by the Pew Center on Global Climate Change, March 2004.

Page 124. Frank quote: Telephone interview, June 22, 2007.

Page 124. Proudfoot quote: Alec Proudfoot, Google.org, "RechargeIT: Plug-In Hybrids."

Page 124. Car companies plan to build plug-in hybrids: Information available on home page of Plug In America. www.pluginamerica.org.

Page 125. Brilliant quote: Google.org, "RechargeIT: Plug-In Hybrids."

Page 126. This tax credit could be paid for by eliminating subsidies to the oil industry: David Sandalow. Recommendations for the federal government purchase order and tax credits for plug-in hybrid buyers were proposed in his book *Freedom from Oil: How the Next President Can End the United States' Oil Addiction* (New York: McGraw-Hill, 2007).

Page 126. "Feebate" legislation: At the time of this writing, California was considering such a move. For more information, see Margot Roosevelt, "Bill Offers Rebates, Exacts Fees Based on Car Emissions," *Los Angeles Times,* February 14, 2008.

Page 127. Seventeen million new cars and trucks are made in the United States each year: John Stoll and Neal Boudette, "December Slump in Vehicle Sales," *Wall Street Journal,* January 4, 2008.

Chapter 7: Growing Gas

Page 129. Joel K. Bourne, Jr., epigraph: "Green Dreams," *National Geographic* (October 2007).

Page 129. Galdikas quote: Telephone interview, October 24, 2007.

Page 130. Orangutans and their intelligence: Jonathan Leake and Roger Dobson, "Chimps Knocked Off the IQ Tree," *Sunday Times,* April 15, 2007.

Page 130. Indonesia and Malaysia produced 87 percent of the world's palm oil: From the U.S. Department of Agriculture (USDA), Foreign Agriculture Service, Commodity Intelligence Report, "Indonesia: Palm Oil Production Prospects Continue to Grow," USDA Web site, Global Crop Production Analysis page (December 31, 2007), www.pecad.fas.usda.gov/ highlights/2007/12/Indonesia_palmoil.

Page 130. Borneo fires, 1997–98: M. J. Wooster and N. Strub, "Study of the 1997 Borneo Fires: Quantitative Analysis Using Global Area Coverage (GAC) Satellite Data," *Global Biogeochemical Cycles* 16, no. 1 (2002), available at American Geophysical Union (AGU) Web site, Publications page (February 12, 2002), www.agu.org/pubs/crossref/2002/2000GB00 1357.shtml. You will access an abstract of the article here; the full article is available to subscribers.

Page 130. Smits quote: Ian MacKinnon, "Palm Oil: The Biofuel of the Future Driving an Ecological Disaster Now," *The Guardian*, April 4, 2007.

Page 131. UNEP and Orangutans: United Nations Environment Programme, World Conservation Monitoring Centre (UNEP-WCMC), "The Last Stand of the Orangutan," UNEP-WCMC Web site, Information Resources page (February 2007), www.unep-wcmc .org/resources/publications/LastStand.htm.

Page 131. Biodiesel produces up to ten times the greenhouse gases: "Biofuel Less Sustainable Than Realized," Wetlands International press release (August 12, 2006), www.wetlands .org/news.aspx?ID=804eddfb-4492-4749-85a9-5db67c2f1bb8.

Page 132. If all corn were devoted to ethanol it would only replace 12 percent of gasoline: Jason Hill et al., "Environmental, Economic, and Energetic Costs and Benefits of Biodiesel and Ethanol Biofuels," Proceedings of the National Academy of Sciences (PNAS) Web site archives (June 2, 2006), www.pnas.org/cgi/reprint/0604600103v1/, p. 1.

Page 132. Global biodiesel and ethanol production: Crystal Davis, "March 2007 Monthly Update, Global Biofuel Trends," World Resources Institute (WRI), EarthTrends Environmental Information, Updates page (April 6, 2007), http://earthtrends.wri.org/updates/node/180.

Page 134. Ethanol production in the United States totaled nearly 5 billion gallons: Renewable Fuels Association (RFA), "From Niche to Nation: Ethanol Industry Outlook, 2006," RFA Web site, Industry Statistics page, www.ethanolrfa.org/industry/statistics.

Page 134. New ethanol refineries: Renewable Fuels Association, "Ethanol Industry Outlook, 2007: Building New Horizons," RFA Web site, Annual Industry Outlook page (February 2007), www.ethanolrfa.org/objects/pdf/outlook/RFA_Outlook_2007.pdf.

Page 134. Production of ethanol and biodiesel has tripled: William Coyle, "The Future of Biofuels: A Global Perspective," U.S. Department of Agriculture, Economic Research Service Web site, *Amber Waves* 5, no. 5 (November 2007): 1, available at www.ers.usda.gov/ AmberWaves/November07/PDF/Biofuels.pdf.

Page 134. EU commits to use biofuels for transportation: Despite wide criticism, the EU confirmed its goal in early 2008. David Cronin, "Climate Change: EU Persists with Biofuels," Inter Press Service News Agency Web site (Brussels, January 23, 2008), http://ww.ipsnews .net/news.asp?idnews=40890. For one percent statistic, see article by James Kanter, "Europe May Ban Imports of Some Biofuel Crops," *New York Times*, January 15, 2008.

Page 134. Iowa State University study: Simla Tokgoz et al., "Emerging Biofuels: Outlook of Effects on U.S. Grain, Oilseed, and Livestock Markets," Center for Agricultural and Rural Development (CARD), Iowa State University, CARD Web site, Publications page (July 2007), www.card.iastate.edu/publications/synopsis.aspx?id=1050.

Page 134. Advisories about rising food prices: Food and Agriculture Organization (FAO) press release, "FAO Forecasts Continued High Cereal Prices," FAO Web site (November 7, 2007), www.fao.org/newsroom/en/news/2007/1000697/index.html.

Page 134. Nearly 2.5 billion people live off less than $2 a day: World Bank, *"World Development Report 2008: Agriculture for Development,"* World Bank Web site, Data and Research page (October 2007), http://go.worldbank.org/ZJIAOSUFU0.

Pages 134–35. Brown quote: Lester R. Brown, "Massive Diversion of U.S. Grain to Fuel Cars Is Raising World Food Prices," Earth Policy Institute Web site, Eco-Economy Updates page (March, 21, 2007), www.earth-policy.org/Updates/2007/Update65.htm.

Page 135. More than 450 pounds of corn are needed to fill an SUV: C. Ford Runge and Benjamin Senauer, "How Biofuels Could Starve the Poor," *Foreign Affairs* (May–June 2007), available at Foreign Affairs Web site, www.foreignaffairs.org/20070501faessay86305/c-ford-runge-benjamin-senauer/how-biofuels-could-starve-the-poor.html.

Page 135. UN warns of food shortages: Javier Blas and Jenny Wiggins, "UN Warns It Cannot Feed the World," *Financial Times,* July 15, 2007.

Page 135. Jean Ziegler quote: Grant Ferrett, "Biofuels 'Crime Against Humanity,'" BBC News (October 27, 2007), http://news.bbc.co.uk/2/hi/americas/7065061.stm. Remarks were made at a press conference at the UN headquarters in New York.

Page 135. Eighteen thousand kids die everyday: Associated Press, "18,000 children Die Every Day of Hunger, U.N. Says," *USA Today,* February 17, 2007.

Page 135. ADM and Watergate: Tom Philpott, "Give Green, Go Yellow: How Cash and Corporate Pressure Pushed Ethanol to the Fore," *Grist: Environmental News and Commentary* (December 6, 2006), www.grist.org/news/maindish/2006/12/06/ADM.

Page 135. ADM leads United States in ethanol production: Antonio Regalado, "Sugar Rush: Ethanol Giants Struggle to Crack Brazil Market," *Wall Street Journal,* September 10, 2007.

Page 135. ADM receives billions of dollars in ethanol subsidies: Sasha Lilley, "Green Fuel's Dirty Secret," CorpWatch Web site, Energy page (June 1, 2006), www.corpwatch.org/article.php?id=13646.

Page 135. Cato Institute quote: James Bovard, "Archer Daniels Midland: A Case Study in Corporate Welfare," *Cato Policy Analysis,* no. 241 (September 26, 1995), available at the Cato Institute Web site, Publications page, www.cato.org/pubs/pas/pa-241.html.

Page 136. Toptiro quote: Institute for Agriculture and Trade Policy (IATP), "Biofuels and Development." Account from speech given by Mr. Toptiro to IATP staff, Minneapolis, November 2007.

Page 136. ADM's position regarding the antislavery pact: Based on meetings in which the author was involved and his personal knowledge of events.

Page 136. Cargill contributes to deforestation: Greenpeace, "How the Palm Oil Industry Is Cooking the Climate," Greenpeace Web site, Press Centre page (November 2007), www.greenpeace.org/international/press/reports/cooking-the-climate-full.

Page 136. ADM invests in Wilmar: A joint publication of Milieudefensie (Friends of the Earth Netherlands), Lembaga Gemawan, and KONTAK Rakyat Borneo: "Policy, Practice, Pride and Prejudice: Review of Legal, Environmental and Social Practices of Oil Palm Plantation Companies of the Wilmar Group in Sambas District, West Kalimantan Indonesia," Redapes.org, Orangutan Outreach blog archive (July 2007), http://redapes.org/news-updates/policy-practice-pride-and-prejudice-review-of-legal-environmental-and-social-practices-of-oil-palm-plantation-companies-of-the-wilmar-group-in-sambas-district-west-kalimantan-indonesia.

Page 137. More displaced citizens in Colombia than in any other country except Sudan: Christian Aid, "Human Tide: The Real Migration Process," Global Policy Forum Web site, Social and Economic Policy page (May 2007), www.globalpolicy.org/socecon/envronmt/climate/2007/0514humantide.pdf.

Page 137. Many palm plantations have been established illegally: Ibid., p. 28.

Page 137. Milvia Dias quote: Christian Aid report, "Human Tide," p. 31.

Page 137. "If you don't negotiate with us": Tony Allen-Mills, "Biofuel Gangs Kill for Profit," *London Sunday Times,* June 3, 2007.

Page 138. Up to 5 million indigenous people will be displaced: Justin Bergman, "Biofuels Displace Indigenous People," Associated Press, May 15, 2007, available at Mongabay.com, http://news.mongabay.com/2007/0516-indigenous.html.

Page 138. Indigenous people being pushed from their land: Biofuelwatch, Transnational Institute, et al., "Agrofuels: Towards a Reality in Nine Key Areas," Carbon Trade Watch Web site, Publications page (June 2007), www.carbontradewatch.org/pubs/Agrofuels.pdf.

Page 138. Villager in West Kalimantan loses farm: James Painter, "Losing Land to Palm Oil in Kalimantan," BBC News (August 3, 2007), http://news.bbc.co.uk/2/hi/asia-pacific/6927890.stm.

Page 138. Dead zone in Gulf of Mexico: Associated Press, " 'Dead zone' in Gulf of Mexico among Top 3 Ever Mapped," Cnn.com (July 29, 2007), www.cnn.com/2007/TECH/science/07/29/dead.zone.ap/index.html.

Page 139. Nitrates in drinking water cause health effects: Environmental Protection Agency (EPA), "Consumer Fact Sheet on Nitrates/Nitrites," EPA Web site, Ground Water and Drinking Water page (November 28, 2006), www.epa.gov/OGWDW/contaminants/dw_contamfs/nitrates.html.

Page 139. Researchers believe that ethanol has a positive energy balance: Food and Water Watch and the Network for New Energy Choices, in collaboration with the Institute for Energy and the Environment at Vermont Law School, "The Rush to Ethanol: Not All Biofuels Are Created Equal," analysis and recommendations for U.S. biofuels projects, Network for New Energy Choices Web site, Uploads page (2007), www.newenergychoices.org/uploads/RushToEthanol-rep.pdf.

Page 139. About 20 percent of greenhouse gas emissions come from land use changes: Intergovernmental Panel on Climate Change, "Summary for Policymakers: Land Use, Land Use Change, and Forestry," U.S. Environmental Protection Agency Web site,

Yosemite page, http://yosemite.epa.gov/OAR/globalwarming.nsf/UniqueKeyLookup/ SHSU5BVRTK/$File/sum_lulucf.pdf/, pp. 11–15.

Pages 139–40. Science examined the life-cycle impacts of many agrofuel sources: Timothy Searchinger et al., "Use of U.S. Croplands for Biofuels Increases Greenhouse Gas Emissions from Land Use Change," *Science,* February 29, 2008, p. 1238; Joseph Fargione et al., "Land Clearing and the Biofuel Carbon Debt," *Science,* February 29, 2008, p. 1235.

Page 140. Wetlands International study: "Bio-fuel Less Sustainable Than Realised," Wetlands International press release, December 8, 2006.

Pages 140–41. Wright quotes: Telephone interview, August 23, 2007.

Page 141. Biofuel provides less than 5 percent of all production: U.S. gasoline consumption totals 140 billion annually. Biofuel production is currently at less than 6 billion gallons. Comparatively, only approximately 100 million gallons of restaurant waste oil are generated each year. Steve Hargreaves, "Can Vegetable-Oil Cars Save the World?" Cnnmoney.com (July 24, 2006), http://money.cnn.com/2006/07/21/news/economy/vegetable_cars/index.htm.

Page 141. Pacific Biodiesel: For a list of places to buy Pacific Biodiesel, visit the Pacific Biodiesel Web site, www.biodiesel.com/index.php/fuel_sales/where_to_buy_biodiesel.

Page 142. Sustainable Biodiesel Alliance requirements: Read more about the Sustainable Biodiesel Alliance's requirements at their Web site, Mission page, www.sustainablebio dieselalliance.com/principles.html.

Page 143. Quante quote: Telephone interview, July 6, 2007.

Page 144. Kholsa quote: Amanda Griscom Little, "Something Ventured, Something Gained," *Grist: Environmental News and Commentary* (December 8, 2006), www.grist.org/news/ maindish/2006/12/08/little.

Chapter 8: Greening the Grid

Page 146. Tim Pawlenty epigraph: In a speech on May 25, 2007, when he signed the Next Generation Energy Act of 2007.

Page 147. Harvey Wasserman calls industries King CONG: Harvey Wasserman, "Totally Boom/ Doom Solartopian Green by 2030," Free Press, Columns page (June 26, 2007), http:// freepress.org/columns.php?strFunc=display&strID=1557&strYear=2007&strAuthor=7.

Page 147. One report documented that fifty-nine proposed coal plants were rejected: "Coal Plants Cancelled in 2007," Source Watch, Project of the Center for Media and Democracy, www.sourcewatch.org/index.php?title=Coal_plants_cancelled_in_2007.

Page 148. Wide range of research groups show how the U.S. economy can be carbon-free and nuclear-free: Several reports have been released in just the last year detailing the gains to be found in energy efficiency and renewables. They include: McKinsey and Company, "Reducing Greenhouse Gas Emissions: How Much and at What Cost?" McKinsey and Company Website, Special Initiative: Climate Change page (December 2007), www.mckinsey.com/clientservice/ccsi/pdf/US_ghg_final_report.pdf/; Arjun

Makhijani, "Carbon-Free and Nuclear-Free: A Roadmap for U.S. Energy Policy," Institute for Energy and Environmental Research (IEER), Joint Project of the Nuclear Policy Research Institute and the Institute for Energy and Environmental Research (July 2007), www.ieer.org/carbonfree/CarbonFreeNuclearFree.pdf/, p. 9; American Solar Energy Society (ASES), "Tackling Climate Change in the U.S.: Potential Carbon Emissions Reductions from Energy Efficiency and Renewable Energy," ASES Web site (January 2007), www.ases.org/climatechange/climate_change.pdf/, p. 5; Ken Zweibel, James Mason, and Vasilis Fthenakis, "A Solar Grand Plan," *Scientific American,* January 2008, p. 73.

Page 148. In 2006, 2.4 percent of the United States' electricity was generated by renewables: Energy Information Administration (EIA), "Electric Power Overview," EIA Web site, Electricity page (October 22, 2007), www.eia.doe.gov/cneaf/electricity/page/prim2/toc2.html.

Page 148. Union of Concerned Scientists estimates on increasing renewable energy: Union of Concerned Scientists (UCS), "Cashing In on Clean Energy: A National Renewable Electricity Standard Will Benefit the Economy and the Environment," UCS-USA Web site, Clean Energy Policies page (2007), www.ucsusa.org/clean_energy/clean_energy_policies/cashing-in.html.

Pages 148–49. Apollo Alliance 2004 report: Jointly produced by the Institute for America's Future and the Center on Wisconsin Strategy, "The Apollo Jobs Report: For Good Jobs and Energy Independence New Energy for America," Apollo Alliance Web site, Jobs page (January 2004), www.apolloalliance.org/jobs.php.

Page 149. A typical coal plant costs $1 billion to build: National Energy Technology Laboratory (NETL), "Tracking New Coal-Fired Power Plants," NETL Web site, Coal and Power Systems page (May 1, 2007), www.netl.doe.gov/coal/refshelf/ncp.pdf.

Page 149. University of California report: Daniel M. Kammen, Kamal Kapadia, and Matthias Fripp, "Report of the Renewable and Appropriate Energy Laboratory—Putting Renewables to Work: How Many Jobs Can the Clean Energy Industry Generate?" University of California, Berkeley (April 13, 2004; corrected January 31, 2006), available at the United Nations Environment Programme Web site, Civil Society page, http://unep.org/civil_society/GCSF9/pdfs/karmen-energy-jobs.pdf. The paper analyzes thirteen independent reports and studies regarding the economic and employment impacts of renewable energy.

Page 149. John Edwards quote: John Edwards 2008 press release, "Edwards Initiative Would Train 150,000 American Workers a Year for 'Green Collar' Jobs," John Edwards 08 Web site, News page (July 13, 2007), www.johnedwards.com/news/headlines/20070713-green-collar-jobs.

Page 149. Jones quote: Telephone interview, December 8, 2007.

Page 150. McGeoy quotes: Telephone interview, December 8, 2007.

Page 150. The average American home uses 938 kilowatt hours on a monthly basis: Energy Information Administration, "Frequently Asked Questions: Electricity," EIA Web site, Frequently Asked Questions page, http://tonto.eia.doe.gov/ask/electricity_faqs.asp#electricity_use_home.

Page 151. Oil produces less than 2 percent of the nation's electricity: Energy Information Administration, "Electric Power Overview," EIA Web site, Electricity page (October 22, 2007), www.eia.doe.gov/cneaf/electricity/epa/epa_sum.html.

Page 151. Coal provided nearly 50 percent of U.S. power in 2006, and other statistics on energy sources: Ibid.

Page 151. A typical coal-fired power plant is often described in terms of the maximum number of megawatts, etc.:American Wind Energy Association (AWEA), "Wind Power Today," AWEA Web site, Publications page, www.awea.org/pubs/factsheets/WindPowerToday _2007.pdf/; Clifford Krauss, "Move Over Oil, There's Money in Texas Wind," *New York Times,* February 23, 2008.

Page 151. The total capacity for U.S. coal plants is 313,000 megawatts: Energy Information Administration, table 2.1, "Existing Net Summer Capacity by Energy Source and Producer Type, 1995 through 2006 (Megawatts)," EIA Web site, Electricity page (October 22, 2007), www.eia.doe.gov/cneaf/electricity/epa/epat2p1.html.

Page 151. There are about 500 coal-fired power plants with 1,493 individual generators using coal as a predominant fuel source: Energy Information Administration, "Frequently Asked Questions: Electricity," EIA Web site, Frequently Asked Questions page, http:// tonto.eia.doe.gov/ask/electricity_faqs.asp.

Page 152. Gyr quotes: In-person interview, June 2002, confirmed February 10, 2008.

Page 153. Installed solar PV capacity increased from 1997 to 2006: Earth Policy Institute (EPI), Jonathan Dorn, "Solar Cell Production Jumps 50 Percent in 2007" (December 27, 2007), EPI Web site, Eco-Economy Indicators page, www.earth-policy.org/Indicators/ Solar/2007.htm.

Page 153. The solar industry has grown at a 35 percent annual rate globally since 1998: Greenpeace, "Solar Generation IV, 2007: Solar Electricity for over One Million People and Two Million Jobs by 2020," ed. Crispin Aubrey, Greenpeace Web site, International Reports page (September 3, 2007), www.greenpeace.org/raw/content/international/press/ reports/solar-generation-iv.pdf/, p. 22.

Page 153. The solar industry growth rate akin to PC industry in heyday: Joel Makower, Ron Pernick, and Clint Wilder Clean, "Energy Trends, 2007," Clean Edge Web site, Reports page (March 2007), www.cleanedge.com/reports/Trends2007.pdf.

Page 153. Kennedy quote: In-person interview, August 7, 2007.

Page 153. Google builds largest solar array in the United States: Google, "Google Solar Panel Project," Google Web site, Corporate Information page (July 18, 2007), www.google.com/ corporate/solarpanels/home.

Page 153. Wal-Mart sets goal to use 100 percent renewable power: Lee Scott (current president and chief executive officer of Wal-Mart Stores, Inc.), "Twenty-First Century Leadership," Wal-Mart Watch Web site (October 24, 2005), walmartwatch.com/img/documents/ 21st_Century_Leadership.pdf.

Page 154. Other firms have installed solar arrays on their stores across the country: Information on Staples and their environmental initiatives can be found on their Web site's About Staples page, at www.staples.com/sbd/content/about/soul/energyclimate.html. Information on Whole Foods is at their Company page, at www.wholefoodsmarket.com/company/sustainablefuture.html; and on Walgreens, at the Flex Your Power Web site, www.fypower.org/pdf/Walgreens_PV.pdf.

Page 154. Bradford quote: David Roberts, "The Revolution Will Be Solarized: An Interview with Travis Bradford, author of *Solar Revolution,*" *Grist: Environmental News and Commentary,* Grist Web site, Main Dish page (November 30, 2006), www.grist.org/news/maindish/2006/11/30/roberts/index.html; Makower, Pernick, and Wilder Clean, "Energy Trends, 2007."

Page 154. The solar industry grew at a 55 percent annual rate globally in 2005: Makower, Pernick, and Wilder, "Clean Energy Trends, 2006."

Page 155. Results of California's SB1 legislation of 2007: California Public Utilities Commission (CPUC) staff progress report, "California Solar Initiative," CPUC Web site (January 2008), www.cpuc.ca.gov/puc/Energy/solar.

Page 155. Statistics on states committing to renewable resources: Pew Center on Global Climate Change, "States with Renewable Portfolio Standards," Pew Center Web site, U.S. States and Regions page (August 2007), www.pewclimate.org/what_s_being_done/in_the_states/rps.cfm.

Page 155. Every day, more solar energy falls on the planet in forty minutes: Ken Zweibel, James Mason, and Vasilis Fthenakis, "A Grand Solar Plan," *Scientific American* (January 2008), p. 64.

Page 155. Science magazine 1999 report: John A. Turner, "A Realizable Renewable Energy Future," *Science Magazine,* July 30, 1999.

Page 156. SEGS statistics: John Carey, with Adam Aston, "Solar's Day in the Sun," *Business Week,* October 15, 2007, www.businessweek.com/magazine/content/07_42/b4054053.htm.

Page 156. Solel Energy Systems signed contract in July 2007: Felicity Barringer and Matthew L. Wald, "California Utility Agrees to Buy Power Generated by Solar Array," *New York Times,* July 25, 2007.

Page 156. Ausra has agreement with PG&E: PG&E press release, "PG&E and Ausra Announce 177 Megawatt Solar Thermal Power Agreement," PG&E Web site, News and Alerts page (November 5, 2007), www.pge.com/about/news/mediarelations/newsreleases/q4_2007/071105.shtml.

Page 156. Darbee quote: John Carey with Adam Aston, "Solar's Day in the Sun," *Business Week,* October 15, 2007.

Page 157. Stirling Energy has signed contracts: Barringer and Wald, "California Utility Agrees to Buy Power Generated by Solar Array."

Page 157. The largest PV solar array in North America: Seamus O'Connor, "Solar Panels at Nellis Could Be Win-Win," Air Force Times Web site, Air Force News page (November 19, 2007), www.airforcetimes.com/news/2007/11/airforce_nellis_solar_071119w.

Page 157. Public Service of New Mexico seeks bid for solar array: Jesse Broehl, "New Mexico Solar Market Expected to Boom," Renewable Energy Access Web site, Magazine page (March 13, 2006), www.renewableenergyworld.com/rea/news/story?id=44328.

Page 157. PG&E announces that they will double amount of solar-power purchase: PG&E press release, "PG&E Commits to Double Its Solar Thermal Power Purchases During Clinton Global Initiative," PG&E Web site, News and Alerts page (September 27, 2007), www.pge.com/about/news/mediarelations/newsreleases/q3_2007/070927.shtml.

Page 158. Installed wind power exceeded thirteen thousand megawatts in 2007: American Wind Energy Association (AWEA), "U.S. Wind Energy Projects," AWEA Web site, Resources page (September 30, 2007), www.awea.org/projects.

Page 158. Wind farms compete with coal prices: Makower, Pernick, and Wilder Clean, "Energy Trends, 2006."

Page 158. Sixteen-mile-an-hour wind energy per hour can create 50 percent more wind energy: American Wind Energy Association: "The Economics of Wind Energy," AWEA Web site, Publications page (February 2005), www.awea.org/pubs/factsheets/EconomicsOfWind-Feb2005.pdf.

Page 158. A modern wind turbine can generate fifty-five times more energy: Ibid.

Page 158. A fifty-one-megawatt wind project delivers electricity 40 percent more cheaply: Ibid.

Page 159. The amount of wind energy that is available in states: Makhijani, *Carbon-Free and Nuclear-Free,* p. 31.

Page 159. An average of two to five birds is killed per wind turbine per year: American Wind Energy Association, "Wind Energy and Wildlife: Frequently Asked Questions," AWEA Web site, Publications page, www.awea.org/pubs/factsheets/050629_Wind_Wildlife_FAQ.pdf.

Page 160. Davies quote: Elinor Burkett, "A Mighty Wind," *New York Times Magazine,* June 15, 2003.

Page 160. The advantages of wind technology: American Wind Energy Association, "Wind Energy: The Fuel of the Future Is Ready Today," AWEA Web site, Publications page (2007), www.awea.org/pubs/factsheets/wetoday.pdf.

Page 160. Fortune Small Business says: Justin Martin, "Dan Juhl, Founder, Danmar and Associates, Woodstock, Minn.: As Investors Like Warren Buffett Recognize Wind Power's Potential, This Consultant Is Helping Farmers Cash In," Cnnmoney.com, Fortune Small Business page (June 1, 2003), http://money.cnn.com/magazines/fsb/fsb_archive/2003/06/01/346435/index.htm.

Page 160. Juhl quote: Telephone interview, December 6, 2007.

Page 161. U.S. General Accounting Office study showed that local ownership of wind generates 2.3 times more jobs and 3.1 times economic impact: U.S. Government Accountability Office (USGAO), "Renewable Energy: Wind Power's Contribution to Electric Power Generation and Impact on Farms and Rural Communities," USGAO Web site (September 2004), www.gao.gov/new.items/d04756.pdf/, p. 84.

Page 161. Department of Energy study for Arizona, Colorado, and Michigan: S. Tegen, "Comparing Statewide Economic Impacts of New Generation from Wind, Coal, and Natural Gas in Arizona, Colorado, and Michigan," National Renewable Energy Laboratory Web site (May 2006), www.nrel.gov/docs/fy06osti/37720.pdf/, p. 2.

Page 161. Juhl quote: Telephone interview, December 6, 2007.

Page 162. Solar power in the dark: Marianne Lavelle, "Big Solar Project Planned for Arizona Desert," *U.S. News and World Report,* February 21, 2008.

Page 162. Germany is world's top consumer of solar energy: Rachel Oliver, "All About: Solar Energy," Cnn.com (November 13, 2007), www.cnn.com/2007/WORLD/asiapcf/10/01/solar.energy/index.html#cnnSTCText.

Page 162. California's $0.50 charge: For a description of California's Public Goods Charge and other energy efficiency programs, see "CPUC's Role in Energy Efficiency Programs," at the California Public Utilities Commission Web site, Energy Efficiency Program page, www.cpuc.ca.gov/PUC/energy/eep/cpucrole.htm.

Page 163. In Berkeley, California, a policy was approved enabling homeowners to install rooftop solar: Todd Woody, "Berkeley to Finance Solar Arrays for Homeowners," Green Wombat blog on Cnnmoney.com (October 31, 2007), http://blogs.business2.com/greenwombat/2007/10/berkeley-to-fin.html.

Page 163. Campus Climate Challenge: "The Campus Climate Challenge is a project of more than 30 leading youth organizations throughout the U.S. and Canada. The Challenge leverages the power of young people to organize on college campuses and high schools across Canada and the U.S. to win 100% Clean Energy policies at their schools. The Challenge is growing a generation-wide movement to stop global warming, by reducing the pollution from our high schools and colleges down to zero, and leading our society to a clean energy future." To find out more about the Campus Climate Challenge visit http://climatechallenge.org/about.

Page 163. Sierra Club Cool Cities: Read more about Sierra's Club Cool Cities program on their Web site at: http://coolcities.us/about.php. You can also find more information about specific cities' action plans at seattle.gov: www.seattle.gov/climate/govResources.htm.

Page 165. Lack of public awareness as obstacle: Zweibel, Mason, and Fthenakis, "A Grand Solar Plan," p. 64.

Page 165. Investment of $10 billion per year from 2011 to 2050: Ibid., p. 73.

Page 165. California Energy Commission evaluated the cost of generating new capacity: Study by Energy and Environmental Economics, "CPUC CGH Modeling," http://www.ethree.com/cpuc_ghg_model.html. At this site, select "GHG Calculator v2b"; download this spreadsheet and select the "Gen Cost" tab at the bottom. Look for "All-in Levelized Busbar Cost California." To convert to kilowatt-hour prices, move the decimal point one space to the left.

Page 165. Coal prices rising: Shai Oster and Anne Davis, "China Spurs Coal-Price Surge," *Wall Street Journal,* February 12, 2008, http://online.wsj.com/article/SB120275985736359763.html?mod=hpp_us_pageone. See also the Energy Information Agency's "Average Weekly

Coal Commodity Spot Prices," http://www.eia.doe.gov/cneaf/coal/page/coalnews/
coalmar.html. Cost to build new power plants increase: Bernie Woodall, "US Power Plant
Costs Up 130 Pct since 2000," Reuters, February 14, 2008, www.reuters.com/article/
idUSN1339129420080214.

Page 165. Vinod Khosla quote: Vinod Khosla, "Solar Flare, Sustainable or Not?" slide no. 35
(Solar Power 2006, San Jose, CA, October 16 2006). Khosla's presentation can be accessed
at his Web site at www.khoslaventures.com/resources.html.

Chapter 9: Less Is More

Page 167. Amory Lovins epigraph: David Stipp, "Can This Man Solve America's Energy Crisis?
Amory Lovins Thinks Business and Nature Can Work in Concert to Cut U.S. Reliance on
OPEC," *Fortune,* May 12, 2002.

Page 167. Corbett quote: Bill Browning and Kim Hamilton, "Village Homes: A Model Solar Community Proves Its Worth," *In Context* (Spring 1993), available at Context Institute Web
site, www.context.org/ICLIB/IC35/Browning.htm.

Page 168. Lovins quote: Amory Lovins, "More Profit with Less Carbon," *Scientific American*
(September 2005).

Page 168. McKinsey and Company estimates: McKinsey and Company, "Reducing Greenhouse
Gas Emissions: How Much and at What Cost?" McKinsey and Company Web site, Special
Initiative: Climate Change page (December 2007), www.mckinsey.com/clientservice/
ccsi/pdf/US_ghg_final_report.pdf/, p. xv.

Page 169. Energy efficiency on a date: Patty Limerick and Howard Geller, "What Every West-
erner Should Know about Energy Efficiency and Conservation," Center of the American
West Web site, Publications page (2007), www.centerwest.org/publications/pdf/
energycons.pdf.

Page 170. Efficient systems are cheaper: For cost saving for efficiency, see McKinsey and
Company, "Reducing Greenhouse Gas Emissions," p. xii. For reference regarding energy
efficiency, see the University of California, Berkeley, report by Daniel M. Kammen
Kamal Kapadia and Matthias Fripp, "Report of the Renewable and Appropriate Energy
Laboratory: Putting Renewables to Work: How Many Jobs Can the Clean Energy Industry
Generate?" (April 13, 2004; corrected January 31, 2006), p. 19, http://rael.berkeley.edu/
old-site/renewables.jobs.2006.pdf.

Page 171. Rosenfeld autobiography: Arthur H. Rosenfeld, "The Art of Energy Efficiency:
Protecting the Environment with Better Technology" (1999), available at the California
Energy Commission Web site, Commission Info Page, www.energy.ca.gov/commission/
commissioners/rosenfeld_docs/2000-10_ROSENFELD_AUTOBIO.PDF/, p. 37.

Page 171. Oil statistics from 1977 to 1985: Mark Clayton, "To Boost US Security, an Energy Diet,"
Christian Science Monitor, September 23, 2004. Persian Gulf statistic from Amory Lovins
and L. Hunter Lovins, "Fools Gold in Alaska," *Foreign Affairs,* July–August 2001.

Page 172. California produces savings: California Public Utilities Commission (CPUC) and California Energy Commission (CEC), "Lowering Energy Costs, Protecting Economic Growth, and Protecting the Environment" California Public Utilities Commission Web site, Energy Efficiency Program page (August 2006), ftp://ftp.cpuc.ca.gov/Egy_Efficiency/CalCleanEng-English-Aug2006.pdf/, p. 2.

Page 172. Good news for everyone involved: Ibid., pp. 2, 3.

Page 172. California New Energy Action Plan: Ibid., p. 5.

Page 172. California invests in efficiency projects: CPUC press release, "PUC Launches Ground-breaking Energy Efficiency Effort," CPUC Web site, Press Release page (September 22, 2005), http://docs.cpuc.ca.gov/Published/News_release/49757.htm.

Page 172. Kennedy quote: Ibid.

Page 173. Efficiency program will produce net ratepayer savings: Ibid.

Page 173. California's per capita electricity consumption remains constant: California Energy Commission, "The Loading Order: How Are We Doing?" Independent Energy Producers Annual Meeting, CEC Web site, Publications page (October 10, 2006), www.energy.ca.gov/2006publications/CEC-999-2006-020/CEC-999-2006-020.PDF.

Page 174. Arnold quote: In-person interview, June 27, 2007.

Page 174. Cost of saving energy is half what it costs to produce it: CPUC and CEC, "Lowering Energy Costs, Protecting Economic Growth, and Protecting the Environment," p. 4.

Page 174. Efficiency Vermont: Learn more about Efficiency Vermont on their Web site, the About Us page, at www.efficiencyvermont.com/pages/Common/AboutUs.

Pages 174–75. California, Vermont, and Connecticut tied for first: American Council for an Energy-Efficient Economy (ACEEE), summary of "The State Energy Efficient Scorecard," American Council for an Energy-Efficient Economy, Publications page (June 2007), www.lcv.org/scorecard.

Page 175. Statistics on Bayer, Dupont, and Johnson and Johnson. All these statistics can be found on the Climate Group's Web site at http://theclimategroup.org. To read about the specific case studies mentioned in this text once on the Web site, go to the Low Carbon Solutions page, and then click on Case Studies.

Page 175. "Negawatt revolution": Amory Lovins, "The Negawatt Revolution," *Across the Board: The Conference Board Magazine* 27, no. 9 (September 1990), available at the Rocky Mountain Institute Web site, www.rmi.org/images/PDFs/Energy/E90-20_Negawatt Revolution.pdf.

Page 176. Investments in energy efficiency will pay off: McKinsey and Company, "Reducing U.S. Greenhouse Gas Emissions: How Much at What Cost?" U.S. Greenhouse Gas Abatement Mapping Initiative Executive Report, McKinsey and Company Web site, Special Initiative: Climate Change page (December 2007), www.mckinsey.com/clientservice/ccsi/pdf/US_ghg_final_report.pdf/, p. xvi.

Pages 176–77. Cavanagh quote: Telephone interview, August 21, 2007.

Page 177. Rogers quote: American Public Media, "Getting More Power Out of Using Less," Marketplace (October 23, 2007). Listen to the full story at http://marketplace.publicradio.org/display/web/2007/10/23/power_conservation.

Page 177. Five states have enacted decoupling legislation for electricity: Mark Clayton, "New Math for Utilities: Sell Less, Make More," *Christian Science Monitor,* October 2, 2007.

Page 177. Average light bulb is only 3 percent efficient: Lovins, "More Profit with Less Carbon."

Page 178. Australia bans incandescent light bulbs: BBC News, "Australia Pulls Plug on Old Bulbs" (February 20, 2007), http://news.bbc.co.uk/2/hi/asia-pacific/6378161.stm.

Page 178. Turnbull quote: Ibid.

Page 178. Nevada bill saves money and power: Southwest Energy Efficient Project (SWEEP), "2007 Nevada Legislative Activities," SWEEP Web site (January 28, 2008), www.swenergy.org/legislative/2007/nevada/index.html.

Page 178. U.S. light bulb legislation: Paul Davidson, "It's Lights Out for Traditional Light Bulbs," *USA Today,* December 17, 2007.

Page 179. Steele quote: Telephone interview, November 23, 2007.

Page 179. Ann Arbor, Michigan, converts to LED technology: Tom Gantert, "City to Be First in LED Lights," *Ann Arbor News,* October 17, 2007.

Page 179. Wal-Mart announces it will install LED lighting: Business Wire, "Wal-Mart Uses GE LED Refrigerated Display Lighting to Save Green" (November 16, 2006), www.businesswire.com/portal/site/ge/?ndmViewId=news_view&newsId=2006111 6005286&newsLang=en.

Page 179. Steele quote: Telephone interview, November 23, 2007.

Page 179. Harman's bill: Congresswoman Jane Harman, 36th Congressional District, "Harman Introduces Bill to Phase Out Low-Efficiency Light Bulbs," Jane Harman's Web site, News Archive page (March 15, 2007), www.house.gov/harman/press/archive.shtml.

Page 179. Vampire appliances: Julie Carr Smyth, "Another Kind of 'Vampire' Invades Home This Halloween: Energy Sucking 'Standby Mode,'" Associated Press (October 31, 2007), www.investmentmoats.com/investment-ideas/vampire-electronics-drain-homes-of -energy. Twenty-four coal plants: Lovins, "More Profit, Less Carbon."

Page 180. Mazria quote: Tim Folger, "Blueprint for Disaster?" *OnEarth Magazine* (Summer 2005), National Resources Defense Council (NRDC) Web site, OnEarth page, www.nrdc.org/OnEarth/05sum/livgreen.asp.

Page 180. Architecture 2030: Read more about Architecture 2030 on the Web site at www.architecture2030.org.

Page 181. Mayors sign Architecture 2030 pledge: American Institute of Architects (AIA), "Mayors Adopt AIA Position on Sustainability," *The Angle* 4, no. 15 (June 15, 2006), AIA Web site, Sustainability Articles from *The Angle* page, www.aia.org/nwsltr_angle.cfm ?pagename=angle_nwsltr_20060615&archive=1&#Mayors.

Page 181. Churchill quote: The International Centre for Facilities Web site says that "Churchill used this statement twice, first in 1924 at the English Architectural Association, then in 1943 upon the occasion of requesting that the bombed-out Parliament be rebuilt exactly as before. The first time he said it a little differently: 'There is no doubt whatever about the influence of architecture and structure upon human character and action. We make our buildings and afterwards they make us. They regulate the course of our lives.'" International Centre for Facilities Web site, Quotes page, www.icf-cebe.com/quotes/quotes.html.

Chapter 10: Power Shift

Page 186. Philip Morris report: Arthur D. Little International, "Public Finance Balance of Smoking in the Czech Republic," p. 2 of executive summary. An excerpt: "Public finance saved between 943 mil. CZK and 1,193 mil. CZK (realistic estimate: 1,193 mil. CZK) from reduced health-care costs, savings on pensions and housing costs for the elderly—all related to the early mortality of smokers." Campaign for Tobacco-Free Kids Web site, Reports page (November 28, 2000), http://tobaccofreekids.org/reports/philipmorris/pmczechstudy.pdf.

Page 186. BP rebrands itself: Susan Bryce, "Global Manipulators Move beyond Petroleum," *New Dawn Magazine,* no. 63 (November–December 2000), available online at www.newdawnmagazine.com/articles/Beyond_Petroleum.html.

Page 186: BP ads: Visit Ogilvy Public Relations Web site to learn about the launching of BP's advertising campaign in 2001: "Case Studies: BP; Launching 'Beyond Petroleum' Worldwide," Ogilvy Web site, Case Studies page, www.ogilvypr.com/case-studies/bp.cfm.

Page 186. BP invests more in oil than renewables: Steven Mufson and Juliet Eilperin, "For BP, a Pair of Repairs," *Washington Post,* August 9, 2006.

Page 186. Chevron urges visitors to "join the discussion": Read the full manifesto at Chevron's willyoujoinus.com Web site, www.willyoujoinus.com/register.

Pages 186–187. Chevron ads: See www.willyoujoinus.com, at the Media Gallery page.

Page 187. Walbridge quote: E-mail, March 2, 2008.

Page 188. Global Climate Science Communications Team: Global Climate Science Communications Team, "Action Plan" (April 3, 1998), p. 3. Document can be found at the Environmental Defense Fund Web site, www.environmentaldefense.org/documents/3860_GlobalClimateSciencePlanMemo.pdf.

Page 188. Victory would be achieved: Ibid., p. 3.

Page 188. Media continue to express doubt about climate change: Maxwell Boykoff and Jules M. Boykoff, "Balance as Bias: Global Warming and the U.S. Prestige Press," *Global Environmental Change* 14, no. 2 (September 2004), available at North Arizona University Web site, College of Engineering and Natural Sciences, Environmental Sciences and Education page, www.envsci.nau.edu/sisk/courses/env555/Readings/BoykoffBias.pdf.

Page 189. Mother Jones article: Chris Mooney, "Some Like It Hot," *Mother Jones,* May–June 2005.

Page 189. Exxon donates to think tanks who say climate change is false: "Put a Tiger in Your Think Tank," *Mother Jones* special report, May–June 2005.

Page 189. Exxon donates to American Enterprise Institute: Ibid.

Page 189. Friends of Science: Excerpt from Friends of Science Web page, at the About Us page, www.friendsofscience.org/index.php?id=1.

Page 189. Friends of Science gets its funding from oil companies: from *Globe and Mail* (Toronto): Charles Montgomery, "Meet Mr. Cool: Nurturing Doubt about Climate Change Is Big Business," August 12, 2006.

Page 189. Frank Luntz quote: From the Luntz Research Companies, "Straight Talk" (July 2002), photocopy of memo at the Environmental Working Group (EWG) Web site, www.ewg.org/files/LuntzResearch_environment.pdf. More information from EWG is available at www.ewg.org/node/8684.

Page 192. Eighty percent of population in cities will be able to reject automobile: David Whitehouse, "Half of Humanity Set to Go Urban," BBC News (May 19, 2005), http://news.bbc.co.uk/1/hi/sci/tech/4561183.stm.

Page 193. Foust quote: Clifford Krauss, "Move Over Oil, There's Money in Texas Wind," *New York Times,* February 23, 2008.

Page 194. Chavez quote: "What the Future Holds for Farm Workers and Hispanics," address given to the Commonwealth Club, San Francisco, November 9, 1984, available at the Mindfully.org Web site, www.mindfully.org/Reform/Cesar-Chavez9nov84.htm.

Page 194. Gibbs's book: Lois Marie Gibbs, *Love Canal: My Story* (Albany: State University of New York Press, 1982).

Page 195. America spends $4 billion a week on the war in Iraq: David Leonhardt, "What $1.2 Trillion Can Buy," *New York Times,* January 17, 2007.

Page 195. Hawken quote: The official Web site for *The 11th Hour* (Warner Independent Pictures, 2007) is http://wip.warnerbros.com/11thhour.

Index

renewable energy, 146–65; arguments
against, 146–47; benefits of, 146; demand
for, 163, 165; green-collar jobs, 148–50,
170, 193; for homes/businesses, 152–55,
162–63, 166, 192–93; information
resources, 213; infrastructure for, 164;
investment in, 162–63, 166, 168–70, 172–75;
organizations and programs, 212–13;
power sharing, 163–64; price concerns,
146; prioritizing use of, 143; statistics, 148,
165, 168; storage technologies, 162; taking
action, 166; transition to, 147–48, 161–65,
183–84, 190–96; U.S. attitudes toward, 12.
See also solar energy; wind energy

renewable portfolio standards, 155

respiratory ailments: coal-related, 15, 45, 46,
51–53; oil-related, 33; public pressure to
reduce, 194–95

Rhode Island, 192

Robert W. Scherer Power Plant, 55

Rosenfeld, Art, 167, 170–73

Royal Dutch Shell, 70, 72, 88

royalty payments, to oil companies, 66

rural economies, wind energy, 160–61, 166,
193

Russia, greenhouse gases, 114

Salim, Dr. Emil, 88

San Diego Gas and Electric, 157, 172

Sarayaku, oil exploration, 23, 36

Saro-Wiwa, Ken, 70

Saudi Arabia, 15, 26–27, 78

Save Our Species Alliance, 47–48

Schwarzenegger, Arnold, 13

Scientific Alliance, 189

Sexton, Chelsea, 119, 120–21

Sherburne County Generating Plant, 56

ShoreBank Pacific, EcoDeposits, 91

Silicon Valley Leadership Group, 122

Sims, Jim, 47–48

Socolow, Robert, 171

soils: climate change mitigated by, 139–40;
depleted by agrofuels, 131, 138–39, 142

solar energy: benefits of, 152–55, 156–57;
cost of, 146, 151–52; demand incentives,
163; government support for, 153, 154–55;
green-collar jobs, 148–50, 170; for homes/
businesses, 152–55, 162–63, 166, 192–93;
industrial facilities, 155–57; infrastructure
for, 164; intermittency concerns, 162;
investment in, 162–63, 168–70; power
sharing, 163–64; provider resources, 214;
statistics, 153–55, 165, 168; technologies,
155–56. *See also* renewable energy

Solar Energy Generating Systems (SEGS),
156

Solarex, bought by BP, 186

solid-state lighting (LEDs), 178–79

South America: agrofuels, 132, 136, 137, 140,
142; oil exploration, 22–25, 36, 84

South Dakota, wind energy, 159

Southeast Asia, biodiesel crops, 132

Southern California Edison, 157, 172

Southern Company, 55, 77, 188

soy, biodiesel and, 133, 135–36, 138–39, 142

Spadaro, Jack, 67–69

species, endangered, 13, 47, 129–31, 136

Stirling Energy Systems, 156–57

Subaru, electric vehicles, 124

suburban development, 101–3, 167

sugar cane/sugar beets, 131, 132, 139, 140

sulfur dioxide, from coal plants, 52–53, 56

Sunoco, CEO salaries, 66

Sustainable Biodiesel Alliance, 142

tar sands oil exploration, 30–33, 195

tax breaks: for oil companies, 65–67, 162; for
plug-in/electric vehicles, 126; for solar
energy, 162–63

Tennessee, coal mining, 42

Tesla Motor Company, 122–23

Texas: oil refineries, 34; urban planning, 102, 104, 181; wind energy, 159, 193

Thompson, Tim, 63, 68

tobacco industry, 80–81, 184, 185–86

Toyota: electric vehicles reclaimed by, 112, 113–14; hybrid/plug-in vehicles, 117, 118, 120, 121, 124

trade deficits, oil and, 15

traffic congestion, 100–101

transesterification, biofuels and, 133

transit-oriented development, 102–3

transportation, public, 95–109; airlines, 100; bicycles, 101, 103–6, 192; buses and streetcars, 101–7, 192; commuting, 101–3, 107–9; employees reimbursed for, 92; energy savings from, 107, 108; government funding for, 103; information resources, 208; organizations and programs, 206–8; prioritizing, 143; taking action, 109–10; urban planning and, 102–3, 191–92; walking, 108, 191–92. *See also* railroads

TXU Energy, loans to, 77

Unocal, lawsuit against, 34–35

urban planning: bicycle-friendly communities, 103–6; information resources, 208; New Urbanist movement, 102; organizations and programs, 206–8; suburban sprawl, 101–3; taking action, 109; transit-oriented development, 102–3, 191–92

U.S. Export-Import Bank, 86

Utah, renewable energy programs, 163

utilities: decoupling profits from sales, 176–77; financing for, 75–94; law/safety standard compliance, 61; net metering, 163–64; price caps, 62. *See also* electricity

vehicle-to-grid power (V2G), 123–25

Venezuela, agrofuels, 132

Vermont, 174–75, 177

Virginia, 42, 77, 177

walking, policies to encourage, 108, 191–92

Wal-Mart, green technologies, 153, 179

wars, for oil, 14, 28, 36, 67, 195

Washington (state), 105, 108, 159, 163

water pollution: agrofuels and, 131, 138–39, 142; coal industry and, 30, 32, 43, 44–51, 67–69; health effects, 139; pressure to reduce, 194

water usage, 13, 32

Weill, Sandy, 81, 84, 85

WestLB, 85

West Virginia, coal, 40–44, 67–69, 77, 91

Whitman, Christine Todd, 64–65

Wilmar, palm plantations, 136

wind energy, 157–60; benefits of, 146, 160; cost of, 158–59; demand incentives, 163; generating capacity, 158–59; green-collar jobs, 148–50, 170; infrastructure for, 164; intermittency concerns, 162; investment in, 162–63, 168–70; opposition to, 12, 159–60; power sharing, 163–64; rural economies and, 160–61, 166, 193; statistics, 158. *See also* renewable energy

Wolfensohn, James, 87, 88, 89–90

Wolfowitz, Paul, 89–90

World Bank Extractive Industries Review, 88–90

World Bank Group, 84, 86–90

World Trade Organization, 87

Zipcar, 107, 108

About the Author

Michael Brune is executive director of Rainforest Action Network (RAN). Brune joined RAN to help convince Home Depot to stop selling wood from endangered forests. After a year of creative protests and shareholder advocacy, the company agreed. *Time* magazine called the victory the top environmental story of 1999, and the agreement led to the protection of five million acres in British Columbia's Great Bear Rainforest. Brune provides strategic direction for RAN's programs, which seek to protect endangered forests from extractive industries, support the rights of Indigenous peoples, and fight climate change by reducing the country's dependence on oil and coal. Brune holds B.S. degrees in economics and finance from West Chester University. He lives with his wife and daughter in Alameda, California.